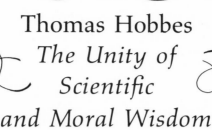

Thomas Hobbes
The Unity of Scientific and Moral Wisdom

There can be no doubt that Thomas Hobbes intended to create a complete philosophical system. In recent years, piecemeal analysis has ignored that intention and reduced his philosophy to an unsystematic jumble of irreconcilable parts. It is generally believed that Hobbes's mechanistic physics is at odds with his notorious egoistic psychology, and that the latter cannot support his prescriptive moral theory. In this book Gary B. Herbert sets forth an entirely new interpretation of Hobbes's philosophy that takes seriously Hobbes's original systematic intention.

The author traces the historical and conceptual development of Hobbes's science, psychology, and politics to reveal how those separate parts of his philosophy were eventually united by developments in his concept of *conatus*. After an analysis of Hobbes's accounts of space, matter, and body, Herbert concludes that, although Hobbes is clearly a materialist, his natural philosophy is not the naïve mechanics it is often thought to be, but a precursor to modern phenomenology.

The book's thorough analysis of Hobbes's account of the passions concludes that it is not simply a reproduction of Aristotle's views—an interpretation that originated with Leo Strauss. Rather, it is a development of the *conatus* concept of his natural philosophy. It is also a refutation of Descartes' account of philosophical and scientific "generosity" and, more generally, part of the seventeenth-century debate over the role of science in matters of morality that culminates in Hobbes's own version of the unity of scientific and moral wisdom.

Through an analysis of Hobbes's doctrine of natural right the author shows how man's passionate concern for his own natural right to life, pursued to its natural limits, is sufficient in itself both to transform him into a paragon of moral virtue and also to serve as the original source of philosophical and scientific desire. Hobbes's political thought is thereby reintegrated with his natural philosophy and psychology in such a way as to constitute a philosophical system.

GARY B. HERBERT is an associate professor of philosophy at Loyola University, New Orleans.

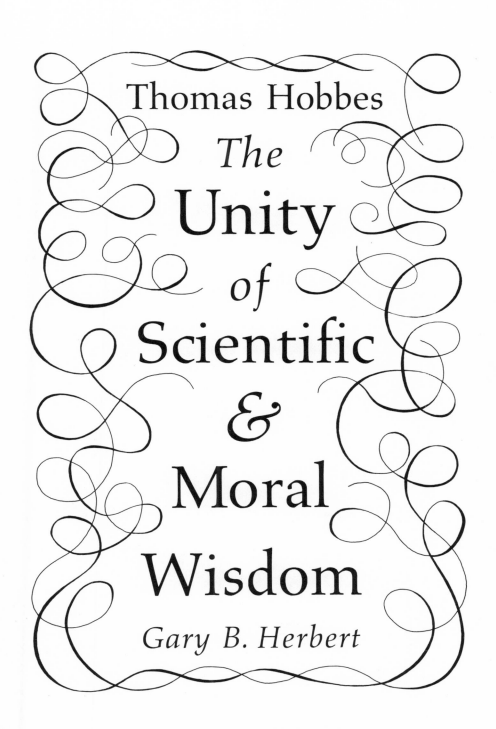

Thomas Hobbes
The
Unity
of
Scientific
&
Moral
Wisdom
Gary B. Herbert

University of British Columbia Press
Vancouver 1989

© The University of British Columbia Press 1989
All rights reserved
Typeset by The Typeworks
Printed in Canada

Canadian Cataloguing in Publication Data

Herbert, Gary B. (Gary Bruce), 1941–
Thomas Hobbes, the unity of scientific
and moral wisdom

Includes bibliographical references and index
ISBN 0-7748-0315-0 (*cloth*)
ISBN 0-7748-0316-9 (*paper*)

1. Hobbes, Thomas, 1588-1679 – Ethics. 2. Science
and ethics. I Title.

B1248.E7H47 1989   192   C89-091065-0

*This book is dedicated
to Stanley Rosen*

Contents

⚮

Preface

The last two decades have witnessed a renaissance of philosophical interest in Thomas Hobbes, the result of which has been an outpouring of studies of his philosophy. If there is anything in particular that distinguishes this renewal of interest in Hobbes, it is the desire to purge his philosophy of its infamous egoism and neutralize the determinist implications of his metaphysical materialism. The problem, according to his contemporary critics, is that his philosophy can produce neither a valid contract theory nor a valid theory of moral obligation so long as human behaviour is governed by the influence of self-interest or fixed by the forces of causal determinacy.

These recent studies have contributed greatly to our knowledge of Hobbes, but at some expense. As a result of these studies, we today know both more and less about Hobbes than ever before. The Hobbes that comes about as a result of these studies is more respectable, more harmless, perhaps philosophically more useful, but also much more unrecognizable. The insight that made him an important philosophical antecedent to Leibniz, Spinoza, and Hegel, as well as to Locke, Rousseau, and numerous others, has been lost. Those elements of his philosophy for which he has become famous have been purged as he has become more respectable. His account of the passions governing all human behaviour has been isolated or, what is worse, inverted. His physics has been reduced to a methodological remnant of the notorious thesis it was originally thought to be. And his intention to produce a complete system of philosophy has been laid aside, a casualty of his contemporary restoration.

The purpose of this book is to work back to a view of Hobbes that relocates him at the inception of a philosophical tradition that leads through Leibniz to Hegel. The intention is to restore Hobbes's thought to its more traditional philosophical location, first, by taking seriously his clearly stated intention to produce a "system" of philosophy, grounded upon physics, working through an egoistic account of human nature to a realistic account of civil association. The argument of the book is that there is a mature philosophical system in Hobbes that can be discovered in those writings that were published on or around 1650 (especially *Leviathan* and *De Corpore*). Those writings show the influence of his eleven-year stay in Paris from 1640 to 1651, during the English civil wars. Hobbes fled England in 1640, anticipating the collapse of Charles I's authority, the inevitable civil chaos, and his own vulnerability as a pro-royalist. During his long stay in Paris, he enjoyed the intellectual company of Maren Mersenne, Pierre Gassendi, Samuel Sorbière, François Bonneau (Du Verdus), and others, and lived at least in the intellectual environs of (and became a philosophical competitor of) René Descartes. One can surmise that this intellectually charged environment contributed to the changes in his philosophy detectable around this time. *Leviathan* is no less distinct from the earlier *De Cive* and *Elements of Law* than *De Corpore* is from his earlier "scholastic" physics.

The primary difficulty in understanding Hobbes "systematically" has always been connecting his physics (which has traditionally been perceived to be a mechanistic materialism) with his theory of sense perception or his psychology (grounded as it is on the primacy of fear and desire). A systematic philosophy would require deriving consciousness from motion, on the one hand, and passion or desire from mere motion, on the other. Hobbes seems never to have been bothered by the problem. The reason for his lack of concern, we will see, is the integrating and mediating function of the gradually evolving concept of "conatus" in his thought. The concept, sometimes translated by Hobbes as "motion," sometimes as "endeavour," depending on the context, runs through every segment of his mature philosophy. Its omnipresence inspired Frithiof Brandt to refer to him as "the philosopher of motion as Descartes is the philosopher of extension."[1] The concept, in its most mature expression, prevents Hobbes's physics from being reducible to a simple mechanistic materialism from which, admittedly, neither consciousness nor desire could be extracted. It also explains why the doctrine of inertia, the centrepiece of seventeenth-century mechanics, has virtually no role to play in Hobbes's philosophy of nature. Hobbes's philosophy, developed out of this concept of "conatus," takes the form of an internally coherent philosophical system that provides us with a dynamic—even dialectical—theory of nature, man, and society. Hobbes's philosophy, so understood, emerges as an important catalyst in the transformation of the "speculative enterprise" of School Philosophy into the historicist enterprise of philosophical modernity, the principle Hobbesian insight of which is that we know only what we make.

Chapter 1 of the book begins with a discussion of Hobbes's philosophical intention, his rejection of the ancients and the relocation of the objective of philosophy in man's mastery of nature. The chapter outlines the general conceptual development that takes place between his earlier and his later writings. Chapter 2 traces this conceptual development as it occurs in his philosophy of nature, following Hobbes's thought through his accounts of body and space, and his disputes with Descartes on these issues. It shows that Hobbes's materialism is phenomenal, rather than metaphysical, in the sense that it does not involve the simple self-identity of externally related objects. Externality is not a relationship between independently existing objects, but rather a product of the reciprocal determinacy of their individuating motions (or "conatus"). As part of this notion of reciprocal determinacy, Hobbes rejects the distinction between the sense objects and things themselves.

The sense in which this natural philosophy can be made consistent with an account of volition, that is, man's liberation from natural necessity, is discussed in chapter 3. Hobbes shows that voluntary motions are a product not of spontaneity but of the transcendence of the immediacy of natural relations that occurs through the mediating and stabilizing function of language.

Chapter 4 analyzes the historical development of Hobbes's account of the passions. His theory of the passions has often been dismissed precipitantly as a mere regurgitation of Aristotle's earlier account. The fact is that Hobbes's theory of the passions is the centrepiece of his philosophical system. The peculiarity of Hobbes's account is brought out in a comparison with that of Descartes which shows the disagreement that existed between them and the implications that follow from their disagreement. An analysis is made of the "dialectic" by which desire proceeds, how it culminates in the seventeenth-century notion of philosophy as the project to make man "master and possessor of nature" and in Hobbes's account of the magnanimous and generous few in whom that mastery reaches its apex. Hobbes's theory issues in an account of "the morality of natural reason" that opens the door to his theory of moral and political existence, and simultaneously anticipates the problems of creativity and paradoxes of historicism that have preoccupied much of contemporary philosophy.

Chapter 5 discusses the philosophical evolution of Hobbes's arguments for natural equality, and considers the sense in which his doctrine of equality follows from—and is consistent with—a physics and psychology that do not preclude the natural inequality of beings. The book concludes with an examination of the philosophical evolution of Hobbes's political philosophy from its earlier origins in an exclusively social idea of volition and desire to those later, mature accounts of the nature of man that ground all human action on the irrepressible, natural character of "conatus" (endeavour). It is that mature account of conatus, or desire, that creates the problem of getting from a Hobbesian state of nature into the social contract. It precludes our relying on unHobbesian trust in others to perform covenants they have made, and thereby shows the way to Hobbes's resolution of the problem.

The conclusion to which the book as a whole aims is that, for Hobbes, the pursuit of morality is not only inseparable from man's irrepressible concern for his self-interest; it is also inseparable from the pursuit of science, insofar as the "unforeseen mischances" that threaten man's welfare cannot be entirely alleviated by civil existence alone. Hobbes is in company with Francis Bacon, René Descartes, and others of his time who recognized that the ultimate benefactor of man will be found in philosophical science. The magnanimity and generosity of the philosophical and scientific few—those who are moved only by a desire for a "continual and indefatigable generation of knowledge"—makes them the true benefactors of mankind. Because of their preoccupation with, and preference for, philosophical and scientific issues, they have the unique characteristic of being morally and politically generous without the threat of sovereign coercion. So understood, Hobbes's philosophy can be seen to be an antecedent of currents of thought in our own times. The pre-eminence and power of philosophical science as Hobbes perceived it anticipates the political power and moral authority of modern technological science and the dangers thereof. Hobbes, of course, could not have been expected to see the dangerous implications of his thought as they occur in a technologically dominated society. It is enough, for our purposes, to re-establish a focus on Hobbes's thought that reintegrates his philosophy with the philosophical, scientific, and political history of his own time.

Acknowledgments

⤛⤜

This book has been published with the generous assistance of a grant from Loyola University. It is due my utmost appreciation.

There are also a number of other people and institutions to whom an expression of gratitude is due for their contributions—direct and indirect— to this book. Appreciation goes to my former teachers, especially to Richard Kennington, who first turned me to Hobbes, and whose scholarly influence is reflected in this book. My deepest debt belongs to Stanley Rosen, for the years during which I was the beneficiary of his almost inexhaustible wisdom, and for the advice, guidance, and inspiration he has given freely since then.

I owe much to the Reverend George Lundy, Executive Vice President of Loyola University, whose assistance and understanding have been utterly essential. A special thanks is owed to Mr. Graeme Matheson, whose careful reading and many valuable suggestions have helped me to locate and remove numerous obscurities from the text, and to James Anderson and Jean Wilson for their patience and helpful advice. Many discerning comments and helpful observations were provided by the anonymous reader for the University of British Columbia Press. Allen Sparks also deserves special thanks for the many hours he spent in preparing the manuscript. Finally, unending gratitude is due my wife, Jane, for her indispensable support and encouragement over the years.

Several editors and publishers have given me permission to draw on materials that have been published previously. "Hobbes's Phenomenology of Space," which appeared in the *Journal of the History of Ideas*, XIVIII (1987), was incorporated into chapter 2. Another article, "Thomas

Hobbes's Dialectic of Desire," in *The New Scholasticism*, L:2 (1976), was drawn upon for use in chapter 4. "Thomas Hobbes's Counterfeit Equality," in *The Southern Journal of Philosophy*, XIV (1976), was used in chapter 5. And, finally, "Thomas Hobbes: The Mediation of Right," which appeared in *Hobbes's Science of Natural Justice*, C. Walton and P.J. Johnson, eds. (The Hague: Martinus Nijhoff 1987), was drawn upon for use in chapter 6. I am grateful for permission to use these materials.

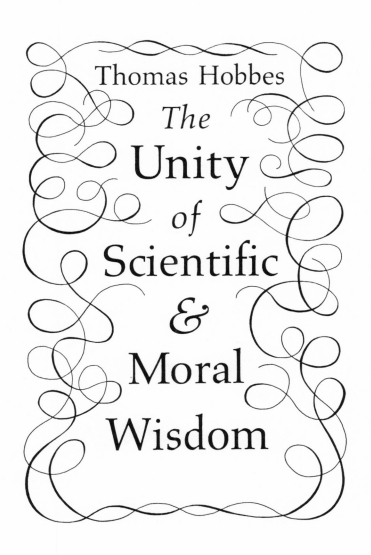

Thomas Hobbes

The

Unity

of

Scientific

&

Moral

Wisdom

1

Hobbes's Philosophical Intention

In his *Introduction* to *Leviathan*, Thomas Hobbes presented to his readers an image of man and nature that was as audacious in its implications for man and society as it was instructive and enlightening. Hobbes made the bold and rather presumptuous claim that an analogy exists between man's creation of the commonwealth and God's creation of the world. "Nature, the art whereby God hath made and governs the world, is by the *art* of man. . . imitated, that it can make an artificial animal."[1] Man has somehow imitated the Divine. Hobbes's portrayal of this act has commonly been called upon by his interpreters as an analogical overview of his whole philosophical system, and rightly so. The terminology that Hobbes used to explain this creation of the artificial animal—the commonwealth—was thoroughly mechanical. That, too, has not been lost on Hobbes's interpreters. The world as he appears to portray it is a thoroughly mechanical place congested with other thoroughly mechanical beings (humans) who are busy constructing still other mechanical beings (commonwealths) not dissimilar from themselves.

There are surprises in store for the reader who carefully works through Hobbes's analogy, and if he does not dismiss the implications, they will serve as a clue to the theory the analogy anticipates. According to the analogy, nature is God's art. This would seem to imply that we ought not confuse nature (God's art) with the world (the product of God's art). Nature is both the genesis of that complex of springs, strings, and wheels which, Hobbes tells us, constitutes the world, and its governing principle. If there is anything more we can know about the Creation, Hobbes does not tell us here, at least not directly.

The suggestion that mankind has imitated God's creative art obviously draws on the biblical claim that man has been made in God's image. It tends to provide a veneer of theological respectability for Hobbes. Whether the respectability is justified or not is another matter. The closer one inspects the analogy, the clearer it becomes that God loses his Divine transcendence in this portrayal. Hobbes, of course, would not make this point conspicuous.

One actually learns more about the nature of God's creative art and His relation to the world He creates by concentrating on the implications that the second half of Hobbes's analogy has for the first. Man's imitation of the Divine art turns out to be an imitation by man of himself, "that rational and most excellent work of nature" (Lev., Intro.), Leviathan has been created by man in his own image. If the analogy holds, it suggests that the world of springs, strings, and wheels which God has created (and of which man is an integral part) is God's self-imitation too!

According to the analogy, man is not only the *artificer* of Leviathan; he is also its *matter*. The imagery is compelling. It silently instructs us that God, the author of the world, is also materially indistinguishable from the world. His formal difference from the world, that is, as its creator, would seem only to identify Him with the principles of mathematical physics, in the image of which only a world of springs, strings, and wheels could be made. Of course, God must be more than the mathematical orderliness of the world. According to Hobbes, He is also its genesis, its Author. Since mechanical principles do not put themselves in motion, the simple identification of God with the principles of mathematical physics is not altogether justifiable. Nonetheless, little room is left for the personal involvement of a biblical God. The obvious atheistic implications of Hobbes's analogy were not lost on his more devout contemporaries. They were sufficient to cause his villification. Before long, "Hobbesism" came to be regarded as a virtual synonym for atheism in England, and Hobbes himself as a valet to the devil.

As compelling as the *Introduction* is in promoting a conception of Hobbes as the great seventeenth-century mechanist, it is also very misleading. The more it is pressed, the more its imagery fails to convey the theory it presumably contains. I am not suggesting here that Hobbes failed to write what he intended but, rather, that his Introduction is not the uncomplicated synopsis that it is usually taken to be. I am suggesting that the *Introduction* contains the dissembled components of a theory very unlike the mechanical one for which he has been given philosophical credit. Later in this chapter we will return to Hobbes's analogical account to see how difficulties internal to the imagery it uses will lead the wary reader to see that it cannot consistently be read as an uncomplicated introduction to a merely mechanistic theory. Nor, I will add, can it be read consistently as an overview of an analogically, or merely methodologically, unified philosophical system. Hobbes's philosophy, in the final analysis, is more dynamic than it is analogical. At the level of his psychology and politics especially, it is not so much mechanical as it is dialectical.

THE MEDICINAL REINTERPRETATION

A backdrop for the interpretation being proposed here can be provided by examining the more traditional and orthodox approach to Hobbes's philosophy. There was no dispute among Hobbes's readers in the last century about whether his intention to produce a complete philosophical *system* should not be the opening into his philosophy. That traditional view of Hobbes's philosophy will be examined, then contrasted with some of the more recent and innovative interpretations that deny the usefulness of taking seriously Hobbes's intention to be systematic.

With very few exceptions, Hobbes's commentators have assumed that the mechanical terminology and imagery he used is authoritative. Coupled with his clearly stated intention to produce a philosophical system, Hobbes has emerged as philosophy's paradigmatic mechanistic-materialist. His own clearly stated intention was to produce a single, coherent, all-inclusive system of philosophy—to be called *The Elements of Philosophy*—grounded on the principles of natural science, progressing systematically through the science of human nature to its culmination in a science of the principles of civil association. The three Elements which together were to constitute his system were *De Corpore*, *De Homine*, and *De Cive*.

Clearly stated though Hobbes's intention is, it is difficult to accept it as an altogether accurate account of what he did. There is no more persuasive reason for challenging the orthodox interpretation than the discrepancy between Hobbes's stated intention to create a system and the remarkably unsystematic character of what he wrote. It seems obvious that the three Elements of his system are uncomplementary. If one begins with what is generally taken to be his mechanistic materialism, there is no legitimate way to arrive at the egoistic psychology that is fundamental to his theory of human nature, for the simple reason that desire cannot be accounted for as a function of simple mechanical motion. And whether one begins from his mechanistic materialism or from his egoistic psychology, there seems to be no route to what is often considered to be the capstone of Hobbes's political theory, his theory of moral obligation, since mechanical motions are not social, and egoistically determinate desire is not other-directed, not concerned with establishing a more considerate relationship with others.

The lack of continuity in Hobbes's philosophy is sometimes dramatized by noting the disproportion that exists between his intention to produce a philosophical system and the unsystematic order in which he published the separate Elements of his tripartite system. Hobbes published the third and final part of his system, *De Cive*, first, in 1642, and published the foundation of the system, *De Corpore*, last, in 1655. What we might take to be the initial version of the second part of his system, *Human Nature*, was published in 1650 as the first part of *The Elements of Law*. In other words, Hobbes reversed the systematic order of his philosophical Elements in their publication. This has been taken by some as evidence that his political philosophy and his theory of human nature do not depend on his natural philosophy as Hobbes would have us believe. His critics have sought other foundations for the separate Elements of his system, foundations which may have crept into his thinking unawares.

Hobbes provided his own explanation as to why he deserted in publication the systematic order of the Elements of his system, but few have found it satisfactory. In the Epistle Dedicatory to *De Cive*, he wrote:

> Whilst I contrive, order, pensively and slowly compose these matters, (for I only do reason, I dispute not), it so happened in the interim, that my country some few years before the civil wars did rage, was boiling hot with questions concerning the rights of dominion, and the obedience due from subjects, the true forerunners of an approaching war; and was the cause which (all other matters deferred) ripened, and plucked from me this third part. Therefore, it happens that what was last in order, is yet come forth first in time, and the rather, because I saw that grounded on its own principles sufficiently known by experience it would not stand in need of the former sections. (De Cive, Epist. Ded.)

Hobbes's *explanation* for the prior publication of *De Cive* was, in other words, that it was induced by the provocative nature of the subject at the time, and also because of the imminent prospect of civil war in England. There was a need for a reasonable, but decisive, statement on critical issues, such as the obligation due to a sovereign from his subjects, and the limits of that obligation. But Hobbes's explanation for the prior publication of *De Cive* is not wholly convincing. His *justification* of its premature publication, that is, his philosophical defense of the decision to depart from a systematic development of his philosophy, was his conviction that *De Cive*'s argument is both persuasive and salutary, and that its persuasiveness derives from the self-evident status of the principles from which it is argued. He did not say that the principles are philosophically self-evident; they remain in need of a foundation. But, for those of his addressees for whom *De Cive* would be politically salutary, its first principles could be trusted to look sensible. They seemed to be corroborated by experience.

Nonetheless, Hobbes's explanation for the prior publication of *De Cive* is not an admission that he had abandoned the systematic aspects of his undertaking or that anything less than a systematic account would do. How then are we to explain the conspicuous incongruity of the Elements of his system? Is it possible that he was unaware of the incoherency of his philosophical system? There is, to be sure, some ground for arguing that Hobbes was himself confused and that his arguments, even though long regarded as paradigms of clarity, are not unambiguous. His writings may reveal not just one, but a multiplicity of intentions and assumptions that may not be entirely compatible. Living as he did at the dawn of the modern revolution is philosophy, one might suspect that some of the complexity of his thought would arise from the complex and contradictory character of his rejection of the philosophical tradition that preceded him. From the perspective of subsequent philosophy, what issued from Hobbes's pen might be expected to be in some ways excessive and in others insufficiently radical. He might be expected simultaneously to reject and borrow from the classical tradition.

One might also suspect that the paradoxical character of Hobbes's philosophy may be due partly to the fact that his works were not written straightforwardly, that he liberally employed innuendo and double intent, living as he did in a time of political turbulence and religious intolerance. There can be no serious doubt that a capacity for dissembling was a vital prerequisite for those who wished to publish safely in matters of natural philosophy in Hobbes's time. Hobbes repeats the thought of his one-time employer, Sir Francis Bacon, that nakedness of mind is no less uncomely than nakedness of body,[2] except that Hobbes uses more tasteful imagery to make the point. He likens the failure to dissimulate, that is, to use discretion in revealing one's thoughts, to an abuse of wine. It is, he says, as if a person should present himself before good company after having tumbled in the dirt (Lev., ch. 8, p. 59). We can anticipate, then, that a sober Hobbes will have laundered his writings before presenting them to the public. In short, the apparent clarity and straightforwardness of Hobbes's writings may be misleading, if not illusory, and the general appreciation of his philosophical intent oversimplified. This does not in itself resolve the problem of clarifying Hobbes's intention and understanding his philosophical system systematically. If a philosophical system is founded upon principles with which it is incompatible, it is not enough to say that the incompatibility is a product of prudential deceits. That leaves unanswered the questions, what are the real foundations and how are we to approach the philosophical theory they are said to found?

And so we come to what is often considered to be the central paradox in Hobbes's philosophy: his insistence that philosophy should be systematic contrasts with the apparent ambivalence of his own commitment to the systematic nature of his undertaking. It is not really so strange, then, that there should have arisen a broad range of mutually exclusive, often contradictory, interpretations of his thought.

The greater number of recent commentaries on Hobbes have sought to resolve the problem that his ambivalence presents by appealing to the medicinal efficacy of piecemeal-analysis, that is, by severing the Elements of philosophy from one another and joining them to elements or principles with which they can be identified more conveniently. The integrity of Hobbes's ethics, for example, has been preserved by dissociating what many of his interpreters refer to as his moral theory from his psychological egoism and attaching it, instead, to some combination of theology or natural law theory,[3] a humanism,[4] or an analytical methodology.[5] The predominant interest of those concerned with rescuing Hobbes's moral theory has been a concern for the logical or conceptual integrity of the argument for moral obligation that they have found in his political writings. Hobbes's infamous egoism is given only a supporting role; it is a validating condition, some say, employed in the application of Hobbes's theory, which unfortunately also undermines the theory's logical validity.[6]

Hobbes's political philosophy, as distinct from his moral philosophy, has been rescued by disconnecting it from his mechanistic materialism and reattaching it, instead, to a moral attitude, that is, to the bourgeois antithesis of vanity and fear that was gradually coming to replace the earlier aristocratic moral attitude in seventeenth-century England.[7] Leo Strauss, the author of this interpretation, went so far as to suggest that the mechanistic-materialistic physics and the mechanistic-materialistic psychology that play so important a role in such later writings as *Leviathan* actually compromise and undermine his original moral insights. The moral neutrality of the power generated by motions in a mechanistic-materialistic universe invalidates any theory which would subordinate power to the morally praised or blamed objectives of men acting from fear and vanity. Hobbes's less scientific, earlier writings, it is claimed, turn out to be more accurate statements of his political thought and its moral foundations than the later.

Strangely enough, there is no spokesman for the primacy of Hobbes's egoistic psychology. This is especially odd since there is probably no idea that is more commonly associated with Hobbes than his portrayal of avaricious man. But the passions that motivate and guide the behaviour of Hobbes's natural man are in these accounts more often than not removed from their place of importance. One exception to this approach to Hobbes's psychology can be found in Leo Strauss's interpretation. But even Strauss traces Hobbes's treatment of the passions to the characteristic moral attitude of seventeenth-century bourgeois man. It is not an account that can consistently be connected to his physics. Consequently, Hobbes's physics fades in importance for Strauss.

Hobbes's natural philosophy has been looked upon as unimportant even by those who have made it the focus of their attention. The definitive interpretation of Hobbes's physics was offered by Frithiof Brandt,[8] who maintained that it was not a possible foundation for any moral, legal or political theory. At best, he maintained, it provides a basis for a mechanistic account of vision. But it can have no role as an integral part of a larger philosophical system.

Other major recent interpretations of Hobbes's philosophy have taken his systematic intentions seriously, but they have concluded either that: he failed in his attempt to be systematic because of the epistemological limitations of his philosophy, his inability to get from nature to subjective experience, or from experience to nature,[9] or that the different Elements of his system only suggest one another or have only an analogical relationship to one another.[10]

The principal problem with the major reinterpretations of Hobbes's philosophy is that they ignore the very problem to which Hobbes's philosophy expressly addresses itself, that is, the problem of providing a theory of man and the world which does not divide the world into a variety of unrelated parts, which does not leave unexplained any major part of the real world, and which does not unite the parts of appealing to some principle (say, "separated essences") that is outside the theory and consequently outside the world as well. Recent interpretations have been enormously valuable in disclosing different aspects of Hobbes's thought; but they have improperly abstracted from his own intention. However difficult the task may be, one cannot arrive at an adequate interpretation of Hobbes's thought without taking seriously his intention to be systematic, that is, his intention to ground the principles of human nature and political association on the principles of a natural philosophy. A genuine interpretation of Hobbes's thought must attempt to integrate the parts of his philosophical system in a manner consistent with that intention. To dismiss it is to transform Hobbes's philosophy into something more respectable, a surrogate for philosophers with different intentions. Certainly there is nothing in what he wrote that can be taken as an admission that he had abandoned his systematic intentions. The objective of the present study will be to undertake just this reintegration of his thought without merely combining incompatibles on the basis of their somehow being suggestive of one another or their having an analogical relationship. Rather, it will search for the underlying principles, if any, which give Hobbes's *oeuvre* the consistency and coherency of a system.

HOBBES'S REJECTION OF ANTIQUITY

One cannot accurately comprehend Hobbes's philosophical intention without considering it against the backdrop of traditional political, moral and speculative philosophy, at least as Hobbes himself perceived it. In fact, one might reasonably argue that Hobbes's rejection of the ancients, and with them those moderns who preserved the fundamental features of ancient speculative philosophy, provided the catalyst for much of his own slowly maturing philosophical theory.

The Critique of Ancient Moral Philosophy

Hobbes's criticism of the ancients is most obvious from his condemnation of the idealism of Greek moral and political philosophy. He maintained that traditional moral and political philosophy was more appropriately called a "dream" than a science. The tradition, he said, tended to treat moral virtue as the single non-coercive cause of political restraint, as if the appeal of moral virtue would be sufficient in itself to guarantee the moral dignity of man and subdue the perversities of his private inclinations. Traditional moral philosophy does not take into account the modest appeal that moral ideals have for the greatest majority of men. It fails to appreciate the fact that man is by nature a private animal, dependably concerned, above all, with his own personal welfare. When the private well-being of a man is jeopardized or even appears to him to be jeopardized, the hold that moral education and social conventions have on him loosens very quickly. The more primitive forces of fear and desire take over.

As a result of what is often called his pessimistic view of human nature (what Leo Strauss referred to as his "rejection of the morality of obedience"),[11] Hobbes was widely and contemptuously perceived as a purveyor of irreverent ideas, a slanderer of the Divine Image in man. His ideas were so repugnant to many thinkers of his time that they vilified him with broadsides that contained more invective than argument. He was "the monster of Malmsbury," "the *pontifex maximus* of infidelity," and many other terribly wicked things.[12]

Hobbes hardly lived up to his villainous reputation. His reply to his detractors was to discover the villainy they attributed to him in their own behaviour. His critique of the ancients can be looked upon as an oblique criticism of those of his contemporaries whom he could not openly criticize without further jeopardizing his own welfare. The point of his rejection of traditional moral and political philosophy (and, simultaneously, the point that his rejection should have had for his critics) is not simply that the appeal of virtue as a motive for action is usually ineffective in subduing man's excessively egoistic behaviour. It is even more his point that where the appeal of virtue is effective, it is also vicious. Virtue has a capacity for serving as the conduit of desire in such a way that virtue and desire virtually coalesce. Virtue can transform itself into moral fanaticism, where nothing remains to temper virtue's desire. Traditional moral theories, Hobbes said, are "hermaphrodite opinions" (De Cive, Preface, p. xiii), partly right, insofar as the appeal of virtue is an appeal to something much more lofty than private desire, but also partly wrong, insofar as in the name of lofty virtue, men are caught up in contention, bloodshed, and war. Men are directed onto the paths of sedition and warfare in the name of political and moral idealism. Virtue's seductive appeal makes men lose sight of everything that is conducive to life; it causes men to grasp at something entirely beyond the moral and political reach of mankind. Paradoxically, it returns man to the condition of nature, where life can be expected to be "solitary, poor, nasty, brutish and short" (Lev., ch. 13, p. 113). Worst of all, it does so deceptively. Men do not easily perceive the malignancy of their actions when they undertake those actions in the name of justice and righteousness. Hence the thinly veiled criticism of the seditious effects of both School doctrines and Christian morality. Hobbes writes:

> But evil men under pretext that God can do anything, are so bold as to say any thing when it serves their turn, though they think it untrue; it is the part of a wise man, to believe them no farther than right reason makes that which they say, appear credible. If this superstitious fear of spirits were taken away, and with it, prognostics from dreams, false prophecies, and many other things depending thereon, by which crafty ambitious persons abuse the simple people, men would be much more fitted than they are for civil obedience (Lev., ch. 2, p. 10).

Hobbes reasoned that the seditious aspects of moral and political idealism might be avoided and a peaceful order maintained if the laws of civil society were grounded on the lowest, most reliable, natural inclinations of men rather than dangled like fruits of Tantalus from society's highest moral ideals. The most natural and dependable inclinations of men are those that reflect the concern they have for their own well-being. Man's concern for himself is not easily distracted. He is, in short, a preeminently private being. He is not a social being in the sense of being naturally sociable. It is his nature to dissociate his own well-being from that of his fellow citizens and his society and to prefer it in every case. In Hobbes's terminology, while man is born in *need* of society, he is not born *fit* for society (De Cive, ch. 1, p. 2). To the extent that he is capable of satisfying this need, man is a *political* being. His political nature is, in effect, his ability to compensate for his otherwise unsociable and contentious inclinations. The domain of politics, in other words, is a domain of art or construction.

Whether Hobbes's criticism of ancient moral and political theory is fair to the ancients is not at issue here. It might even be argued legitimately that there is more of Plato's political philosophy in Hobbes than Hobbes would want to admit. Certainly his criticism of Aristotle's doctrine of separated essences and its effect on men, frightening them from obedience to the laws of their countries, is less a criticism of Aristotle (to whom it does not really apply) than it is a thinly veiled criticism of the separation of spiritual and political authority that is fundamental to Christian morality.

Hobbes believed that enlightening men regarding their needs rather than their moral obligations would ultimately be sufficient to make them fit for society. Were men to realize that the greatest threats to their own well-being were kindled, paradoxically, by their own suspicious behaviour as they sought the power required to withstand those threats, that realization would evoke fear and desire in them. Hobbes saw fear and desire as the initial determinate forms of *conatus*, that is, of that smallest and most fundamental motion that constitutes life. Fear and desire represent *conatus* raised to the level of consciousness. Moreover, he saw in these twin passions the precondition (if not the source) of man's rational behaviour. One's fear, if it is great enough, can dissuade him from rash actions. And one's desire to augment his well-being, if it is enlightened by (and therefore made more moderate by) his fear will lead him to compensate for the anticipated, that is, potential, threats that fear initially reveals. The desire to compensate, Hobbes thought, will direct men to the desirability of civil association and, therefore, to the social contract. A moral and political education that focuses on those things that would satisfy man's most enlightened fears and desires, rather than prescribing ascetic-seeming ideals, will be persuasive to a degree unmatched by any previous moral philosophy. It will not have as its side-effect the viciousness that accompanies excessive moral and political idealism. Thus educated, man might be transformed into a flawless paragon of civic virtue.

Man's decision to leave the state of nature is a *natural* decision. Nature, Hobbes might be thought to say, is self-transforming in man. In the act of transforming nature, man transforms himself. Civil society is, in effect, nature rendered reasonable. Civil man is the rational expression of natural man, of the man who has found rational means to express the passions that he exhibits self-destructively in the natural condition. The un-mediated separation of human action and desire from any consideration of ideals not only makes any account of virtues merely ideal; it also makes any account of political things merely prudential. Hobbes realized that it would not be sufficient to replace ancient moral idealism with a prudential political realism. Hobbes did not merely borrow a page from Machiavelli. Rather, he realized what many of his interpreters maintain he did not realize–that politics grounded on prudence alone will culminate in the un-mitigated bestiality of a sovereign whose absolute authority has no other source than his own absolute power. Hobbes's intent was to avoid this ex-treme without appealing to its opposite, that is, moral idealism.

Ultimately, it will be shown how Hobbes's critique of the ancients and his attempt to arrive at an integrated account of nature, man and political life contains a presentiment of the dialectic of self-interest, or abstract right, found in G.W.F. Hegel's *Philosophy of Right,* where the truth of what is one's right is to be discovered in duty, where self-interest and moral self-consciousness are abstract, unmediated and ultimately unintelligible except insofar as they are understood to be reciprocally de-pendent moments of what Hegel calls the concrete ethical life.

Critique of Ancient Metaphysics

Hobbes did not think that the dilemma of the ancients in attempting to prescribe virtue for the non-virtuous was merely the product of their naive moral idealism. He recognized in the ancient moral dilemma a deeper problem whose origin is to be found in the doctrine of separated essences. He associated that problem, somewhat debatably, with the metaphysics of Aristotle. Hobbes rejected the doctrine as the produce of "senseless and in-significant language" (Lev., ch. 46, p. 686; ch. 4, p. 27). The unmediated separation of essences and the material world they are supposed to order makes any account of essences merely formal and any account of the mate-rial world subject to all varieties of linguistic absurdity. Man's ability to generate words for his ignorance is virtually unlimited.

Hobbes's criticism of the doctrine of separated essences is never clearly directed against Plato, and is only directed against Aristotle to the extent that Aristotle is associated with School Philosophy. We might assume that Hobbes's true antagonists are those who presume the existence of beings (e.g., God, incorporeal substance) whose infinite or universal character precludes the possibility of their determinate reality. His pious admission that we cannot conceive the greatness and infinite power of God, that the name of God is only for the sake of our honouring him (Lev., ch. 3, p. 17), ought not be mistaken for a statement of belief. More correctly, it is

Hobbes's modestly veiled statement of disbelief in anything that is not determinate.

Hobbes is through and through a materialist, but not (as we shall see) in the unreflective modes provided by ancient atomism or even modern mechanistic materialism. Hobbes held firm to the thought that *to be* means *to be something*, that is, to be determinate. There is nothing that is neither here nor there, neither this nor that. In short, he rejected the logic of a *summum genus*. On the other hand, his claim that physical reality is reducible to motion, not to simple bodies, and that motion is not simply the spatio-temporal change of position attributed to otherwise inert bodies but, rather, is *conatus*, makes it impossible to interpret him as a naive atomist. The function of *conatus* in his account of determinate reality makes his physics a dynamics.

Hobbes is also very definitely a monist. He recognized that the dualism in Cartesian philosophy leaves us with a problem of transcendence no less severe than that which had troubled ancient and School philosophy. The world falls too easily into unrelated halves. Hobbes sought to avoid this dilemma, once again, with an account of motion conceived as *conatus*. He produced a physics in which all individuation, all determinacy, whether physical, mental, or moral, comes about from the immanent workings of nature conceived as *conatus*. Hobbes produced a theory which made opposition characteristic of nature and, in that way, was able to attribute a dynamically determined purposiveness to natural motions. The theory anticipates the dialectics of much later philosophical thought. Of course, opposition is inconceivable where there is no endeavour or intent confronting another endeavour or intent. Things moving in a mechanistically ordered universe may collide, but they never oppose one another.

This suggestion—that Hobbes is not, in the end, a mechanist—is bound to meet with objections from many of Hobbes's readers. Hobbes, it will be protested, is the paradigmatic mechanist! And, is not mechanics the very antithesis of dialectic? While mechanics may have given birth to dynamics in its modern form, was it not also replaced by dynamics, but not until Newton? Was not Hobbes merely the heir of the Cartesian-Galilean theory of inertia, the foundational principle of modern mechanics?

Certainly it is true that Hobbes's language does not include all the terminology we have come to expect in dynamics or dialectics. But one really should not expect that, given the fact that he is writing during a time dominated by the newly emerging mechanical sciences on the one hand, and by the deductive logic of School Philosophy on the other. The mechanical terminology he employed is misleading if it is taken as the measure of his philosophical system.

The really basic question for students of Hobbes is how he thought a philosophically competent mediation of the natural, the human, and the political was possible. Once again, we can learn something about Hobbes's intention to produce a philosophical system by returning to the analogy in
his *Introduction* to *Leviathan*. The analogy provides one with at least a
partial clue to the direction Hobbes's thought was to take. We have already
seen that the analogy does not say too much about nature per se, except
that God is both the matter and artificer of nature, that nature arises from
God's self-generating imitation of Himself. The imagery does not easily
lend itself to a mechanics.

As the *Introduction* proceeds, we are given several lists of attributes
that, presumably, explain the analogical relationship between God's art,
the world, man, and Leviathan. The lists include curious discrepancies that
are too obvious, too consistent with one another, and too suggestive, I believe, to have been merely accidental. They, too, have the effect of making
the analogy less amenable to a mechanical interpretation. A diagram of his
explanatory lists will give us something like this:

God's art	: World	::		Man	: Leviathan (nature)
?	springs	heart	[soul]		sovereignty
?	strings	nerves	joints		judiciary & executive
?	wheels	joints	nerves		reward & punishment

Hobbes's original anatomical list identifies man with his most important
organic parts—the heart, the nerves, and joints, in that order of priority.
The heart, we are told, is a spring. In *De Corpore*, Hobbes associates the
heart with the passions, that is, with appetite and aversion, and with the
generation of pleasure and pain (De Corp., ch. 25, art. 12). It helps to give
a clue to his intention. The priority of the heart on the list may suggest the
condition that prevails when the heart, human passion, orders all relationships. That is, it suggests the natural condition. The nerves and joints are
identified respectively with strings and wheels that give motion to the
body, but their impetus is received from the heart.

In his *second* anatomical list (shown above), which he uses to illustrate
the correlative characteristics of the commonwealth, changes have been introduced without comment. I doubt that they are inadvertent. The fundamental parts of the commonwealth—sovereignty, the magistrates and judiciary, and (in a departure from his preference for material components)
reward and punishment—are represented respectively by the soul, the
joints, and the nerves. What is worthy of notice is that Hobbes has re-

placed the heart in this second anatomical list with the soul at the same time that we have moved from man as a creature of the natural world to man as a citizen of the commonwealth. This indicates, I would suggest, a fundamental change in the locus of order from the individual to the sovereign, but what is more important, from desire to law, from rights to obligation. It suggests the elevation of reason over passion as the prerequisite of civil society, but it also suggests that reason and passion are not entirely exclusive faculties. Man transforms himself into a social being by creating Leviathan just as God transforms Himself into nature by creating the world.

Concomitant with this switch, and as if to draw attention to it, Hobbes inverts the order of priority of joints and nerves in the list. The reason for the inversion is apparent if we consider what these two anatomical entities represent respectively. The priority of nerves (reward and punishment) to joints (magistrates and judiciary) in the original list indicates the subordination of law to right or desire in the condition of nature. The unlimited pursuit of one's natural right, even to the point of self-destruction, is the law among pre-political man. The emergence of the commonwealth, however, depends on the priority of joints to nerves, or the subordination of rights to law, or unmediated reward and punishment to executive and judicial authority. The reversal serves to corroborate the intentional character of Hobbes's substitution of soul for heart in his second list.

What the analogy suggests is the self-transformation of desire and simultaneous generation of civil association. Civil reasonableness is the rational expansion of fear and desire, nothing more. The analogy directs our attention almost exclusively to the generation of civil association and the transformation of man into the reasonable animal. It seems almost to forget the natural condition out of which man has emerged, as if, with the generation of Leviathan, his emergence had been complete. However, the terms Hobbes uses to describe the strength and weakness of the state, namely, health, sickness, and death, brings us back to the fact civil society does not remove man completely from the natural condition. There are obstacles to human felicity that reasonableness and mere civil association cannot remove. Nature remains a not-altogether-benevolent complex of springs, strings, and wheels, which is not to say that nature is something mechanical, but that it is not purposively directed toward satisfying man's utmost needs. Man may master what is brutal in human nature by contracting with others to form civil society, and by doing so may give himself a measure of security. But if he is to guarantee his well-being, he will have to return his attention to nature, to anticipate the "unforeseen mischances" (Lev., ch. 44, p. 604) that await him, for example, sickness and death. Civil association alone will not rescue man from such maladies. If he is to be his own benefactor, the self-generated imitation of himself, he must make an assault on nature. He must make himself the master and possessor of nature per se. His mastery of nature will depend, of course, on the accessibility of nature to man's will, or, more specifically, on the identity of the Divine and the temporal, the identification of God with a scientifically predictable and manipulable nature. This is, in effect, what Hobbes has silently suggested in his subtle analogy, and what he has established as his philosophical intention.

THE CONCEPTUAL DEVELOPMENT OF HOBBES'S PHILOSOPHY

The preceding overview of Hobbes's systematic intentions admittedly teases a great deal from a very short *Introduction*, much of it in need of considerable support. Providing that support, as well as drawing out more fully the nature and implications of Hobbes's thought, will be the task of subsequent chapters. Something else remains to be done, however, before this synoptic introduction is complete.

Hobbes's philosophical system matured only gradually. Although the earliest of his works certainly contribute to the progress and development of his mature philosophical system, they should not be confused with the parts, or Elements, of that philosophical system. One will not successfully comprehend Hobbes's philosophy without some effort to comprehend its complex process of maturation. Heretofore, Hobbes's interpreters have not shown much interest in this matter. Leo Strauss is unusual in this regard. He traced the evolutionary development of Hobbes's political theory, but he ignored any correlative development in Hobbes's physics and, therefore, he ignored the systematic intention. This distorts the conclusions of what is otherwise a classic in the literature on Hobbes. In later writings, Strauss abandoned his original humanist interpretation of Hobbes and acknowledged the importance of his philosophy of nature for the rest of his philosophy. [13] He promised us a future work, to be written with Alexandre Kojéve, which may have corrected this defect; but, to my knowledge, no such work was ever written.

There is, in fact, a clearly discernible evolution in the axioms of Hobbes's civil philosophy, and that evolution has its concomitant in an evolution of the axioms of his natural philosophy. The concomitant evolution of his political theory and his natural philosophy is, I believe, the result of a gradually emerging conception of nature per se, one which takes its bearings in an evolving conception of human nature. As his thought matures, his conception of nature, man, and civil existence becomes progressively more dynamic and, in a certain qualified sense, dialectical.

More specifically, the theoretical principles of *Leviathan*, Hobbes's most mature account of his politics and philosophy of human nature, are significantly different from those of his earlier *Elements of Law* and *De Cive*. Likewise, Hobbes's *De Corpore* is fundamentally different from his earlier writings in natural philosophy such as his unpublished "Little Treatise." When one takes this process of development into consideration, what emerges is an altogether novel philosophical system, the elements of which are to be found in those writings that appear in or around 1650, the most important of which are *Leviathan* (1651) and *De Corpore* (1655). It is this system that the present study is concerned to uncover. It is a philosophical system that has been for the most part obscured by the very forcefulness of the earliest and most persuasive formulations of Hobbes's ideas. In anticipation of the more careful examination of this mature philosophical system in the following chapters, I will concentrate for the remainder of this chapter on a somewhat more elaborate overview of the conceptual development of Hobbes's philosophy; a brief examination of what is meant by saying that Hobbes's philosophy issues in a psychology and a politics that are dialectical; and an indication of what happens when Hobbes's philosophy is read in the light of this conceptual development. Stated most succinctly, his thought culminates in the identity of scientific and moral wisdom.

The Early Writings

Hobbes's earliest writings on political philosophy were the peculiar product of his rejection of ancient political theory. The Preface to his translation of Thucydides' *Peloponnesian War* (1929) praises Thucydides and, in the process, recalls a suggestion made by Machiavelli that one would do better to imitate the practices of the ancients than to imitate their theory. According to Hobbes, it is prudence that functions as the virtue of the man of wisdom, and prudence is experience, knowledge of history. Neither philosophy, nor science, nor moral axioms will provide man with what is needed to insure his virtue or moral perfection as it is judged by his fellow citizens.

The political realism of the Preface was reaffirmed eleven years later in *The Elements of Law,* a book which was circulated originally in 1640, but not published until 1650, and then in two parts, *Human Nature* and *De Corpore Politico.* In this work Hobbes compares life to a race, suggesting the unavoidably competitive and contentious character of human nature. But the contentiousness Hobbes observes is not yet given any foundation in a theory of nature per se. Men compete for honours and dominance over other men only for the sake of recognition. This holds true even for the battles waged among philosophers and scientists. Hobbes seems to give little thought to the possibility that the pursuit of subtle victories in the ongoing dialectic of philosophical master and slave reduces philosophy to fashionable sophistry.

The reason Hobbes's early political philosophy is entirely unrelated to his early natural philosophy is that natural philosophy does not accommodate itself easily to the image of life as a race. In *Leviathan,* published a decade after *The Elements of Law,* Hobbes will explain that natural philosophy is not perceived by very many men to be eminent. The reason for its lack of eminence is obvious. The greater part of mankind is not sufficiently educated to appreciate such heady stuff, and cannot acknowledge the accomplishments of those who have made advances in natural philosophy. The scientist's accomplishments will not win much for him in the race for honours. As we shall subsequently see, Hobbes's solution to this problem will involve his abandoning the image of life as a race.

The unrelated character of Hobbes's early philosophy of nature and his early political theory has its real origins in the fact that there are no provisions in the early natural philosophy to account for the competitive tenacity in man that his political philosophy makes central. Hobbes's natural philosophy had its first expression in his unpublished *Short Tract on First Principles,* sometimes referred to as *The Little Treatise* (1630–7). In it, Hobbes developed a not-too-sophisticated mechanistic materialism. The fundamental principle governing all change was traced to local motion. Hobbes put himself in the camp of modern physics by denying purposiveness and intention to nature.

There is, in short, a hiatus between Hobbes's early political realism and his early mechanistic philosophy of nature. The humanistic and mechanistic dimensions of his earliest thought cannot be brought together; and Hobbes really made no attempt at it. Ultimately, the elements of Hobbes's philosophy will be integrated with the aid of an account of *conatus.* He will give us an account of the dynamic individuation of motion, on the one hand, and an account of the dynamic individuation of passion on the other, in each case explained by an appeal to *conatus.* Both the philosophical elements—the political theory and the physics—will be significantly altered by the new account.

The Mature Writings

In the more mature writings (those appearing from around 1650), Hobbes reformulated his thought to reconcile the separate dimensions of his philosophy and generate a genuine philosophical system. The principle of reconciliation turned out to be Hobbes's gradually evolving concept of *conatus.* The concept has been something of a mystery to students of

Hobbes's thought. It first appeared in *The Elements of Law*, not as a synonym for appetite, as is sometimes said, but, rather, as a concept for "solicitation," that is, for an intentionality that is in itself indeterminate, that never manifests itself except as attraction or repulsion. It is visible only as appetite, aversion, fear, pleasure, or love, and always as appetite for, aversion to, or fear of something (Ele. of Law, ch. 7, par. 2, p. 31). Years later, in *Leviathan*, the concept was extended to include an account of both perception and thought, with the result that the passivity of rational calculation and perception characteristic of mechanistic accounts of human nature gave way to a more dynamic conception of reason and participation. The concept served to mediate the opposition of reason and desire that Hobbes took to be a limiting characteristic of ancient moral philosophy. *Conatus*, or endeavour, became the very nature of reason and sense, no less than it is the nature of appetite and desire.

The maturation of Hobbes's natural philosophy came about with the further extension of the *conatus* concept, which was originally a concept in his psychology. He broadened the concept by identifying what was essential to the *conatus* conception in ideas already contained in his early physics, and by reformulating them to establish an identity of motion, perception, thought, and the passions. At the most fundamental level they are not separate and distinct faculties but functions of the same *conatus*.

It is well known that Hobbes's mature account of nature adamantly insists that there is nothing other than body. There is, however, some confusion as to what he meant. This much is certain, that the idea of an indeterminate reality, that is, an infinite being or a disembodied universal, was to Hobbes sheer nonsense. It is nowhere and, consequently, it is nothing. From this materialist identification of reality with body, Hobbes proceeded to dissolve body into motion, and then to identify all motion with *conatus*. Here is where confusion begins to occur for students of Hobbes. *Conatus* is not for Hobbes some primitive substance or metaphysical force. It is simply the reciprocally determinate relationship of two entities whose identities are established by that reciprocal determinacy. If one ignores this reduction of motion to *conatus*, what Hobbes writes will look very much like a mechanistic materialism that cannot be reconciled with either his psychology or his political philosophy. If one fails to appreciate the centrality of the *conatus* concept, or the peculiarity of Hobbes's treatment of it, one will not be able to understand how Hobbes could have thought he had produced an integrated system of philosophy. One will not perceive the dynamical character of Hobbesian physics and the dialectic that it produces at the level of psychology and politics.

It is necessary to explain what is meant here by saying that Hobbes's philosophy is dialectical, especially since the orthodox view would have it that a more undialectical philosopher has never writ! The term "dialectical" is notorious for its ambiguity, and it probably confuses more often than it clarifies. By dialectical, in the context of Hobbes's philosophy, I do not mean a method of philosophical disputation which, because of its ability to refine opinions and ideas by challenging and counterchallenging them, gradually discloses ideas that are more true, or more representative of reality. Rather, the term is used here to refer to the negatively determinate interdependence of all reality, where reality is a self-individuating process, the product of its own internal oppositions and contradictions. In a dialectical theory of reality, nothing exists that is independent of, or indifferent to, this process, or therefore to any other determinate being. A dialectical theory is, then, an explicit repudiation of the inert, or passive, existence of beings or forces as they are represented in a mechanistic materialism; or the externality and neutrality of concepts as they are found in modern mathematical physics. In psychology it would involve a rejection of radical individualism, that is, of man as the "existential atom" who can be understood in isolation from others, but without necessarily doing away with the ego and opposition of interests. In political philosophy it would imply a rejection of the concept of inalienable rights, at least in the rigid or dogmatic sense that rights are *a priori* and inert, stubbornly but passively persistent in an otherwise morally indifferent external world. This is not to say, however, that a more dynamic conception of right does not have a vital role to play in Hobbes's philosophy.

THE UNITY OF SCIENTIFIC AND MORAL WISDOM

Perhaps the most interesting result of the interpretation of Hobbes's philosophy given here is that his political theory loses its place as the culminating Element of his philosophical system. This is not to say that his political theory is not important; for it is true that Hobbes's political philosophy is his highest accomplishment. But it is not the theoretical completion of his philosophical system.

If one thinks through Hobbes's philosophical treatment of political association and does not too quickly superimpose the prudential remarks found in his early writings on his mature thought, the necessity of this conclusion will be evident. Man, for Hobbes, is pre-eminently a natural being. He is a social being only in a secondary sense. His needs exist prior to (they are not generated by) his civil or social sense. They are an extension of his natural *conatus*, and are found, Hobbes says, "even in the embryo" (De Corp., ch. 25, art. 12). Hobbes reduces man's fetal needs to two: the irresistible desire for self-preservation, that is, unending life, and the desire for an unlimited augmentation of his well-being, that is, felicity.

Because man's twin needs are natural and, therefore, in a certain sense unlimited, their complete satisfaction cannot be obtained through the finite benefits gained by living in a peaceful society. Neither market commodities nor mere peace are sufficient for providing man with the entirely good life.

The problem man faces is that the fetal impulse which characterizes human need inevitably—even dialectically—betrays itself, harming itself by the very act by which it pursues its benefit. The acquisition of wealth, political power, and glory, though they are the means to the good life, are the inevitable contributing causes of man's downfall. Wealth incites the envy of others; political power creates suspicion; glory produces resentment. Whatever the situation, the ultimate result is latent warfare.

Nevertheless, the act of contracting with others, which is responsible for man's ability to accumulate wealth and acquire power and glory, has an important contributing function in his emancipation. By virtue of his act of contracting with others, man alienates himself from nature and partly liberates himself from its indifference to his welfare. Of course, man's decision to leave the state of nature is itself a *natural*, not a civil, decision. Nature, one might say, is self-transforming; man, as a mode of nature, transforms nature and in so doing transforms himself. Or, in the light of the analogy in Hobbes's *Introduction* to *Leviathan*, humanity emerges in opposition to its origins, the creative fiat being at once the act by which man is *made* and is *cast out* of nature. He is brought into being by his own self-generating principle of conservation.

Civil society is, then, nature rendered reasonable. Civil man is the prudentially reasonable expression of natural man. He is the man who has found a reasonable means to express (if not to satisfy thoroughly) the passions that he self-destructively exhibits in the natural condition. He ceases to be self-destructive.

However, man's alienation from nature is also, paradoxically, an alienation of his right to seek the unqualified acquisition of his own good, that is, the complete satisfaction of his fetal desire for preservation and, especially, the augmentation of his well-being. He must restrict his desire, refrain from claiming a right to the property and power of others. Even so, while human well-being is augmented by the act of contracting, it is not thereby guaranteed. Political existence, however convenient it may be, does not fully satisfy the irresistible urge man has to provide for his future preservation and welfare. It cannot guarantee him against disease and other natural calamities.

The present study will show how, in Hobbes's mature writings, the good life, felicity, emerges only when men learn "to imitate the creation" (De Corp., Epist. Ded., p. xiii). Although man's abandonment of the natural condition accounts for his liberation from the tyranny of nature, the good life is achieved only when man returns his attention to nature and endeavours to reshape it according to the image of his own will, thereby making himself the measure, and so the master, of all things. Understanding Hobbes's liberation of man from the natural condition requires that we first return to his physics.

The limitation of the efforts of man, implicit in Hobbes's theory, is that, in his effort to master nature, man alters his own nature as well, and as a result is left in a perpetual state of disharmony with nature. When man restructures nature, he restructures his problems, but does not necessarily resolve them. Hobbes's solution to this fundamental and seemingly irresolvable opposition of man and nature is not presented straightforwardly. Obliquely, he shows that only a magnanimous and philosophical few, inspired by "great designs," and in pursuit of "the great and master delight," can obtain the freedom and felicity that constitute the good life.

Ultimately, the dialectic of the human *conatus* culminates in the identification of the man of moral wisdom with the man of scientific wisdom. The just man is he who obeys the laws without having to experience the judicial threats of sovereign power. He obeys the laws, however, not merely to preserve life, and certainly not because he is a paradigm of selflessness and altruism, but, rather, because it makes possible his "continual and indefatigable generation of knowledge" (Lev., ch. 6, p. 45). In the indefatigability of his assault upon his natural origins, the philosopher recreates nature by restructuring it in the image of his own nature. He makes himself its master and possessor.

The implication of this transformation of the philosophical enterprise, as Hobbes presents it, is that philosophical wisdom can no longer be understood as a product of the liberation of reason from the encumbrances of the passions. Rather, it is the extension of a dynamic within nature itself, understood as *conatus*. Philosophy, for Hobbes, is a pre-eminently natural undertaking. At least it is for the mature Hobbes. By picturing the desire for wisdom as a natural desire and, so, as a movement within nature to complete its innate tendencies, Hobbes's own philosophy takes on certain aspects anticipatory of nineteenth-century philosophies of history. In the words of Leo Strauss, "Hobbes... opens up the way to Hegel."[14]

2

Hobbes's
Philosophy of
Nature

In his very fine study of Hobbes's natural philosophy, Frithiof Brandt remarked that Hobbes "wrote mechanics like a philosopher."[1] The comment was not intended as a compliment. It was meant to suggest that Hobbes's physics fell outside the mainstream of modern mechanics due largely to his failure to purge it of antiquated concepts carried over from School metaphysics and, more specifically, his failure to comprehend and appreciate the significance of the doctrine of inertia, the foundation of the new mathematical physics. Brandt's remark reflects the general consensus of scholars that Hobbes's physics is unremarkable and not due special attention as a contribution to the history of modern science. The criticism is not without merit. It calls to mind the backhand compliment paid Hobbes by his contemporary and antagonist, René Descartes, who said that Hobbes's "ability in morals was far greater than in metaphysics and physics."[2]

Whether or not Hobbes's physics is notable in itself, Hobbes believed it was an integral part of his philosophical system, that somehow his psychology and his political and moral theory were all united with it. Since what Hobbes thought he had done ought to play a part in one's interpretation of what he did, in fact, do, any study of his psychology and political theory ought not omit a careful consideration of his physics.

The criticism of Hobbes's natural philosophy is especially interesting insofar as it is a presentiment of the orthodox approach to his philosophy as a whole, the principal problem of which is the integration of the various elements of his system. It is almost never disputed that Hobbes's natural philosophy is thoroughly mechanistic. The need for integrating the elements of his system makes it difficult to resist the implications that mechanism would seem to have for a theory of human nature and political philosophy as well. More commonly, it is argued that Hobbes intended to extend the principles of mechanics to the study of human nature and political association. Richard Peter's observation sums up the consensus of opinion. He maintains that, "Hobbes ruthlessly... pushed the mechanical model into the innermost sanctuaries of human intimacy, endeavour and decision."[3]

The principal difficulty with this approach to Hobbes's philosophy is that some of the undeniably major ingredients in his psychology and politics resist a rigidly mechanical interpretation. It is hard to see how subjectivity, egoism and a doctrine of rights—all major components of his philosophical system—can enter into the mechanical theory consistently. Subjectivity is not a mechanical phenomenon. And machines cannot coherently be thought of as having either desires or rights.

Difficulties such as these have not escaped Hobbes's interpreters. The emotive and moral elements are dealt with most often, the difficulties resolved, by not taking seriously those components that are incompatible with a mechanical interpretation in one of two ways. Either they are taken to be the *real* origins of his psychology and political philosophy, in which case Hobbes's mechanics turns out to be an unfortunate preoccupation of little interest to us, or they are taken to be a *lapsus calami*, an inadvertent slip into normative or emotive terminology, perhaps through the use of terms that are vague and equivocal, such as the word "endeavour" which would be inconsistent with his main mechanistic line of thought. Because mechanism, when applied to the study of man, gives us no way to speak meaningfully about "qualitative" differences between men, the mechanistic interpretation of Hobbes's philosophy tends to draw those who hold it to Hobbes's theory of natural equality as the axiom of his system. Once we have accepted the premise that all men are by nature equal, the principles of bourgeois morality seem to follow with facility. Hobbes begins to look like the author of a moral-democratic doctrine.[4]

The fact is, Hobbes's writings lend themselves to all sorts of interpretations. The implications of his mechanics, when juxtaposed with other nonmechanical ideas in his thought, have made his writings a virtual cornucopia for innovative analyses.

To be sure, Hobbes sought to give an entirely coherent account of the world as a material continuum in such a way as theoretically to make possible a universal science. He is, without doubt, a thoroughgoing materialist whose terminology is for the most part that of the mechanistic sciences of his day. But while Hobbes involved himself in the seventeenth-century controversy in physics, he nevertheless employed concepts which placed him outside the main developments in mechanics. Most notable here is

Hobbes's concept of *conatus*. His mature natural philosophy is not a simple mechanics. Failure to see this is the principal source of the supposed fragmentation of Hobbes's philosophical system into so many unrelated parts.

This is not to say that Hobbes's system is a success. The parts of his system are held together by a common concept, *conatus*. The unity of the *conatus* concept is itself a problem. The *conatus* that grounds Hobbes's physics is only debatably the same as the *conatus* governing his psychology and his political philosophy. In his attempt to give us a System of Elements, all grounded on a single, homogeneous *conatus* concept, Hobbes actually arrived at an idea of the unity of scientific and moral wisdom. The pursuit of morality is ultimately inseparable from the pursuit of science, and vice versa. One might call science and political or moral wisdom different modes of the same Hobbesian undertaking.

BODIES

There has been a persistent tendency among Hobbes's readers to perceive him as a materialist in the tradition of Epicurean atomism. Indeed, a renaissance in Epicurean atomism was a lively part of seventeenth-century science. There are problems when one locates Hobbes too comfortably in that tradition. On a first reading, Hobbes does, indeed, sound conspicuously like an atomist. He states that "everything that is, is body," and develops the thought by stating, "The *subject* of Philosophy, or the matter it treats of, is every body of which we can conceive any generation and which we may, by any consideration thereof, compare with other bodies, or which is capable of composition and resolution; that is to say, every body of whose generation or properties we can have any knowledge" (De Corp., ch. 1, art. 8, p. 10).

When this description of the subject-matter of philosophy is taken together with Hobbes's definition of body, as, "that, which having no dependence upon our thought, is coincident or coextended with some part of space" (De Corp., ch. 8, art. 1, p. 102), we have the makings of an easily understood materialistic metaphysics that is thoroughly mechanical. Hobbes lends more weight to this interpretation when he occasionally speaks of atoms as the constituent matter of the universe. "The whole of space between heaven and earth," he says, "is filled with small atoms" (De Corp., ch. 26, art. 5, p. 426). Understandably some have maintained that "Hobbes's materialism... is essentially that of historical atomism as formulated in its main features by the Democriteans."[5]

Nonetheless, this interpretation of Hobbes's natural philosophy will not withstand a careful analysis. Hobbes's physics has no provision for objects whose existence is independent of (or external to) other objects. His physics is thoroughly dynamical. There are also reasons of historical perspective for rejecting the atomistic interpretation of Hobbes. The seventeenth-century renaissance of Epicureanism with which Hobbes is often associated, was not, itself, a recrudescence of premodern atomism. Seventeenth-century physics tended to abstract from the metaphysical issues of the ancients and their commitment to the existence of absolutely solid bodies which, somehow, can be known. The "points" or "particles" of seventeenth-century mathematical physics were more the conceptual prerequisites of modern physics than its metaphysical foundations. While "points" may have been referred to as the parts of which visible bodies are composed, there was little effort made to argue that they are the metaphysical ultimates of nature. Rather, they are the postulates necessary for establishing the locus of motion.[6] In *De Corpore*, for example, Hobbes identified the distance between the earth and the Sun as a mere point when compared with the distance of the fixed stars to the earth (De Corp., ch. 17, art. 1, pp. 446–7). Likewise with the objects about us. Hobbes says, "There is no impossible smallness of bodies" (De Corp., ch. 27, art. 1, p. 446; ch. 7, art. 13, p. 100).[7] There is, rather, an infinite divisibility of magnitude.

This disclaimer would not be necessary were it not for the fact that the more naive interpretation of Hobbes's physics serves rather often as a filter through which Hobbes's philosophy is read. Few have appreciated sufficiently the nature of the development that Hobbes's natural philosophy underwent from 1630 to 1655. The concept of nature that formed the basis of his earliest and most mechanical writings gradually transformed itself into the inherently dynamic concept of *conatus*. That concept serves as the mediating force of his philosophical system.

The intention of the present chapter is to examine the development of Hobbes's concept of nature in his writings and its function in his mature natural philosophy. To that purpose, we will begin with a short digression, or preparatory overview of the revolutionary transformation from Aristotelian physics to the mathematical physics of the seventeenth century. That revolutionary transformation was the historical backdrop to Hobbes's philosophical efforts, whether he was an integral part of the revolutionary development of mathematical physics or not.

DIGRESSION: THE HISTORICAL BACKDROP

Issues in seventeenth-century physics cannot effectively be understood without connecting them with Aristotelian physics, either affirmatively as with School philosophy, or negatively, as with the main lines of development in mathematical physics. By Hobbes's time, the principles of Aristotelian physics had been repudiated by those at the forefront of the significant developments in physics. However, the principles that would govern a newer, more enlightened physics had not yet effectively been exposed. Time and again in the long search for the first principles of a new physics, Aristotelian principles were to creep back into the theories of his modern repudiators. It turned out to be easier to refute Aristotle than to liberate physics from his authority.

According to Aristotle, all change in the natural world is governed by the interaction of two sets of contraries: (hot:cold) and (dry:moist). The contraries serve as the determining limits of the primary elements that compose the world: fire (hot and dry), air (hot and moist), water (cold and moist) and earth (cold and dry.)[8] The contraries themselves are subject to change. Hot can become cold, dry can become moist, and so on. When such changes occur, one primary element is transformed into another, different element. Water (cold, moist), for example, is transformed into air (hot, moist) by the simple expedient of heating it.

The characteristics of the primary elements are such as to organize them into a natural, cosmic order. Unlike the primary bodies of Greek atomism, every Aristotelian element has its natural place where it would be were the world perfectly ordered.[9] In the natural order of things, the heaviest of elements (earth) belongs at the center of the world, and the lighter elements (water, air, and fire in that order) form successively higher layers. The natural order is in itself altogether fixed, static, and final. But because of the transformation of elements (via the transformation of contraries) it has not been sustained. Any element that finds itself out of its natural place because of its transformation will tend to return to its proper place with an unrelenting obstinacy. Such motion is referred to by Aristotle as natural motion,[10] and is visible in the phenomenon of "weight."[11] All movements contrary to the natural motions of the elements Aristotle referred to as "compulsory movement,"[12] or an unnatural or violent movement,[13] such as when earth is heaved up into the air.

Motion is process. What is cold is always potentially hot, and what is moist is potentially dry. Consequently, water (cold, moist) is always potentially air (hot, moist) and earth (cold, dry). As such, it is also potentially light (as air would be) and potentially heavy (as earth would be).[14] The terms "potentially" and "actuality" are used in two different ways here. When natural elements and the compounds of those elements either rise or descend seeking their natural places, or realizing their natural activity, this is locomotion. On the other hand, when, through the reciprocal conversion of contraries one element is transformed into another, for example, when water is transformed into air as it is heated, making the potentially hot actually hot, we have alteration. Alteration, of course, promotes locomotion.

Aristotle maintains that no motion is ever instantaneous. "Everything that is in motion must be moved by something. For if it has not the source of its motion in itself it is evident that it is moved by something other than itself."[15] The cause of the natural motion of an element is in itself, that is, its weight, and it seeks its natural place. However, when things are moved violently, contrary to their natural motions, the cause must be from something else that is in contact with that thing.[16] Violent, unnatural motion presupposes that a natural motion has been interrupted! Once the cause of movement has broken its contact with the body that it has moved contra-naturally, the moved body resumes its original natural motion.

The natural continuum is kept in constant motion because of the alteration of elements, that is, the transformation of one element into another through the conversion of contraries (e.g., hot to cold) and consequent transformation of weight (e.g., light to heavy). This alteration of elements occurs because of the influence of the motion of celestial bodies, for example, the sun as it alternately approaches the earth and recedes, thus causing an alteration of the seasons, the heating (and evaporation) of water, etc.[17] Consequently, for Aristotelian physics, motion becomes "the characteristic fact of nature. . . . "[18] Any investigation into nature, therefore, will be an investigation of movement.

For centuries, Aristotle's physics served as the authoritative natural philosophy. Its status did not begin to change until scholarly opinion fixed its attention on two phenomena conspicuous for their irreconcilability with Aristotle's physics: projectile motion and the acceleration of freely falling bodies. Projectile motion was a perplexing phenomenon to one who accepted Aristotle's claim that violent or non-natural motion requires the immediate presence of a body that is capable of interrupting natural motion. If that is so, how can one account for the fact that a batted ball, once it leaves the bat (and, hence, loses contact with the cause of its violent motion) does not immediately resume its natural motion, that is, fall straight downward? What causes the projectile to maintain its contra-natural motion?

Aristotle was not unaware of the phenomenon or the problem;[19] neither did he lack a solution. He suggested that the original cause of contra-natural motion transfers to the air or water through which a projectile moves the power to move it or to continue moving it. The air through which the ball is batted fills in behind and pushes the ball forward. But, Aristotle also knew that the medium (e.g., the air) impedes the movement of things as well.[20] The medium must both cause and impede the motion of the projectile. This confusion of causes led scholarly opinion to look with growing doubt on Aristotle's claim that the cause of motion must be in constant contact with the things moved. Projectile motion remained a problem.

The acceleration of freely falling bodies, the second of the two phenomena that scholarly attention focused upon, also caused scepticism. Why would a freely falling body gather speed as it falls? What would account for the increase in its speed? Aristotle knew that a natural element, for example, earth, "moves more quickly the nearer it is to" its natural place.[21] But, why? Its natural cause (weight) would not logically be capable of explaining both the velocity of the original fall *and* its acceleration. The problem of attributing contrary effects to one cause emerged again.

By the fourteenth century a solution to Aristotle's twin problem was found in what was called *impetus physics.* It was suggested by John Buridan and others that there must be a motive force (impetus) that is transferred from the mover to the moved object when they come into contact. The motion of the moving body could then be explained by this immanent force being transferred from the first body to the second. The explanation had the effect of removing the cause of a projectile's motion from the medium and returning it to the original body from which it received its motion.

Though impetus physics was suggestive enough to have been accepted early on by Galileo, it had clear limitations. It was more a metaphysics than a physics, and it never offered an account of impetus itself—what it is, or why it can do what it does. It contributed little to solving the problem of acceleration of freely falling bodies other than to equivocate suggestively between impetus as mere motion and impetus as impulse, impatience.

Perhaps the most significant contribution to the development of physics in the fourteenth century was provided by the nominalist critique of abstract forces. William of Ockham "denied the existence of motion as an entity separate from the moving body, indicating rather that motion was a term standing for a series of statements that the moving body is now here, now here, etc."[22] Ockham, in other words, abandoned Aristotelian dynamics for an account of motion that would require only extension, only the succession of places through which a moved body would pass. This purely kinematic explanation of motion does not concern itself with the time required for traversing a given distance. Motion becomes a series of displacements. The old Aristotelian problem of accounting for projectile motion was consequently transformed into the new problem of accounting for the velocity of a projectile at a given instant, that is, the intensive or instantaneous velocity of an object. Some scholars argued that "instantaneous motion is neither swift nor slow, because swift or slow are defined in time,"[23] which kinematic theory does not consider. Consequently it cannot be. This problem was solved by adopting the terminology of hypotheticals. The velocity at a given instant would be determined by the space a body *would* traverse in a given amount of time *if* it maintained the same velocity throughout that time. Unfortunately, this explanation presumes the thing it purports to explain, the velocity.

The idea that originated with Ockham in the fourteenth century did not really bear fruit until the seventeenth, and then only with substantial change. The dramatic change in physics occurred when Galileo, a representative of impetus theory early in his career, turned to a purely mathematical approach to physical phenomena, an approach suggested originally by Ockham's nominalist account of motion. The purely mathematical approach to motion led, eventually, to the famous doctrine of inertia, first stated explicitly not by Galileo, but by René Descartes. In 1644, in his *Principles of Philosophy*, Descartes maintained as his first law of nature "that each thing as far as in it lies, continues always in the same state; and that which is once moved always continues so to move."[24] Motion was conceived by Descartes as the state of a moving body, a state from which it will not deviate unless acted upon by some other body. Descartes, in effect, took motion to be a regular pattern of displacements, "the action by which any body passes from one place to another."[25] Following Galileo's lead, Descartes speculated that all nature could be made accessible through mathematical science. He wrote, "I do not accept or desire any other principle in Physics than in Geometry or abstract Mathematics, because all the phenomena of nature may be explained by their means, and sure demonstrations can be given of them."[26]

Accounting for the acceleration of freely falling bodies was a more difficult problem for the new mathematical physics than the problem of projectile motion. The most popular solution of the time was offered by the physicist, Dr. William Gilbert. Gilbert claimed that the earth is a magnet, that bodies fall because of terrestrial attraction.[27] His suggestion was made more persuasive, I suspect, because of the scholarly fascination at the time with the inexplicable properties of magnets. The properties of magnets were inexplicable especially because the notion of attraction could not easily be accommodated to the purely kinematic theories of Galileo, Descartes, and others who had accepted the principles of mathematical physics. Descartes certainly did admire the reasonableness of the explanation such a theory would provide for acceleration in falling bodies. The velocity attained by a falling body is maintained by the body; the magnetic attraction of the earth at every subsequent instant adds to the initial velocity of the falling body. Velocity accumulates. The problem of explaining the acceleration of freely falling bodies was thereby solved, but not in such a way that it contributed to the progress of purely kinetic physics.

Because all motion is locomotion, and since locomotion is nothing more than the action by which a body moves from one place to another, all changes in the velocity of a body must come from another body external to the moved body. Because all change is accounted for as a result of external relationships, Cartesian physics would not admit the influence of mystical or metaphysical forces such as "impetus" or "magnetical virtue." Bodies must be conceived as indifferent to their conditions, indifferent to whether they are in motion or at rest. Bodies are inert. They initiate no change and are not changed by change. The rigorously mathematical Cartesian physics is, then, correctly referred to as a kinematics; it cannot, strictly speaking, be called a dynamics.[28]

The preceding account is, admittedly, a sketchy overview of developments in physics. Only those things have been pointed out that are, in one way or another, helpful to our locating Hobbes's natural philosophy. There may be figures in the history of philosophical science that can stand alone, that can be read without an elaborate historical introduction. Hobbes is not one of them. To make an investigation of Hobbes's physics, one must first be aware of the fact that it is generally assumed that Hobbes adopted the Galilean-Cartesian doctrine of inertia, and that his physics falls squarely in the tradition of seventeenth-century mathematical physics. This assumption is mistaken.

HOBBES'S NATURAL PHILOSOPHY

Hobbes certainly did participate in the controversy in physics that took place in the seventeenth century. He was also obviously a man who desired and enjoyed the recognition of other well-known scholars and men of position, and that must have inspired his desire to enter the philosophical controversy. His earliest writings in natural philosophy coincide with his trip to the continent from 1634 to 1637. His travels were taken as the tutor to the son of William Cavendish. His patron, the second Earl of Devonshire, had, himself, been Hobbes's pupil from 1610 to 1628. Hobbes's visit to the continent, his third, was a formative influence on him, first, because it brought him into personal acquaintance with Galileo in Italy and, second (and perhaps more important), because it brought him into the company of the circle of scholars in France that had been drawn together by Marin Mersenne. It was in the company of those same people that Hobbes began to compose his later, more mature physics, *De Corpore*, during his eleven-year absence from England during the Civil War.

One must resist concluding from the fact that Hobbes belonged to a circle that included René Descartes that he was simply one of the minor representatives of seventeenth-century mathematical physics. Mersenne's circle was not all that philosophically homogeneous. Connecting Hobbes too closely to Descartes tends to conceal those elements of his natural philosophy that kept him outside the main current of developments in physics at the time and that served as the basis of what he thought would be a unification of all the elements of his philosophy. It is not accidental that Descartes did not write political theory; for it is hard to reconcile political theory with a rigorous mathematical physics. Hobbes, on the other hand, did write a physics, and, unlike Descartes, he claimed it as the foundation of a political theory.

The Early Natural Philosophy

The earliest of Hobbes's writings on natural philosophy, an unpublished *Short Tract on First Principles*, often referred to as *The Little Treatise*, is believed to have been written between 1630 and 1637, when Hobbes was already over forty years old. It was about this time that Hobbes, in 1636, visited Galileo in Italy and most likely came away influenced. *The Little Treatise* was the focal point of one major controversy over the proper interpretation of Hobbes's philosophical intentions. The work was ignored by Leo Strauss in his "humanist" interpretation of Hobbes. Strauss's claim that the work is "of no great interest"[29] was vigorously disputed later by Michael Oakeshott and J.W.N. Watkins. Watkins argued that *The Little Treatise* represents "a condensed, preliminary statement of Hobbes's cosmology, psychology and ethics." He added that, "With one exception its ideas survived, essentially unaltered, into his later philosophical and political writings."[30]

Watkins, I believe, is correct in seeing in this early writing an indication of Hobbes's synoptic interest and intent. His claim that its ideas go essentially unaltered in Hobbes's later writings, however, is something of an overstatement. *The Little Treatise* is an early attempt at developing a theory which avoids appeal to immaterial intelligibles, to the "separated essences" of School metaphysics, which are supposed to structure the world without being in it because they are universal. It was also intended as a repudiation of Aristotelian physics. The intended audience of *The Little Treatise* is School metaphysicians. Hobbes has not yet taken up the battle with mathematical physicists of his own time, and his writings at this time reflect that fact.

Hobbes's rejection of separated essences never lost its prominence in his writings. The separated essences of School doctrines, he said, were the products of little more than "inconstant signification" (Lev., ch. 4, pp. 28,

20), or a misuse of language. In *Leviathan*, in 1651, Hobbes stated that man, unlike other creatures, enjoys the "privilege of absurdity" (Lev., ch. 5, p. 33), a privilege which "has the quality not only to hide the truth but also to make men think they have it and desist from further search" (Lev., ch. 46, p. 686). Hobbes thought that School metaphysicians had exercised the privilege with speculative abandon in their insistence upon these Aristotelian essences.

In opposition to School doctrines, *The Little Treatise* locates the fundamental principle governing all change and all order in local motion. "Nothing can move itself."[31] All motion results from the immediate influence of an agent acting on (touching) a patient. "That which now resteth, cannot be moved, unless it be touched by some Agent."[32] Oddly enough, this view does not seem to Hobbes to preclude the possibility of a "power inherent"[33] in the agent by which a patient is acted on at a distance. An agent, through its active power inherent, can act upon (touch) a patient causing it to move without having moved itself. Its action at a distance is not purposive, Hobbes says, and it will act on all patients equally. The active power inherent takes the form of a corporeal emanation of species, tiny particles of the agent that are corporeal yet manifest and convey all the properties of the agent, which, Hobbes says, "are moved locally,"[34] which effect by touch, and which emanate from their agents continually and "in infinitum." This power inherent to influence at distance is associated with the effect of the sun, moon and stars, but is also evident from "the Experience of Magneticall virtue."[35] Hobbes briefly considers the possibility of a mediumistic doctrine of influence at a distance (which he will later adopt), but makes nothing of it. Bodies must somehow touch to affect one another.

"Corporeal species" (species emitted by an agent, that move locally, that affect by touch, i.e. impact, and that cause only local motion in the patient as their effect) exhibit characteristics of attraction and repulsion toward one another, or "conveniency and disconveniency."[36] Hobbes adopts the idea of attraction and repulsion at this time only to explain the phenomena of magnetism and the transfer of vibrational energy from one string of a musical instrument to that of another. The idea suggests that Hobbes had been influenced by impetus physics, perhaps by Galileo who was at this time a spokesman for impetus physics. It is also likely that Hobbes's idea of "the power inherent" was influenced by the general interest in the properties of magnetism. It is hard to construct an image of a world governed by such forces. Bodies would collide with other bodies, with the effect of attracting them rather than propelling them away. Striking would be a form of pulling.

In the final section of *The Little Treatise*, Hobbes extends his principles of mechanics to animate behaviour, that is, animal spirits and phantasma. Here the most obvious difficulties of his early mechanics become evident. Only motion is imparted to the patient, but something more than motion (phantasma, images) occurs. The species that emanate from agents contribute nothing but motion to the patients which they act upon. When motions are imparted by species to animal spirits, we have what Hobbes calls the "object of sense,"[37] that is, colour, light, heat, and so on. When the motion that has been imparted to the animal spirit is mediated by the brain, as in dreams and remembering, where the object sensed is absent, Hobbes calls the motion a "phantasma."

Hobbes does not appear to wonder about this qualitative effect of motion and the causal leap it requires. We are told that all animated behaviour (sense perception, understanding, and appetite) is the *passive* result of the actions of corporeal species emanating from agents which, by emanating species every which way, impart their motions to the animate body. Appetite is described as a passive motion of the animal spirits *toward* the object by which they are moved. It appears that the inherent power of attraction and repulsion belongs to more than heavenly bodies and magnets. Appetite and will are considered accidents of motion, not faculties. Neither appetite nor will can initiate motion. Their passive motion is described by Hobbes as the patient's desire for the agent as Good. This means the inherent power to move man to desire can be found in anything that can be desired, feared, loved, hated. Without his making an issue of it in *The Little Treatise*, the inherent power becomes the most pervasive power in the universe. It is this inherent power, and the objects in which it resides (everything and anything), that cause men to act.

By the time of *Tractatus Opticus* (1644) and the *English Optical Treatise* (1646) Hobbes had begun to redefine his theory of motion, abandoning *The Little Treatise*'s doctrine of the emanation of corporeal species for a contraction/dilation theory of motion.[38] By virtue of its alternating contraction and dilation, he argued, the sun presses upon the air, or the medium, around it, and that pressure is conveyed all the way to the eye of man where, because of the pressure it places on the retina, vision occurs. In a letter from Hobbes to Sir Charles Cavendish, dated 8 February 1641, Hobbes admitted some confusion about contraction and dilation. He said, "For the cause of such reciprocation, it is hard to guess what it is. It may well be the reaction of the medium. For though the mediu yeld [sic], yet it resisteth to: for there can be no passion without reaction."[39] Hobbes caught himself up in some circular reasoning here. The motions of the medium are explained by the contraction and dilation of the sun; the motions of the sun are explained, in their turn by the motions (the reaction) of the medium! One might liken it to the pressure produced by pushing an overturned cup down beneath a body of water. The water below both pushes upon the air inside the cup and is pushed by it. Whether Hobbes's explanation makes sense or not, the fact is he has introduced an idea of reciprocal determination or reciprocal causation which substitutes for the properties of attraction and repulsion belonging to the "power inherent" in his *Little Treatise*. His explanation of contraction and dilation duplicates his explanation of the "power inherent" that is apparent in "magneticall virtue." Hobbes professed ignorance about that also,[40] but once again believed it would be found to be caused by reciprocal motions within the lodestone interacting with the medium around it.

The companions to Hobbes's new theory of contraction and dilation were the concept of a medium or "spiritus internus" (rejected in *The Little Treatise*) by which motions might be transmitted and through which one body might affect another instantaneously at a distance, and a subjectivity of species (not merely the subjectivity of sense qualities) that makes real qualitative differences between objects entirely subjective. This idea will be impossible to reconcile with a mechanical theory that depends on the externality of objects, that is, on their objective differences. These two concepts generated a controversy between Hobbes and René Descartes. Both claimed authorship.[41] As a result of the controversy, and from that time onward, Hobbes and Descartes held less than amicable thoughts of one another.

Hobbes's doctrine of the subjectivity of species raises a problem that is perplexing: How can one combine such a doctrine with a theory that assumes the objectivity of objects? That is, how can an object exist independently of perception when the principle of its individuation, its very species, the cause of its being something in particular, is subjective and perceptual? The most common opinion of Hobbes's critics is that he does maintain the subjectivity of species from this time on, along with the objectivity of objects, that he assumed things exist independently of our perception of them and that, oddly enough, "he does not seem to have been at all troubled about" the problem it raises.[42]

If Hobbes is not troubled about the problem of objects existing independently of sense experience, when their principle of individuation is subjective, I suspect it was not because he was oblivious to it, but rather because it was not a problem affecting his physics. The problem is put behind him, at least to Hobbes's mind, by his abandoning the externality (or indifference) of objects—an idea associated with primitive materialism—for an idea of reciprocal determinacy. In his *English Optics*, Hobbes argued for the metaphysical priority of motion to bodies. "There is," he says, "no body independent of motion. There is in all bodies that have any consistency so as to not be fluid and subtle in the highest degree, a certain internal motion or agitation of parts by which that body differs specifically from bodies of another kind."[43]

Hobbes is altogether clear in expressing his view that motion is the principle of individuation for body. The idea of the simple self-identity of an independently existing body in absolute space has no role whatsoever in his mature physics. Unfortunately, that is the paradigm most often used for understanding his physics.

Some light can be shed on Hobbes's idea if we look at it from the perspective of his dispute with Descartes regarding optics. In explaining the transmission of light from luminous bodies, Descartes supposed the existence of a transparent medium which fills the interstices of the world. According to Descartes, light is not transmitted by something material moving through the medium. Rather, it is a pressure propagated through the medium. This pressure is not itself motion; it is only an inclination to move. "It is," Descartes says, "necessary to distinguish between movement, and action or inclination to move."[44]

Hobbes disagreed with this Cartesian distinction between movement and the inclination to move. Even the beginning of motion is motion. In his *English Optics*, Hobbes opposed Descartes by saying:

> So that light is nothing but a fancie, made by the lucid object by such pressure as I have even now described. But this pressure is really & actually a locall motion of the parts, both of the lucid object which comes a little forward every way, and also of the organ, that is to say, of the spiritts in the hart, & ye parts of the braine and of the optique nerve (though the said motion bee imperceptible) and is not a meere inclination. For all inclination if it bee pressure or endeavor is actually a motion and progression of something out of its place, pressure cannot otherwise bee conceived.[45]

Hobbes appears to be arguing that bodies, whether luminous or not, are distinguished from others, that is, are determinate, because of internal motions, and that light and vision occur because of the reciprocal determinacy of motions. Later, in *De Corpore*, Hobbes will define light as an "endeavor outwards" caused by the reaction of the heart to pressures propagated from outside (De Corp., ch. 27, art. 2, p. 448). This makes light a "fancie," that is, a phenomenal object.

Hobbes wants to give a physical or materialistic account of the generation of light by appealing to the effect of local motion in a medium (e.g., air), and without calling upon the Cartesian notion of "inclination." A luminous body broadcasts pressure from its contraction/dilation in every direction. Light is perceived, and consequently the luminous body becomes determinately a luminous body, when the motions of the luminous body interact with the motions of an organ of vision. The motions may be so small as to be imperceptible, so failure to detect them, for example, in the eye itself, will not refute the hypothesis.

The intensity of a motion, Hobbes maintains, is relative to the intensity of a counter-motion. That is, one motion becomes determinate because of its relation to other motions, and the relationship takes the form of resistance and opposition. What Hobbes suggests is a dynamic concept of difference. Externality does not disappear from Hobbes's philosophy as it does in Leibniz's, but the simple self-identity of externally related objects does.

That the theory has fundamental defects is not to be denied. Most obvious is the simple circularity it requires. The determinacy (i.e., separate existence) of bodies is due to the reciprocal relatedness of motions which are, in turn, internally located, that is, located within bodies! Whether the theory is consistent or not, the fact is, Hobbes does consistently maintain the dynamic idea of reciprocal determination. He would appear to be on the borderline of a thoroughgoing phenomenology.

In this regard, one would do well not to ignore the possible influence of Marin Mersenne, Hobbes's close acquaintance and friend. In 1625, in *La Vérité des Sciences*, Mersenne responded to the sixteenth- and seventeenth century *conatus* critics of philosophical science who argued sceptically that nothing can be known with certainty. Mersenne claimed that, though we cannot know with certainty the real natures of things, we can know with certainty the appearances of those things. A science of phenomenal objects is possible.[46] Whether due to Mersenne's influence or not, Hobbes adopted this phenomenalism and, having rejected the clean distinction between appearances and things, may be said to have been one of the first to go beyond phenomenalism to phenomenology.

Another change in Hobbes's philosophy by the time of the *English Optics* (one that is intimately connected with the previous changes) concerns the locus of sense perception. Whereas in *The Little Treatise* (1630–7) and in the *Elements of Law* (1640) the brain was identified as the passive locus of sense-reaction, in the *English Optics* (1646), as well as in *Leviathan* (1651), the heart served as the locus of sense-perception. At the same time, Hobbes extended the use of the *conatus* concept beyond its original employment in *The Elements of Law* (1640) where it referred to "solicitation," that is, to the attraction and repulsion that manifests itself phenomenally either as appetite, pleasure and love, or as aversion and fear (El. of Law, ch. 7, par. 2, pp. 31–2). In *Leviathan* it is also used to explain the process of sense perception and thought. These two changes are interrelated and suggestive of a major change in Hobbes's philosophical thinking.

This change will be the subject of the following chapter. Suffice it to say that shortly before 1650 a significant change in Hobbes's philosophical views occurred, and that the change is relevant for our understanding of his subsequent theory of human nature and his political philosophy.

Hobbes's Mature Natural Philosophy

In *De Corpore* we have the last and most mature account of Hobbes's philosophy of nature. The work, published in 1655, but worked on for almost a decade prior to that, gives the appearance of being a patchwork product. It consists of four parts: Part I: "Logic" (or philosophical methodology); Part II: "The First Grounds of Philosophy" (the principal concepts of mechanics, such as space and time, body and accident, cause and effect); Part III: "The Proportions of Motions and Magnitudes" (Hobbes's expansion of geometry into natural philosophy which, incidentally, he never really carries through); and Part IV: "Physics, or the Phenomena of Nature" (Hobbes's account of sensation and physical phenomena, for example, motions and magnitudes no longer considered in abstraction from their phenomenal occurrences).

Parts III and IV are of especial interest to us insofar as they contain a number of significant changes in his natural philosophy. The contraction-dilation hypothesis adopted by Hobbes in *Tractatus Opticus* to explain how motion is initiated and transmitted through a fluid medium is now abandoned for a "simple-circular" theory of motion.[47] Also, the concept of vacuity is rejected, though it is not refuted. And, most important, the concept of *conatus*, or "endeavour," which first appeared in *The Elements of Law* and later in *Leviathan* is now extended to account for all natural motion whatsoever. The consequence of this last change is that his physics is absorbed into the developing idea of *conatus* and the dynamic theory of nature and man that Hobbes is slowly arriving at. Our concern in the following pages will be to examine the nature and function of this concept in Hobbes's natural philosophy. It is around (or because of) this concept that the greatest confusion over his physics is centred.

Hobbes's treatment of *conatus* has been pretty much a puzzle to his readers because it seems to repeat the ambivalent characteristics that the concept of "impetus" had for fourteenth-century physics. Hobbes always defines *conatus* as motion, but treats it (in one place) as a principle of psychology and at another place as a principle of physics. Here is the source of confusion surrounding Hobbes's physics. His first definition of *conatus*, in 1640, took it to be a principle of psychology or animal motion. He writes:

This motion, in which consisteth *pleasure* or *pain*, is also a *solicitation* or provocation either to draw *near* to the thing that pleaseth; or to *retire* from the thing that displeaseth; and this solicitation is the *endeavour* or internal beginning of *animal* motion, which when the object delighteth, is called *appetite;* when it *displeaseth*, it is called *aversion*, in respect of the displeasure *expected, fear*. So that *pleasure, love* and *appetite*, which is also called desire, are *divers names* for divers considerations of the *same thing*. (El. of Law, ch. 7, par. 2, pp. 31–2)

While *conatus* was defined as the principle of animal motion in *The Elements of Law*, it appeared fifteen years later in *De Corpore* as the first principle for what appears to be a mathematical physics. He wrote that *conatus* is, "motion made in less space and time than can be given; that is, less than can be determined or assigned by exposition or number; that is, motion made through the length of a point, and in an instant or point of time" (De Corp., ch. 15, art. 2, p. 206).

The problem, of course, is to reconcile these two definitions. The orthodox approach to *De Corpore* has been to acknowledge Hobbes's indebtedness to Descartes and Galileo for the doctrine of inertia, and to understand Hobbes's intent, therefore, as residing squarely within Galilean-Cartesian science.[48] More specifically, the mathematical treatment of motion as one finds it in the mathematical physics of Descartes and Galileo eradicated entirely the purposiveness of Aristotelian physics. Motion is only a term which stands for a series of statements that a body is here, now here, now here, etc. The Galilean-Cartesian account abandons Aristotelian teleology for an idea of motion that would require only extension, only the succession of places through which a body could pass, as its conceptual prerequisite. Descartes and Galileo, then, produced a purely kinematic theory of motion.

This mathematized theory of motion suffered its own peculiar problems. The purely kinematic explanation of motion did not concern itself with the time for traversing a given distance. Motion was conceived as a series of displacements. Unexplainable in the terms of this theory was the velocity of a body (projectile) at a given instant, that is, the intensive or instantaneous velocity of an object. If a body moves through a duration of time, surely it must also move in each instant of that duration. It cannot, of course, unless some duration of time, however brief, is involved. That is precisely what was not involved in the nominalist account of motion.

Descartes and Galileo resolved this dilemma with the famous Law of Inertia. In 1644, in his *Principles of Philosophy*, Descartes offered the law as his first law of nature, "that each thing as far as in it lies, continues always in the same state; and that which is once moved always continues so to move."[49] Inertia is not, itself, mere motion. Descartes maintained "that it is necessary to distinguish between movement, and the action or inclination to move."[50] The orthodox approach to Hobbes's theory is to assume that his *conatus* is simply a name he gives for that force or tendency in an instant of time. In short, it is perceived as the Hobbesian word for "inertia." There are, however, difficulties with this interpretation. We have already seen that Hobbes would not accept Descartes' distinction between movement and the inclination to move. As Gabbey has stated, he appears to have allowed no room for the notion of inertia, any inertial force whatsoever, in his physics. He defines the principle in Part II of *De Corpore* (De Corp., ch. 8, art. 9, p. 115), but makes no significant use of it after that. Frithiof Brandt noticed Hobbes's puzzling neglect of the principle. He wrote: "the principle of inertia plays an astonishingly small part in Hobbes's natural philosophy. . . it is briefly mentioned in half a page, and there is no indication that Hobbes was especially interested in it."[51] Brandt concludes from this that Hobbes apparently did not see the consequences of Descartes' principle. Brandt's conclusion fits with his indecision regarding whether Hobbes's concept of *conatus* was purely kinematic or dynamic. His solution is to fudge the issue by saying it was both.

One must take issue with Brandt's conclusion. I would argue that Hobbes made no use of the inertia principle because his physics does not call for it as a foundational idea. This is not because he substituted for inertia some volitional force (impetus) with which inertia cannot be reconciled,[52] but because he produced a dynamic, relational account of identity and difference to which a doctrine of inertia had little to contribute. Hobbes certainly wanted to accommodate to his natural philosophy as much of the mathematical physics of his day that he could, but he never sacrificed the ideas crucial to a dynamics for the sake of that accommodation. Hence his arguments with Descartes over inclination and his "neglect" of the principle of inertia.

Hobbes insists that nothing can move itself. This can easily be taken to be a statement from a purely mechanical account of motion, that is, "kinematics." It isn't. Even the *conatus*, the beginning of motion, is defined as the reciprocally determined determinant of motion. In physics, it is the visible phenomenon of pressure, just as in psychology, it is the visible phenomenon of fear and desire, that convinces Hobbes of this. This is not to say that *conatus* is pressure. Hobbes distinguishes the two. Pressure occurs when two bodies, having opposite endeavours, meet. The endeavour of either in that situation can then be said to be pressure. What it would mean to say that there is a *conatus* or endeavour in a medium where there is no opposition or resistance is hard to say, just as it would be hard to say that a body in infinitely extended and utterly empty space has, or does not have, any velocity. Hobbes does say that an endeavour will proceed as far as the medium. If the medium is infinite, the endeavour will proceed infinitely (De Corp., ch. 22, art. 9, p. 341). But, were there no resistance, it would also be infinitely indeterminate. *Conatus* is reciprocally determinate. Just as there is no difference of bodies apart from their determining motions, so for Hobbes, is there no difference between motions apart from their determining *conatus,* and no difference between any two *conatus,* the first beginnings of motion, apart from their opposition and mutual resistance.

Part of the confusion surrounding Hobbes's philosophy of nature stems from the fact that his terminology is sometimes confusing. One can easily be misled by his claim that "Place is nothing out of the mind, nor magnitude anything within it" (De Corp., ch. 8, art. 5, p. 105), or again, that "This magnitude does not depend on our cogitation as imaginary space doth" (De Corp., ch. 8, art. 4, p. 105). This distinction that Hobbes makes between imaginary space (or, place) and magnitude (or, extension) is most often taken to be a simple distinction between "imaginary magnitude" and "real magnitude."[53] Imaginary space (imaginary magnitude) is phantasmal, or merely relative, space, that is, place, while extension, or real magnitude, is real space, outside of and independent of mind.

This interpretation of Hobbes's account of space collapses when one considers Hobbes's additional qualification "that a body keeps always the same *magnitude,* both when it is at rest, and when it is moved; but when it is moved, it does not keep the same *place*" (De Corp. ch. 8, art. 5, p. 105). If, in this passage, body refers to a real (i.e., extended) body, and not some phantasm, and place refers to imaginary space (imaginary magnitude), as Hobbes suggests, it would be impossible to account for the reality of motion. If we read this passage in the light of the ordinary interpretation of Hobbes's account—distinguishing between imaginary magnitude (place) and real magnitude (which a body always keeps)—the ordinary interpretation fails. If a body "keeps always the same magnitude," then extension (real magnitude) cannot be for Hobbes the same as real (or, absolute) space, void of extended bodies. The ordinary interpretation would require that one think in terms of real, that is, extended, bodies moving about from place to place, meaning by that, moving through space which has only phantasmal or imaginary existence. This would leave us with an account that makes motion illusory.

Hobbes's distinction between imaginary space and extension arises in the context of a dispute with René Descartes, and probably cannot be comprehended fully in abstraction from that dispute. Hobbes makes scattered, rather oblique references in *De Corpore* and elsewhere to Descartes (De Corp., ch. 7, art. 2, p. 93; ch. 9, art. 7, p. 125), often without naming him directly, but there is little doubt that Hobbes had Descartes in mind. He criticizes Descartes for failing to draw the obvious conclusions suggested by the premises with which he begins. Descartes builds his theory on the doctrine that body and extension are identical, but fails to draw the conclusion, obvious to Hobbes, that space is thereby made phantasmal, that is, subjective.

Hobbes takes it to be nonsense that, "[w] should take a space or extension for a body or thing extended and thence conclude because space is every where imaginable, Therefore bodie is in every space. For who knows not that Extension is one thing, and the extended another, as hunger is one thing, and that which is hungry is another."[54] This passage, taken from Hobbes's unpublished *Minute* or *First Draught of the Optics*, from 1646, is augmented and developed later in *De Corpore*. There, Hobbes writes:

> For no man calls it space for being already filled, but because it may be filled; nor does any man think bodies carry their places away with them, but that the same space contains sometimes one, sometimes another body; which could not be if space should always accompany the body which is once in it. And this is of itself so manifest, that I should not think it needed any explaining at all, but that I find space to be falsely defined by certain philosophers, who infer from thence... that the world is infinite (for taking *space* to be the extension of bodies, and thinking extension may increase continually, he infers that bodies may be infinitely extended.) (De Corp., ch. 7, art. 2, p. 93)

In this passage, Hobbes uses the terms "space" and "place" interchangeably. Shortly, he will make an important distinction between the two concepts, space and place. There is consequently room for all sorts of confusion and misinterpretation. The point to see here, however, is that Hobbes does not so much disagree with Descartes' definition of space (here, identical with "place") and extension as he does fault with the failure to see the result that space is thereby made phantasmal. In Hobbes's words, "[T]hose that, by making *place* to be of the same nature with *real space*, would from thence maintain it to be immovable, they also make place, though they do not perceive they make it so, to be a mere phantasm" (De Corp., ch. 8, art. 5, p. 105).

What Hobbes's criticism entails, that is, what positive argument lies behind his disagreement, has, for the most part, been overlooked by his critics. It has been suggested that Hobbes anticipated Kant in his treatment of space and time, insofar as he was the first to assert the subjective nature of both (De Corp., ch. 7, art. 2–3).[55] Problems arise when it is assumed, nonetheless, that the spatial (or phantasmal) object is for Hobbes opposed to an objective and independently existing thing-in-itself which is unknowable. The more carefully one examines Hobbes's account, the more difficult it is to maintain this ordinary view.

Hobbes's account of space is inseparable from his account of body. Body, according to Hobbes, is not the same as extension (magnitude). Rather, extension is an *accident* of body, Hobbes explains, without which body cannot be thought. "There are certain accidents," Hobbes writes, "which can never perish except the body perish also; for no body can be conceived to be without extension, or without figure" (De Corp., ch. 8, art. 3). He explains, "Magnitude is the peculiar accident of every body." (De Corp., ch. 8, art. 5, p. 105). Hobbes's phenomenological indifference to the division between an inner, subjective world and an inaccessible outer, objective world, is indicated in his remark, "[T]hey answer best that define an *accident* to be *the manner by which any body is conceived;* which is all one as if they should say, *an accident is that faculty of any body, by which it works in us a conception of itself*" (De Corp., ch. 8, art. 2, p. 103).

The implication of these remarks is that body is entirely phenomenal. This conclusion is somewhat anticipatory. It depends in part on the more careful analysis of Hobbes's account of space which is to follow. Hobbes's accounts of body and space are not really separable. By way of anticipation, and without stretching matters too much, one might argue that Hobbes's account of space follows from a phenomenological reduction of his own phenomenal notion of body.

Space

Hobbes began Part II of *De Corpore* with his own version of Cartesian hyperbolic doubt. He wrote, "In the teaching of natural philosophy, I cannot begin better. . . than from privation; that is, from feigning the world to be annihilated" (De Corp., ch. 7, art. 1, p. 91).

Hobbes is not maintaining that there is no externality, but only that perceptions and conceptions are not, themselves, evidence of it. He maintains that, "we compute nothing but our own phantasms" (De Corp., ch. 7, art. 1, p. 92), and that men do all their calculations and perceivings "sitting still in our closets or in the dark" (De Corp., ch. 7, art. 1, p. 92). A thing viewed from the darkness of Hobbes's closet may be considered to be either an internal accident of mind or, he says, a "species of external things, not as really existing, but appearing only to exist, or to have a being without us" (De Corp., ch. 7, art. 1, p. 92).

Space is the *appearance* of externality, *"the phantasm of a thing exist-ing without the mind simply"* (De Corp., ch. 7, art. 2). In Part IV of *De Corpore* and in *Leviathan* Hobbes refers to space as the conceptual accom-paniment of the outward endeavour of sense motions that constitutes a body. It is the phantasm of a thing *appearing* to exist outside the mind that arises when we abstract from both *what* the thing is, that is, its identifying characteristics, and *where* it is, that is, its place. It is, in effect, a pure in-tuition of space. Hobbes has a presentiment of Kant's treatment of space as the outer form of sensuous intuition, but without any notion of its exist-ing *a priori*:

> If therefore we remember, or have a phantasm of anything that was in the world before the supposed annihilation of the same; and consider, not that the thing was such or such, but only that it has a being with-out the mind, we have presently a conception of that we call *space;* an imaginary space indeed, because a mere phantasm, yet that very thing which all men call so. (De Corp., ch. 7, art. 2, p. 93)

Space is the product of a double abstraction: from the specific location, or place and the specific attributes, for example, magnitude, of a phantas-mal object. These latter two features from which Hobbes abstracts to ar-rive at his concept of space are also concepts of space, these being the more specifically defined imaginary space (place) and real space (extension or magnitude).

Imaginary Space

Imaginary space (place) is, according to Hobbes, merely phantasmal, rela-tional, or "relative" space. If one simply abstracts from the specific at-tributes of a phantasmal object, that is, what it is that is placed, its mag-nitude, but not its specific location (the place itself), he will get an idea of what Hobbes intends by imaginary space. It is a precondition of a thing's being conceivable that it be some place (Lev., p. 675). This fits with Hobbes's denial of the possibility of "separated essences" or incorporeal substances. Whatever is, or whatever can be thought, must be in some specific place. It must be determinate. Kant would call this a precondition of possible experience. Hobbes tells us that imaginary space (place) is "an effect of our imagination" and "an accident of the mind" (De Corp., ch. 8, art. 4, p. 105). It is to be "called the *place* of that body" (De Corp., ch. 8, art. 5, p. 105), and, as such, is nothing outside the mind. Place is the im-movable locus of movement, without which movement cannot be comprehended. "[F]or, seeing that which is moved, is understood to be carried from place to place, if place were moved, it would also be carried from place to place, so that one place must have another place, and that place another place, and so on indefinitely, which is ridiculous" (De Corp., ch. 8, art. 5, pp. 105-6).

Real Space

Real space Hobbes calls extension or magnitude. It is in talking about real space, as opposed to imaginary space, that Hobbes would appear to mislead many of his readers, that is, cause them to believe that he is talking about something (real space) that actually exists independently of mind. In fact, real space is no less imaginary than imaginary space. It is an idea one arrives at when one abstracts only from the specific location, or place, but not from the magnitude of the individual object, its "what."

In *De Corpore*, Hobbes says, "The *extension* of a body, is the same thing with the magnitude of it, or that which some call *real* space" (De Corp., ch. 8, art. 5, p. 105). He adds, in disagreement with Descartes, that extension is not the same as body, though every body keeps the same extension or magnitude as it changes place. Extension is an accident of body, the necessary or defining accident of body. One might want to refer to extension as a discursive *a priori* that mathematically delimits body without locating it in any particular place, but without which the act of locating does not make sense. I believe this is what Hobbes has in mind when he states that "magnitude is the cause [rather than the effect] of [our imagination]," in contradistinction to imaginary space which, he says, is "an effect of our imagination" (De Corp., ch. 8, art. 4, p. 105). It is the precondition of delimitation or individuation which, because it is not itself an image but, rather, the precondition of any perceived image, is nothing within the mind. That is to say, it is not something one can actually see. It is "an accident which can never perish except the body perish also; for no body can be conceived to be without extension" (De Corp., Part II, ch. 8, art. 3). Hobbes explains, "A body, and the magnitude, and the place thereof, are divided by one and the same act of the mind; for to divide an extended body, and the extension thereof, and the idea of that extension, which is place, is the same with dividing any one of them; because they are coincident, and it cannot be done but by the mind, that is by the division of space" (De Corp., ch. 8, art. 8, p. 108).

The division of space to which Hobbes refers, and the resulting separation of body, magnitude, and place, is illustrated in the following chart:

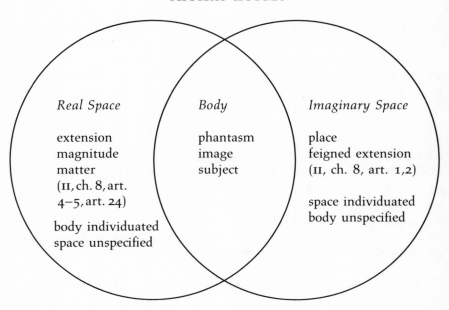

Real Space

extension
magnitude
matter
(II, ch. 8, art.
4–5, art. 24)

body individuated
space unspecified

Body

phantasm
image
subject

Imaginary Space

place
feigned extension
(II, ch. 8, art. 1,2)

space individuated
body unspecified

As the chart suggests, when real space (extension) is placed, one gets the concept of a perceived object, that is, body (the mathematically measurable bodies of modern mathematical physics). Hobbes is altogether clear in rejecting as nonsense the idea that there may be an extended thing that is in no place. Only determinate beings exist, and the first criterion of their existence is that they be somewhere. Hobbes is a phenomenalist insofar as he does not consider individuation, or determinate being, independent of the individuating functions of perception and conception. A body or thing is necessarily a subject. A thing, he says, is called a subject because it is subject to, or placed in, imaginary space and is, for that reason, capable not only of being perceived by sense but also understood by reason (De Corp., ch. 8, art. 1, p. 102).

If one reverses the procedure and conceives place, that is, imaginary space, as extended (i.e., coincident with the concept of real space, that is, extension or magnitude) one gets the idea of "solid space," or, Newtonian space. Hobbes writes:

> That space, by which word I here understand imaginary space, which is coincident with the magnitude of any body, is called the *place* of that body; and the body itself is that which we call the *thing placed*. Now *place*, and the *magnitude* of the thing placed, differ. First in this, that a body keeps always the same *magnitude*, both when it is at rest, and when it is moved; but when it is moved, it does not keep the same

place... place is immovable; for, seeing that which is moved, is understood to be carried from place to place, if place were moved, it would also be carried from place to place, so that one place must have another place, and that place another place, and so on infinitely, which is ridiculous. (De Corp., ch. 8, art 5, p. 105)

Immovable place is Hobbes's counterpart to the idea of absolute space, or solid space. Hobbes writes, "the nature of *place* does not consist in the *superfices of the ambient,* but in *solid space*" (De Corp., ch. 8, art. 5, p. 106). Against it, the motions of isolated bodies can be detected and measured. But space, so conceived, is only phantasmal, the result of what one might call a phenomenological reduction. Hobbes describes the procedure one would follow to arrive at this idea of solid, or absolute, space:

Though there be no body which has not some magnitude, yet if, when any body is moved, the magnitude of it be not at all considered, the way it makes is called a *line,* or one single dimension; and the space, through which it passeth, is called *length;* and the body itself, a *point;* in which sense the earth is called a *point,* and the way of its yearly revolution, the *ecliptic line.* But if a body, which is moved, be considered as *long,* and be supposed to be so moved, as that all the several parts of it be understood to make several lines, then the way of every part of that body is called *breadth,* and the space which is made is called *superfices,* consisting of two dimensions, one whereof to every several part of the other is applied whole. Again, if a body be considered as having *superfices,* and be understood to be so moved, that all the several parts of it describe several lines, then the way of every part of that body is called *thickness* or *depth,* and the space which is made is called *solid,* consisting of three dimensions, any two whereof are applied whole to every several parts of the third. (De Corp., ch. 8, art. 12)

"Superfices," according to the *Oxford English Dictionary,* is "a magnitude of two dimensions having only length and breadth; that which forms the boundary, or one of the boundaries of a solid, or separates one part of space from another; a surface." Solid, or three dimensional space (or, in Hobbes's terms, immovable place) is a phantasm got by imagining the movements of a two-dimensional superfices. That two-dimensional superfices is, itself, the phantasmal product of a reduction of the phenomenal object to a body lacking all magnitude, which is put in imaginary motion. Hobbes, in effect, agrees with an unnamed "other" to whom he refers who claims that, "real space is made immovable by the understanding; as when, under the superfices of running water, we imagine other and other water to come by continual succession, that superfices fixed there by the understanding, is the *immovable place* of the river" (De Corp., ch. 8, art. 5, p. 106).

Hobbes concludes his *De Corpore* discussion of space with the some-times misleading remark that "space, or place, that is possessed by a body, is called *full*, and that which is not so possessed, is called *empty*" (De Corp., ch. 8, art. 6, p. 107). The comment might tempt one to fall back upon the Epicurean account of space and body, which was enjoying a renaissance in the seventeenth century, and approach Hobbes's physics from its naïve notion of externality. It is important to see that what Hobbes means here by empty space, or again by solid space, is not ac-curately identified with the idea of radical externality, objective space, or, in Hobbes's terms, the vacuum. In his earlier writings, even as late as the *English Optics* (1646) Hobbes accepted the possibility of a vacuum, but by the time of *De Corpore* it had been abandoned. It is true that in two sentences in Part II of *De Corpore* Hobbes attacks what he calls a childish argument used by some to refute the possibility of the vacuum (De Corp., ch. 8, art. 9), but that should not be disproportionately emphasized. His own laborious (twelve-page) refutation of various proofs of the vacuum from Lucretius to his own time makes his own position clear (De Corp., ch. 26, art. 2–4). An explanation of the universe can be developed ade-quately without calling on that hypothesis. There is no valid sense in which we can take Hobbes to have included as an integral part of his natu-ral philosophy the actual existence of radical externality. This is not to say that externalty is eliminated in Hobbes's account. Rather, it is there as it is in Kant's philosophy, that is, in a way that prevents the division of the world into the inner accessible part and the outer, inaccessible part.

In this sense, at least, Hobbes is not a materialist. Hobbes's materialism is through and through phenomenal. Individuation is not something Hobbes conceives as part of a universe external to man, which man some-how tries to comprehend. Space, imaginary space (place), real space (mag-nitude or extension), and solid space are all accidents of body, different ways in which body is conceived, and are accessible only through an act of phenomenological analysis.

BODY AS PHENOMENON

The above observations regarding the conceptual ingredients of Hobbes's idea of body bring us back to his dual claim—the claim with which this section began—that the object of philosophical knowledge is bodies of which we can conceive the generation, but that bodies are things, and are not generated. How are we to reconcile this apparent contradiction in Hobbes's thought?

Hobbes uses the terms "body," "thing," and "object" interchangeably. Bodies are things, and things are "whatever we name" (De Corp., ch. 2, art. 6, p. 18). More precisely, "Body is a simple *name*, being put for that first single conception... " (De Corp., ch. 2, art. 14, p. 24). Hobbes explains that "seeing names ordered in speech... are signs of our conceptions, it is manifest they are not signs of the things themselves" (De Corp., ch. 2, art. 5, p. 17). The function of naming and the act of conceiving will be given more careful consideration in the next chapter. The present references to naming are intended only to locate the nature of body and to show that, independent of the acts of naming and conceiving, it is nothing. Body is described physiologically by Hobbes as the outward endeavour (or motion) of sense, that is, the phenomenal presence of the sense that an object is outside of mind or sense.

Body, as a name for the sensation of externality, is not in itself an object of experience. Body becomes an object of experience by becoming subjectivized, that is, by accumulating qualitative determinations which are themselves contingent additions. In *Leviathan*, Hobbes writes, "though the nature of that we conceive be the same, yet the diversity of our reception, in respect of different constitution of body, and prejudices of opinion, gives everything a tincture of our different passions" (Lev., ch. 4, p. 28).

Again, Hobbes says that "the object is one thing, the image or fancy is another" (Lev., ch. 1, pp. 2–3). The object becomes imaged, or the magnitude gets placed, by the constructive faculty of human comprehension. The generation of body is, then, the generation of those accidents which individuate body. That is, the generation of body is, in effect, the construction of images.

Because body is a function of *conatus*, the natural motion that would be indeterminate if it did not receive its determinacy reciprocally as it opposes other natural motions (including the motions of sense and passion), body is indivisible. As *conatus*, body is unextended. Unextended, it is indivisible, and therefore is capable of performing the rational function of an Epicurean atom, that is, of providing the rational universe with indissoluble limits, and so "salving the phenomena" (De Corp., ch. 27, Art. 1, p. 447) without the aid of the idea of indivisible material extension. In its function, though not in its account, body is like the "point" in Cartesian or Newtonian mathematical physics.

Body, then, is the name for that interaction of motions that, because of the peculiar nature of sense (as we shall subsequently see) is a kind of stasis. Experience is not possible until things begin to stand still, to maintain their individuation (and therefore their difference from other things) for more than an instant.

In *De Corpore,* chapter 8, Hobbes argues in a manner that has led some to claim he makes motion a secondary rather than a primary quality of body. That could be taken to mean that motion is incidental to body, that body exists first and only then is moved. This would reinforce the mechanistic, materialistic interpretation of Hobbes's physics. In this passage, Hobbes gives two lists of the accidents belonging to bodies. He writes: "there are certain accidents which can never perish except the body perish also; for no body can be conceived to be without *extension,* or without *figure.* All other accidents, which are not common to all bodies, but peculiar to some only, as *to be at rest, to be moved, colour, hardness,* and the like, do perish continually, and are succeeded by others; yet so, as that the body never perisheth" (De Corp., ch. 8, art. 3, p. 104).

Motion, in this list, is treated separately from extension, and would appear to have a secondary status. But, as Hobbes elaborates the distinction, the status of motion and rest gets changed.

> And as far as the opinion that some may have, that all other accidents are not in their bodies in the same manner that *extension, motion, rest,* or *figure,* are in the same; for example, that colour, heat, odour, virtue, vice, and the like, are otherwise in them, and, as they say, *inherent;* I desire they would suspend their judgment for the present, and expect a little, till it be found out by ratiocination, whether these very accidents are not also certain motions either of the mind of the perceiver, or of the bodies themselves which are perceived; for in the search of this, a greatest part of natural philosophy consist. (De Corp., ch. 8, art. 3, p. 104).

The discrepancy between the two lists in the status given to motion and rest is indicative, I believe, of the peculiar nature of motion. Motion is not mentioned with extension and figure in the first list as a primary accident of body, but is mentioned with them in the second list. Motion is a secondary quality of body insofar as bodies may be either in motion or rest. Motion in this sense is not a necessary attribute of body. A body may remain in one place, never relinquishing it for another. It may remain at rest. However, rest is itself a mode of motion; it is "virtual motion."[56] Consequently, motion belongs with extension in this list of conceptual prerequisites of body and, in fact, must even precede it. Since every static quality, every quality that can be either perceived or conceived, and therefore every quality capable of individuating body, is a product of *conatus, conatus,* as the "smallest motion," must retain its priority. It is because of this that Hobbes's physics has been called a "pure kinetics."[57] Frithiof Brandt observed that "when Hobbes has been and is still called a materialist, this is in a certain sense misleading. The concept of matter plays an exceedingly small part and has a constant tendency to disappear. Hobbes should more correctly be called a motionalist, if we may be permitted to coin such a word. He is the philosopher of motion as Descartes is the philosopher of extension."[58]

Brandt's observation, which is surely correct, becomes more difficult to understand if it is simply incorporated into the traditional view of Hobbes's natural philosophy, and taken to reflect a rigorous mechanics. Mechanics makes no provision for the generation of bodies from pure motion. The individuated world of things could not be accounted for if motion were the exclusive primary in a mechanics.

The reduction of all phenomena, all bodies, all difference to motion by Hobbes has led J.W.N. Watkins to write that "Even the most dead-seeming chunk of inert matter is, one might almost say, brought to life by this idea, transformed into something humming silently with incipient motion."[59]

Watkins adds the suggestive and, I believe, accurate claim that Hobbes serves as the philosophical precursor to Leibniz, and even influences Leibniz' conception of the monad of energy as the basic constituent of the universe. For Hobbes, motion is not merely mechanical (though it may be discussed mechanically). The smallest and most fundamental of motions, *conatus*, is an endeavour. It is the nature of this smallest of motions to oppose and resist other motions (De Corp., ch. 25, art. 2, p. 391). Nature, so characterized, is opposition, resistance. Resistance already plays an integral role in the mathematical physics of Descartes, insofar as it is an adjunct of the doctrine of inertia. In Cartesian physics, a medium or another body may resist the movement of a given body, but the original body's motion is "inert." That is, the body itself is indifferent to the resistance or to any change in its motion. There is resistance, but no opposition. For Hobbes, on the other hand, resistance is not passive; it is dynamic and determining. Bodies come into being only through the interaction of motion, and motions are determinate only in opposition to other motions. The Cartesian doctrine of inertia has little to contribute to Hobbes's more dynamic theory.[60]

The difficulties involved in thinking Hobbes's physics consistently through ought not keep one from recognizing that the concept of *conatus* is fundamental, and that the concept includes reciprocal determinacy. His theory makes opposition an integral part of identity, that is, an integral part of the nature of body.

Hobbes, Leibniz, and Some Observations from Hegel

It is with regard to Hobbes's idea of *conatus* that his philosophy bears a certain resemblance to that of Leibniz, on whose early writings Hobbes had a conspicuous influence.[61] Not the least interesting is the fact that Leibniz's metaphysics drew a wealth of commentary and criticism from Hegel, who does not seem to be very familiar with (at least he does not comment on) Hobbes's *De Corpore*. To the extent that Hobbes and Leibniz agree, one might abstract from Hegel's criticism of Leibniz and (with due caution observed) apply that criticism to Hobbes's philosophy. With the help of a comparison with Leibniz and a careful extraction of Hegel's critical remarks, we can gain a better insight into Hobbes's overall philosophical intent.

For Leibniz, as for Hobbes, nature (substance) is real insofar as it is a unity, a one (for Hobbes, a body). However, reality only emerges with the exposure of *difference* within unity. Whatever is real owes its reality to the fact that it is both one (a unity) and unique (differentiated). This idea Leibniz expresses in his principle of the identity of indiscernibles. Nature, or substance, is an infinite multiplicity of differentiated individuals, which Leibniz calls monads, or in his early writings, following the influence of Hobbes, *conatus*. Leibniz's monad is, in short, Hobbes's *conatus*, with notable differences in the process of its individuation. Leibniz, following Hobbes, maintained that it is part of the nature of the *conatus* (monad) that it is not extended. In his *Theory of Abstract Motion*, he writes: "Conatus is to motion as a point to space, or as one to infinity, for it is the beginning and the end of motion."[62]

Leibniz argued that indivisibles, or unextended beings, must exist, at least as a precondition for our conceiving the beginning and the end of any motion or any body. By beginning and end is meant the determinate dimensions that make it meaningful to say something exists. An infinitely small body, or an infinitely diminishing motion, is not merely next to nothing. It *is* nothing, since no characteristics can be attributed to it, for example, length, duration, without making it divisible, that is, finite. Were it divisible, there would be a smaller part possible; hence, it would not be infinite. Looked at from a reversed perspective, no matter how many infinitely divisible points we might put together, we would never have enough to constitute even the smallest of lengths, since to add the infinitely small is to add nothing. Leibniz makes it clear that the *conatus*, or monad, is not an extended being. He writes, "the nature of body consists, not in extension, but in an action which is related to the extended, for I hold that there can be no body without effort"[63]

The monad is a non-extended, indivisible being that is somehow associated with effort. Thus far, Leibniz's remarks keep him very close to Hobbes. In a certain sense, both Hobbes and Leibniz fall with the sphere of influence of traditional Aristotelianism. For Aristotle, being manifests itself as *energeia* or *entelechia*. A being is its work; it is what it does. However, while it is meaningful for Aristotle to talk about being as a whole, the idea of a whole is absent in Hobbes's philosophy (making him, in this regard at least, more a Protagorean), and is only externally superimposed in Leibniz's philosophy. In his *Lectures on the History of Philosophy*, Hegel remarked that, unlike Spinoza, who began with the oneness of substance, Leibniz began with the monad, the radically individuated substance, or *existence for self*.[64]

Leibniz followed Hobbes's lead in this and suffers the same dilemma Hobbes faced. Existence-for-self, or radical individuation, precludes the idea of a rational whole. This is all the more a problem for Hobbes because *conatus* is not, as it is for Leibniz, a self-related ("windowless") force, but an endeavour that is reciprocally related to other endeavours. Its identity (its determinacy) is a product of its relation to other endeavours (motions) that are themselves determined by the same relation. The difficulty this creates for Hobbes is obvious; determinacy becomes paradoxical. X is what it is only because of its determining relationship to Y. The same holds for Y. The existence of each is fixed by its relationship to the other, but neither can establish any relationship to the other unless the other is itself already fixed. Furthermore, we cannot avoid arriving at another form of the problem mentioned earlier, the problem of getting a whole from an aggregate of infinitely divisible parts. For Hobbes, parts are not so much infinitely divisible as they are totally indeterminate apart from the whole (the others). The difficulty as it exists for Hobbes can be seen more clearly if we look once again to his account of *conatus*.

Conatus as described by Hobbes is always reactive. All action is reaction; it is visible to us as opposition and resistance. To say this is to say that there is in all things a sensitivity to all other things. They are dynamic, not merely kinematic. We can see this in the broader use Hobbes makes of the phenomenon of "sense." Hobbes prefers to reserve the term "sense" for those reactions in which there is self-consciousness, but he is clear in maintaining that it is not wrong to use the term to explain relations in which self-consciousness does not occur. "But though all sense, as I have said, be made by reaction, nevertheless it is not necessary that every thing that reacteth should have sense" (De Corp., ch. 25, art. 5, p. 393).

Hobbes adds that if reaction in general is to be called sense, then it follows that all bodies must be understood as "endued with sense," and that "by reaction of bodies inanimate a phantasm might be made" (De Corp., ch. 25, art. 5, p. 393). Such inanimate reactions would be infected with immediacy, however. They would cease as soon as the object lost contact, or as soon as the *conatus* was removed from its reciprocal relation with another *conatus*. It is the immediacy of reaction that identifies motion and distinguishes it from sense.

Even this must be qualified, for Hobbes clearly indicates in *De Corpore* that both animate and inanimate objects are liberated from immediacy to the extent that a reaction is transformed into habit, which, he says, is "a generation of motion, not of motion simply, but an easy conducting of the moved body in a certain and designed way... attained by weakening of such endeavour as divert its motion... by the long continuance of action, or by actions often repeated" (De Corp., ch. 22, art. 20, pp. 348–9). Hobbes explains that when the lath of a cross-bow is bent and held in that bent position for a long time it acquires a habit so strong that it not only will not restore itself to its original position once released, but will require a greater force to bend it back. In short, some reciprocally related determinations of motion outlive their reciprocal relations. They lose their dependency. The motions or endeavours preserve the patterns that resulted from their original opposition. According to Hobbes, one of the endeavours which originally created the opposition (the original sense determinacy) weakens. The reciprocally determined pattern of the other endeavour endures.

All things, then, are sense-perceptive in this broad sense of the term. In most inanimate objects, sense has only a momentary duration and is without influence on subsequent sense. Sense is simply "the retaining of such motion as is made in" a subject (De Corp., ch. 25, art. 5, p. 393), and that retention, when it takes place in the inanimate, is "habit." What distinguishes the animate from the inanimate being is that in the animate, habit manifests itself as consciousness, what Leibniz later calls "apperception," distinguishing it from mere perception or reaction. One must keep in mind that this is not merely a physiological account of sense but a relational account of all determinacy. To confuse one with the other is to transform Hobbes's natural philosophy and his philosophy of man into the mechanistic-materialistic theory with which he is so often associated. And that merely renews the problem of reconciling the incompatible elements of his presumably systematic theory.

Consciousness is not, for Hobbes, an inner, spiritual substance. It is not a faculty of mind. Rather, it is the determinate relation between different *conatus* (whose differences are determined by this relation). It is sensation, reaction, that differs from inanimate reaction insofar as it is "vehement," that is, greater than the action (motion) that provokes it. The fact that the relationship of motions is determined by their comparative vehemence does not seem to discourage Hobbes from the idea that the

vehemence of sense motions is itself determined by the comparative relation of motions! Hobbes has no other means of accounting for this
vehemence. He does occasionally explain it as deriving from the greater
"elasticity" of sense motions, but this would seem to be more substitution
of one word for another than a genuine explanation. This is an issue that
will come up again in the discussion of Hobbes's theory of the passions. It
is sufficient for now to see that conscious sensation is not a passive reaction
in a perceiving body. Rather, it involves a dynamic assertion of self, a
"vehemence" which Hobbes, in one context, refers to as "study," a sense
of "gravity" in which one evaluates and selects those motions which are of
interest to the perceiving subject, elevating them thereby to the level of
perceptions:

> And hence it is, that an earnest studying of one object takes away the
> sense of all other objects, for the present. For study is nothing but a
> possession of the mind, that is to say, a vehement motion made by
> some one object in the organs of sense, which are stupid to all other
> motions as long as this lasteth... From hence it is manifest, that
> every endeavour of the organ outwards, is not to be called sense, but
> that only, which at several times is by vehemence made stronger and
> more predominant than the rest; which deprives us of the sense of
> other phantasms, no otherwise than the sun deprives the rest of the
> stars of light not by hindering their action, but by obscuring and
> hiding them with his excess of brightness. (De Corp., ch. 25, art. 6. p.
> 395)

This act of sense consciousness, whereby one object of sense becomes predominant, is called judgment. Sense is judgment. Without comparing and
distinguishing, phantasms are not distinct. An organism that apprehends
without comparing, without judgment, apprehends nothing. Sense perception, by its very nature, is selective.

Necessarily then, the act of conscious sensation, as distinguished from
mere sense reaction, involves a distinction between consciousness and the
ideas (or objects) of consciousness. The distinction is attributable in
Hobbes's theory to the individuating activity of the *conatus*, or
endeavour, of a perceiving subject. The distinction (absent in empiricist
epistemology) suggests the embryonic beginnings of a doctrine of self
which, unlike the Cartesian doctrine of the substantial priority of self to its
objects (or, at least, the doctrine often attributed to Descartes), is in a way
anticipatory of the Kantian doctrine of the transcendental unity of apperception, by which the "I" is perceived only in and during the active perception of objects of thought. There is this major difference. For Hobbes,

the *unity* of apperception is not transcendental. There is no regulative idea that is the rational precondition of the unity of sense experience. There is only an endeavour, a *conatus*, one might call it an intentionality, that, by virtue of its vehemence, makes itself visible to itself. Hobbes writes, "by what sense shall we take notice of sense? I answer, by the sense itself, namely, by the memory which for some time remains in us of things sensible, though they themselves pass away. For he that perceives that he hath perceived, remembers (De Corp., ch. 25, art. 1, p. 389).

In Hobbes's idea of sense perception, then, we can discriminate three different modes or moments: those virtual or "unconscious" perceptions which are obscured, hidden from our attention by our attention, that is, by our preoccupation with other more vehement and irresistible perceptions; our conscious or vehement perceptions, the perceptions and ideas which capture our attention, obscuring other ideas in the process; and consciousness of consciousness, the reflexive perception *that* one has perceived. The first mode belongs to the animate and inanimate alike, the second two belong to the animate alone, the third to man. Once again, this topic belongs to Hobbes's natural philosophy, since we are concerned with the preconditions for the identity of an object, which is always the product of opposing motions, *conatus*.

A comparison of Hobbes with Leibniz on the issue of perception and consciousness is instructive. The activity (*energeia*) of the monad, Leibniz maintains, is perception. Difference in kinds of perception distinguishes the animate from the inanimate for Leibniz as they do for Hobbes. Leibniz writes:

> No conation without motion lasts longer than a moment except in minds. For what is conation in a moment is the motion of body in time. This opens the door to the true distinction between body and mind, which no one has explained heretofore. For every body is a momentary mind, or one lacking recollection (recordatio), because it does not retain its own conatus and the other contrary one together for longer than a moment. For two things are necessary for sensing pleasure or pain—action and reaction, opposition and then harmony—and there is no sensation without them. Hence body lacks perception of its own actions and passions, it lacks thought.[65]

Leibniz's distinction between body and mind, that is, between mere motion and sense, is very much indebted to that made already by Hobbes, though it would appear that Leibniz would not readily acknowledge it. Everything possesses the power of representation and perception by virtue of its individuating activity as a monad, or *conatus*. Its principle of individuation is *conatus*. The conscious being (or monad) distinguishes itself by its vehemence and, therefore, the distinctness of its perceptions. In his *Lectures on the History of Philosophy*, Hegel commented on Leibniz's theory. His comments apply equally to Hobbes. Consciousness, he wrote, is the very thing that constitutes the distinction of the undistinguished, and that distinction constitutes the determination of consciousness.[66]

According to Hegel, there is for Leibniz (and, we might add, for Hobbes) no individuation apart from the individuating activity of consciousness or being-for-self. But the conscious *conatus* is itself individuated by its activity (if there is a difference between the *conatus* and its activity). And its activity, as desire, cannot be comprehended except reciprocally or reflexively, as a product of the determinate individuation which it evokes.

Thus far, Hegel's remarks apply equally well to Hobbes as to Leibniz. This is not to say that there are no differences between Hobbes and Leibniz. For Hobbes, the natural universe is a continuum of motions, the constituent substance of which (*conatus*) is also motion. The individuating *conatus* is not a solid body that is internally unaffected by its environment as is the case, for example, in crude atomism. According to Hobbes, all relation between one *conatus* and another is radically external, not in the sense that they are indifferent to one another but, rather, in the sense that their relations are contingent and historical, not logical. Because all relation takes the form of opposition of motions that are mutually individuating, there is for Hobbes no simple self-identity that is aloof from, or indifferent to, this reciprocal relation. There is, in other words, no natural thing that is indifferent to those things to which it stands in some relation. Hobbes writes: "For seeing in all sense of external things there is mutual action and reaction, that is, two endeavours opposing one another, it is manifest that the motion of both of them together will be continued every way especially to the confines of both the bodies" (De Corp., ch. 25, art. 10, p. 405).

The difficulty for Hobbes in this account is in the fact that a thing defined by its own *conatus* will be individuated by its own individuating relation to other *conatus*. All identity, then, is dynamically acquired, perhaps even dialectically acquired, in the sense in which dialectic was defined in the first chapter. The peculiar difficulty that this involves for Hobbes is to be found simply in the fact that he does not have a philosophical terminology sufficient to express the account with any clarity. The idea of *conatus*, externally related to other *conatus*, but also individuated by that external relationship, is not easily accommodated by terminology borrowed from the mechanistic sciences.

Admittedly, it is difficult to comprehend a universe that consists of motions that are not the motions *of* solid bodies travelling through space according to some mechanistically transparent procedure. To some extent, we share Hobbes's problem. The *conatus* has no identity, no determinacy, apart from its relation to other *conatus*. Its identity is relational and dynamically derived. It is hard to see, then, how it can serve as the constituting material of a natural continuum. But that is precisely what Hobbes has argued. Hobbes's natural universe is a continuum of reciprocally determined motions. It is an altogether fluid continuum that, because of the relational character of its determinacy, cannot be known in any final, or rational, sense. Hence, Hobbes remarks that "no discourse whatsoever can end in absolute knowledge of fact, past or to come" (Lev., ch. 7, p. 52).

The difficulties of Hobbes's theory are made even more obvious if contrasted with Leibniz's restatement of the theory. Leibniz was to argue, in contradistinction to Hobbes, that no relation is radically external. The monads which are the ultimate constituents of the world are absolutely unconditioned; they are "without windows." Since the monads alone are real, every change in nature must be change within a monad; it must be uncaused or spontaneous change. Leibniz, in short, rejects Hobbes's account of the externality of causation as untenable.

The spontaneity of individual monads is not the consequence of the absence of sufficient reason, or causality. It is, rather, the consequence of their being uninfluenced by anything external to their own determinate natures. The monad is thoroughly shut up in itself. The radically independent character of the monad enables Leibniz to avoid the confusing notion of reciprocal determinacy that is integral to Hobbes's natural philosophy. But it does not help him to account for the unity of the whole. Leibniz's solution to that problem is to begin with the intelligible unity of the whole, that is, to replace the indeterminacy of Hobbes's theory with a preestablished harmony. God, we are told, created all monads from the very beginning in such a way that all things occur with perfect spontaneity within each individual monad. However, the spontaneously occurring events arise in perfect conformity to one another.

Leibniz sought to grasp the intelligible unity of the whole (impossible for Hobbes) without sacrificing its radical heterogeneity. One might argue that his philosophy represents an attempt to overcome the problem of the one and the many by combining the truth of Spinoza's philosophy, that is, its radical universality, with a version of the truth of Hobbes's philosophy, the radical heterogeneity of the universe. That Leibniz's attempt fails is testified to by Hegel, who writes: "The principle of the harmony among the monads does not consequently belong to them, but it is in God, who for that very reason is the Monad of monads, their absolute unity. . . . "[67]

The individual monads are unified by an appeal to the unifying function of God. Every monad is a representation of the universe. But Hegel argues that thought (which "thinks" by differentiating, and therefore represents the multiplicity of monads) and Being (the One, God) cannot be unified without a dissolution of difference, the elimination of thought, or the annihilation of the heterogeneous universe. He writes, "With Leibniz, the extent to which thoughts advance is the extent of the universe; where comprehension ceases, the universe ceases, and God begins. . . . "[68] God is an artificial unity of the world, an externally imposed unity, a "makeshift." Thinking in terms of the way advanced societies eliminate the unwanted products of their own internal activities, Hegel writes, He is "the waste channel into which all contradictions flow."[69] Leibniz, in short, has not resolved the problem created by external relation and reciprocal determinacy in Hobbes's natural philosophy, that is, the problem of giving a rational account of the whole.

Unlike Leibniz, Hobbes did not attempt to resolve the problem of the intelligible unity of the whole. He appealed to no "waste channel" to absorb the disunifying character of natural differences. "Nature dissociates," and it individuates in the process. Identity is a product of dissociating differences. Furthermore, dissociation is itself a form of association, one which precludes a rational grasp of the whole. Consequently, it is inaccurate to identify Hobbes as a rationalist in any simple sense, no less than it is inaccurate to identify him with empiricism, atomism, or mechanism.

Hobbes's natural philosophy is certainly a monistic materialism. It is monistic insofar as it includes no reference to "separated essences" or transcendent principles which supervise and maintain the dissociations and differences within nature and, in the process, order and unify the universe. The order one finds in the natural continuum is transient.

What this means for Hobbes's philosophy is that wisdom in the sense of a complete account of the whole is beyond the limits of human finitude. For that reason it is correct to refer to Hobbes's philosophy as "pessimistic," as many of his commentators do. However, Hobbes's pessimism transforms itself into the optimism of the modern philosophical project because the absence of a fixed universe (the object of a rational account) makes possible man's liberation from nature's dominion. Through his efforts to fix his own horizons, that is, to "imitate the creation" (De Corp., "Epistle to the Reader"), man can make himself the lord of his own domain.

Through his discovery of scientific method, man has revealed in himself a capacity for reshaping nature to satisfy his own needs, that is, to recreate nature in his own image, imitating the original creation. In that way, man makes himself the measure of all things (Lev., ch. 2, p. 4). It is here that we find the most significant aspect of Hobbes's physics. The peculiar nature of man's discourse with nature makes a final reconciliation of the human and the natural in knowledge impossible. In his pursuit of mastery over nature, man alters his own nature, as well as his needs, leaving him in a state of perpetual disharmony with nature. The result of this enduring condition is that the object of man's pursuit—knowledge—is dissociated from wisdom and is identified, instead, with power. Theory is, from this time, identified with practice, that is, with the generation of "theories" that may be used to enable man to master and reorder the natural continuum to serve his own needs.

The links which unite Hobbes's physics with this concept of philosophical mastery are not made thematic in his physics. To explore this development in Hobbes's thought, we will have to turn to his treatment of human nature.

3

The Liberation from Natural Necessity

In his *Introduction* to *Leviathan*, Hobbes maintained that "life is but a motion of limbs . . . " (Lev., Intro., p. ix). His claim would seem to suggest that human nature is reducible to functions that are entirely mechanical. Historically, this is how Hobbes has been read. The consequence has been his reputation as the apostle of mechanism. The reputation is unjustified, however, Neither the concept of life nor the argument by which that concept is developed are, in fact, mechanical. The problem is, a consistently developed mechanical conception of human nature requires the surrender of any notion of human desire or intention, at least as a fundamental principle of human behaviour. That Hobbes does *not* make any such surrender is evident throughout his writings. A special example of the place and function of desire in his account of human nature is his remark in *Leviathan*, "Nor can a man any more live, whose desires are at an end than he, whose senses and imaginations are at a stand. Felicity is a continual progress of desire, from one object to another; the attaining of the former being still but the way to the latter. The cause whereof is, that the object of man's desire, is not to enjoy once only, and for one instant of time; but to assure for ever, the way of his future desire" (Lev., ch. 11, p. 85).

In what is, perhaps, the most infamous remark in the corpus of Hobbes's writings, he concludes, "I put for a general inclination of all mankind, a perpetual and restless desire of power after power, that ceaseth only in death" (Lev., ch. 11, pp. 85–6).

Hobbes's own statements regarding his philosophical intention to develop a system of philosophy make clear the fact that his theory of human nature was intended to mediate (not simply to "bridge") his physics and his political theory. Nonetheless, the theory of human nature which is to mediate physics and politics seems to contain the elements of their contradiction unassimilated. Man appears to be identified by Hobbes as simultaneously a creature of mechanical necessity and a creature of need and desire, without any credible explanation how these two forces might merge. The contradictory relationship of politics and physics would seem to have been resolved by the mediating grace of an internally inconsistent conception of man.

Part of the difficulty involved in making sense out of Hobbes's philosophical system was resolved in the previous chapter with the demechanization of Hobbes's natural philosophy. In his most mature natural philosophy, Hobbes identified motion, or more specifically, the most fundamental and minute constituent of natural motion, with *conatus*. The result is a dynamic and dialectical conception of nature according to which all difference and all individuation is the product of dissociating forces which resist and even oppose one another, individuating *themselves* in the process. This paradoxical thesis was, to be sure, only embryonically conceived by Hobbes. The important issue is to understand how this thesis relates to his mature conceptions of man and political association.

The clue to the integration of Hobbes's physics and his theory of human nature is visible in the fact that, while the *conatus* concept characterizes Hobbes's mature philosophy of nature, it does not originate with his natural philosophy. The *conatus* concept was first used by Hobbes in *The Elements of Law* (1640) where he employed it to signify "solicitation," the most fundamental of the animal motions, which manifests itself as the many different human passions. Later, in Leviathan (1651), the concept was extended to include sense motion (i.e., sense perception) and reason. Not until *De Corpore* (1655) did he use the concept to refer to all motion in general. In other words, while Hobbes's dynamic conception of nature as *conatus* has its *systematic* origins in his physics, it has its *historical* point or origin in his theory of human nature. According to Hobbes, the unavoidable hostility of man toward man is not a conclusion drawn from empirical observations of characteristic human behaviour.[1] Neither is it a phenomenon that occurs because of divisive social and political groupings (cultural or economic hostility), nor again because of human ignorance of the implicit moral obligations of man. It is, Hobbes says, an "inference made from the passions" (Lev., ch. 13., p. 114). It is, in short, an extension of that dynamic, dialectical impulse that is the rudiment of all human thought and action, and, in fact, of all nature.

This "inference made from the passions" that one finds in *Leviathan* is not a part of Hobbes's earlier writings. In *The Elements of Law*, for example, Hobbes appears to have combined the traditional scholastic view of man as the rational animal with a more modern, mechanical conception of man. He writes: "Man's *nature* is the *sum of his natural faculties and powers,* as the faculties of *nutrition, motion, generation, sense, reason,* etc. These powers we do unanimously call *natural,* and are contained in the definition of man, under these words, *animal* and *rational*" (El. of Law, Human Nature, ch. 1, art. 4, p. 2).

In this passage, Hobbes identifies motion as only one of several faculties which together constitute human nature. Hobbes does not identify thought and sense with motion here for the reason that he does not yet conceive motion as *conatus,* that is, as something dynamic, dialectical, as a self-generating agent of delimitation. If one makes the mistake of taking Hobbes's early mechanical conception of motion as the explanatory principle of his subsequent theories of man and polity, one will arrive at a mechanical theory of man and society that has become paradigmatic for much modern social theory. The result is not an adequate index of Hobbes's own thought and, however much it may be part of the orthodox interpretation of Hobbes's philosophy, does not do justice to the complexity involved in it.

The point being made here is that Hobbes does not ground his mature theory of human nature on a crude mechanics. The belief that he does is admittedly almost universal. Unfortunately, the extension of Hobbes's early (and much overemphasized) interest in mechanics to his mature theory of man and politics precludes raising the very question to which Hobbes addressed himself: the problem of reconciling physics and politics. It does worse than that. It reconciles physics and politics by appealing to a conception of human nature, ignoring the fact that the two components of that conception—mechanical movement and volitional activity—remain unreconciled.

Hobbes clearly intended to avoid this conceptual hiatus. Nonetheless, though he intends to reconcile man and nature, purposiveness and causal determinacy, he does not want to dismiss their difference. According to Hobbes, man is a natural being and, in that sense at least, he is part of the natural continuum. At the same time, he is not limited by the purely material possibilities of mere nature. Ultimately, man escapes the natural condition that threatens his continued welfare. That is to say, man becomes an historical being, at least in the broadest sense of that term, in that he transcends the immediacy, or merely transient character, of natural relations. Accounting for this difference of identity of man and nature is precisely the intention of Hobbes's philosophy. Too great an emphasis on the mechanical aspects of Hobbes's physics makes this intention incomprehensible. Understood mechanically, Hobbes appears to be suggesting a very curious doctrine, perhaps best described as an *ego-less egoism*. Room must be made for an account that does not preclude both the identity of and the difference between man and nature. Hobbes himself has no doubt that he has given us an account of a human nature that transcends the immediacy of natural relations, thereby liberating man from natural necessity. That is, he has no doubt that his account of human nature accounts for purposiveness and human volition. Our question is, how?

THE GENERATION OF VOLUNTARY MOTION

The greater number of Hobbes's commentators have addressed his philosophy of man with the paradigm of *vision* in mind rather than the paradigm of *volition*, prompted, most likely, by the many experiments undertaken in this area by both Hobbes and his contemporaries. The inevitable result has been that Hobbes's philosophy has been recast as an epistemological theory that culminates in a formal dualism of the kind most often associated with Descartes. In fact, it is volition rather than vision that is his starting point. By volition here I mean the peculiarly human dimension of *conatus*. It is volition, or voluntary motion, that liberates man from natural necessity. Voluntary motion is, for Hobbes, the result of the dialectical transformation of *conatus*, that is, dynamically determined natural motions, into *endeavour*, or desire, the specifically human *conatus*.

The nature of this transformation is lost if one ignores the distinction Hobbes makes within human endeavour between *vital* motions and *voluntary* motions. Vital motions represent that dimension of human nature by which man is most clearly and directly part of the natural continuum. They represent a natural inertia. They are those motions, "begun in generation, and continued with interruption through their whole life; such as are the *course* of the *blood*, the *pulse*, the *breathing*, the *concoction, nutrition, excretion*, etc. to which motions there needs no help of the imagination" (Lev., ch. 6, p. 38). Voluntary, or animal, motions, on the other hand, Hobbes identifies as "to go, to *speak*, to *move* any of our limbs, in such manner as is first fancied in our minds" (Lev., ch. 6, p. 38).

The question that Hobbes must address and answer for us is: What is the source of voluntary motions and the principle that differentiates them from vital motions? Recent commentators have tended to answer this question and resolve the problem it creates by defining it away. A rather common observation has been that Hobbes's theory is not so much *causal* as it is *explanatory*.[2] If this were true, it would absolve Hobbes from having to reconcile volition with causal necessity. Hobbes becomes, thereby, a rationalist in the most pejorative sense of the term. Ultimately, it leads to a quasi-Kantian or deontological interpretation of Hobbes's theory of human behaviour that emphasizes the rational system it presumably contains to the exclusion of the naturalism, egoism, and political realism that are integral parts of Hobbes's philosophy.

The problem, then, is locating what Hobbes took to be the origin of voluntary motions that liberate men from the natural condition. It is a previously unobserved peculiarity of Hobbes's philosophy that he traces voluntary motions to two sources: imagination and passion. Only the former, imagination, has been given much thematic consideration in this regard. Early in *Leviathan,* Hobbes maintained that "imagination is the first internal beginning of all voluntary motion" (Lev., ch. 6, p. 39). From imagination is derived speech, which Hobbes takes to be "the most noble and profitable invention of all others" (Lev., ch. 4, p. 18), without which man would be altogether incapable of civil association. However, Hobbes also claims that the beginning of voluntary motion is to be found in the passions (El. of Law, ch. 5, art. 14, p. 25; Lev., ch. 6 p. 38), and that it is man's "curiosity'"—an extension of human passion—that distinguishes him from other natural creatures.[3] This confusion of sources of voluntary motion—imagination and passion—makes conspicuous, once again, the question whether the visional or the volitional is the more appropriate paradigm for interpreting Hobbes's philosophy. Ultimately, we shall see, it must be the volitional. Correspondingly, passion, rather than imagination, is the origin of voluntary motion and, therefore, the fundamental principle of all human activity.

In chapter 6 of *Leviathan,* after maintaining that "imagination is the first internal beginning of all voluntary motion," Hobbes adds: "These small beginnings of motion, within the body of man, before they appear in walking, speaking, striking and other visible action, are commonly called ENDEAVOR. This endeavor, when it is toward something which causes it, is called APPETITE, or DESIRE... And when the endeavor is fromward something, it is generally called AVERSION" (Lev., ch. 6, p. 39).

Imagination is the first internal beginning of voluntary motion only in the order of discovery, that is, in our observations of human behaviour. Before it appears in the actions of men, or, perhaps, independent of its manifestation in actual behaviour, volition exists as desire or endeavour. Imagination exists as the focus of desire. This is one way in which we can understand Hobbes remark that desire always needs an object. However, if that is the case, then it is by an examination of imagination (or sense motion in general) and language that one can discover the first beginnings of voluntary motion per se, the passions.

Voluntary motions—thinking, speaking, and, in general, acting purposively—arise out of the peculiar character of the opposition of vital motions in man and the natural continuum. Human mortality and finitude attest to the hostile character of natural forces. No man escapes forever the threat of those forces. No man gets out of life alive. It is not a bias for mechanism that leads Hobbes to begin his chapter on Imagination in *Leviathan* with the axiom of the natural sciences, "when a thing is in motion, it will eternally be in motion, unless somewhat else stay it" (Lev., ch. 2, pp. 3–4). The characteristic motion of man is *life*, vital motion. Vital motion is an inertia that resists absorption into the natural continuum, a *conatus* or endeavour that is found "even in the embryo" (De Corp., ch. 25, art. 12, p. 407). Voluntary motions are the peculiarly human extension of that inertia.

In *Leviathan*, chapter 1, Hobbes gives us what he calls the "natural cause of sense," although it "is not very necessary to the business now at hand" (Lev., ch. 1, p. 1). Ostensibly, this is because he has written about it elsewhere. In fact, the account minimizes the *conative* aspects of sense motion and has to be corrected as the account develops. He writes:

> The cause of sense, is the external body, or object, which presseth the organ proper to each sense, either immediately, as in the taste and touch; or mediately, as in seeing, hearing, and smelling; which pressure, by the mediation of the nerves, and other strings and membranes of the body, continued inward to the brain and heart, causeth there a resistance, or counter-pressure, or endeavor of the heart to deliver itself, which endeavor, because *outward*, seemeth to be some matter without. And this *seeming*, or *fancy* is that which men call sense. (Lev., ch. 1, pp. 1–2)

The integral role of passion or appetite in this process is evident in the fact that Hobbes defines "will"—the term most often associated with the initiation of voluntary action—as "the last appetite in deliberating" (Lev., ch. 6, p. 49), and describes appetite as "a corroboration of vital motion, and a help thereunto" (Lev., ch. 6, p. 42). In short, the instinct for self-preservation (the vital motion) is for Hobbes an embryonic inertia that is fundamental to—and is extended by—the voluntary motions of which man is capable, such as sensing, imagining, speaking, and thinking. It is in the extension of this embryonic inertia in voluntary motions that the initial liberation of man from the immediacy of natural events is to be found.

Sense motions are exclusively reactive, the product of that natural tendency found in all things, but especially in man, to maintain themselves in their original condition (De Corp., ch. 22, art. 13, p. 344). No sense motion is ever spontaneously initiated by a human observer; every sense motion is provoked by external pressures which are "sensed" in the degree that they hinder or augment vital motion (De Corp., ch. 25, art. 13, p. 408).

It is as a result of this opposition of motions that "phantasms" (i.e., images or ideas) arise. The phantasm is an outward reaction of sense which Hobbes identifies with what we would call the phenomenal object, which men generally believe has an existence outside themselves, independent of sense. This tendency to believe that objects are situated outside us, that is, not phenomenal in the last analysis, is the "great deception of sense" (De Corp., ch. 25, art. 2, p. 390). This phantasm, Hobbes says, "is that we commonly call *the object*" (De Corp., ch. 25, art. 2, p. 390). He adds:

> Seeing, therefore, there is in the whole organ, by reason of its own internal natural motion, some resistance or reaction against the motion which is propagated from the object to the innermost part of the organ, there is also in the same organ an endeavour opposite to the endeavour which proceeds from the object; so that when that endeavour inwards is the last action in the act of sense, then, from the reaction, how little soever the duration of it be, a phantasm or idea hath its being; which, by reason that the endeavour is now outwards, doth always appear as something situate without the organ. (De Corp., ch. 25. art. 2, p. 391).

As the phantasm or idea endures, or is liberated from the immediacy of natural events, it takes the form of what, in *De Corpore*, Hobbes calls "habit" (De Corp., ch. 22, art. 20, pp. 349–50). Sense motions, it seems, have a tendency to endure, even after the sense object (the motion propagated from without) has disappeared. The motion propagated from without and the resistance generated from within have a reciprocal dependency that endures. The endurance of this complex motion and reaction is "habit."

Imagination and *memory* are other names that Hobbes gives for this "habituation" that overcomes sense motion. We are told that imagination "is nothing but *decaying sense*" (Lev., ch. 2, p. 4), which is not so much the decay of motion as it is the obscuring of motions by the appearance of other, newer, and oftentimes more vehement sense motions. Memory, on the other hand, is nothing more than imagination that lingers for an indefinite period of time. "So that," he writes, "imagination and memory are but one thing, which for divers considerations hath divers names" (Lev., ch. 2, p. 6). In short, the different mental activities we ascribe to men are different functions of motion understood as *conatus*. Absent entirely from this account is the faculty psychology associated with scholasticism.

One of the principal points of obscurity is Hobbes's apparent treatment of objects as simultaneously phenomenal and non-phenomenal. Sense is caused by "the external body, or object, which presseth the organ proper to each sense. . . " (Lev., ch. 1, pp. 1–2). The idea of a body existing independent of or external to sense, however, is considered by Hobbes to be a deception. Some commentators have suggested that Hobbes naïvely believed that objects exist outside man. It seems terribly unlikely. Hobbes's theory will not permit the idea of an externally existing object, at least in the sense of a thing-in-itself, any more than it will permit the idea that man is epistemologically isolated from the natural world. As we saw in the previous chapter, Hobbes does not separate body and motion, as if motions were accidental to, rather than intrinsic to bodies. He is not an atomist. Furthermore, independent of the counter-motions which resist it, even a natural motion is altogether indeterminate. Though the mechanistic terminology which Hobbes employs resists the suggestion, I do believe it is not far wrong to borrow from Hegelian terminology and refer to the non-phenomenal object in Hobbes's philosophy as the object-in-itself which, in itself, that is, independent of its determinate (determining) relationships to another, is not anything in particular. It is an abstraction.

While imagination and memory are not distinct from sense per se, according to Hobbes, consciousness is. "All phantasms," he says, "are not images" (De Corp., ch. 25, art. 7, p. 396), meaning by that they are not all consciously perceived. There may well be phenomenal objects "which do not at all stir the mind" (De Corp., ch. 25, art. 13, p. 410), what Leibniz later called "petite perceptions." According to the physical account Hobbes gives, consciousness occurs when the phenomenal object (phantasmal motion of sense) penetrates by way of the nerves and brain to the heart. In his *Elements of Law*, the brain, rather than the heart, was given the responsibility for the generation of consciousness. But the brain is merely a passive and reactive organ, whereas the heart is associated by Hobbes with passion and vehemence. In *Leviathan*, where the dynamic conception of human nature fully emerges, Hobbes reverses the respective roles of brain and heart, placing the heart at the foundation of consciousness. Hobbes's emphasis on the role of the heart in his physiological explanation accentuates the centrality of endeavour or *conatus* in human nature and in experience.

When a motion penetrates to the heart, Hobbes says, it is received there in the form of a feeling of either pleasure or pain, which he refers to as "a certain fruition of good or evil" (De Corp., ch. 25, art. 13, p. 410). That is to say, a motion is determined to be pleasurable or painful depending upon whether it helps or hinders the vital motions, those motions without which no other life-motions can endure. The phrase "a certain fruition of good or evil" has baffled no small number of Hobbes's readers unnecessarily. We can understand Hobbes to mean that pleasure and pain are a *fruition* insofar as they are signs—or better yet, symptoms—of the shock that occurs when motions of certain intensities reach the heart. The subsequent reverberations of the heart Hobbes then calls "appetite" and "aversion." The intensity of the motions of appetite and aversion, that is, the degree to which a particular appetite or aversion exceeds another appetite or aversion in its "vehemence," is an index of the degree of human consciousness present.

Consciousness, in other words, is a matter of degree, occurring reflexively. It is always an assertion of self. The purely physical account that Hobbes provides for us is philosophically subordinate to a dynamic and "egoistic" hypothesis. The judgment that a particular sensation (i.e., penetrating motion) is good or evil—meaning by that a help or hindrance to one's vital motions—is not different from the pleasure or pain which expresses the judgment. It is not voluntary in the sense of being willfull or spontaneous. The fact that the will is "the last appetite in deliberating" (Ltv., ch. 6, p. 49) means that it does not precede this process but is, rather, a function of the process. Will is dissolved into appetite or endeavour. Consequently, will and consciousness are matters of degree that may conceivably be more predominant in some observing creatures than in others, and even greater in some human beings than in others.

The presence of pleasure or pain marks the point at which mere sensations or phantasms become images, since with the addition of sufficiently vehement pleasure or pain certain sensations stand out and are, therefore, more notable. Imagination differs from sensation, Hobbes says, in that it is the "appearance" (Lev., ch. 2, p. 4) of what is sensed. There can be, it would seem, no pleasure or pain without consciousness and vice versa, no consciousness without pleasure or pain. The visibility or conspicuousness of a phenomenal object is symptomatic of its significance, that is, its pleasurableness or painfulness, for the observer. Sense is intentional. All phenomenal objects have the character of "pragmata," or objects which to some degree, more or less, are perceived to influence the observer's well-being. It is this characteristic that brings them to one's attention, turning one from other less vehement phantasms.

Hobbes illustrates this characteristic of phenomena with his example of the decay of sense, that is, the "obscuring of it," which he likens to the invisibility of stars obscured by the much brighter light of the sun as it shines. Because they are not predominant, the stars, like our phantasms, are not visible (Lev., ch. 2, p. 5). Again, Hobbes associates consciousness with the activity of "study" which, he maintains, is etymologically related to the term "stupor" (De Corp., ch. 25, art. 6, p. 395).

Though pleasure and pain signify the appearance to consciousness of a phenomenal object, they are not themselves sufficient to explain consciousness. If they were, consciousness would be wholly empirical. Pleasure and pain are phenomenal manifestations of the human *conatus*, the impetus to preserve oneself and augment one's well-being that precedes and preconditions all experience. Human endeavour is an *a priori* inclination, "found *even in the embryo*; which while it is in the womb, moveth its limbs with voluntary motion, for the avoiding of whatsoever troubleth it, or for the pursuing of what pleaseth it" (De Corp., ch. 25, art. 12, p. 407).

It is this embryonic endeavour, or natural inclination, preceding and preconditioning experience, that is at the basis of human experience. This inclination becomes visible, however, only within experience. Infants, for example, "at the beginning and as soon as they are born, have appetite to very few things, as also they avoid very few, by reason of their want of experience and memory; and therefore they have not so great a variety of animal motion as we see in those that are more grown" (De Corp., ch. 25, art. 12, p. 407).[4]

Through the broadening of one's experiences and the gradual diversification of one's interests, the ego becomes more defined, though it is not generated from experience. The Hobbesian ego is neither a substantial nor an empirical ego. It is neither the sum of its phenomenal likes and dislikes nor a substantial entity knowable apart from those phenomenal preferences.

Human endeavour is the sum of two contrary moments, which Hobbes refers to as appetite and aversion, "the first endeavours of animal motion" (De Corp., ch. 25, art. 12, p. 408). The "vicissitude of appetites and aversions" he calls deliberation, insofar as it is varying opinion on whether the same thing "will either be for their good or their hurt" (De Corp., ch. 25, art. 13, p. 408). Appetites and aversions, when they appear as deliberation, Hobbes calls "will" and "unwillingness" (De Corp., ch. 25, art. 13, p. 409). There is, in short, no autonomously functioning will in Hobbes's philosophy. Will is reduced to appetite, which, in turn, is a manifestation of *conatus*. "The same thing is called both will and appetite; but the consideration of them, namely, before and after deliberation, is divers" (De Corp., ch. 25, art. 13, p. 409). Hobbes labours consistently to avoid any reference to faculties that would commit him to a two-substance doctrine or to the immateriality of mind.

LANGUAGE AND UNDERSTANDING

Hobbes's theory of the nature of understanding follows from his functional account of consciousness. In *Leviathan*, we are told that understanding is "imagination that is raised in man, or any other creature endued with the faculty of imagining, by words, or other voluntary signs... " (Lev., ch. 2, p. 11). And, he adds that this is a capacity that is "common to man and beast" (Lev., ch. 2, p. 11). Man's ability to understand differs from that of the beast by virtue of the fact that the words, or voluntary signs, that raise imagination do so in the form of affirmations and negations; what we would call judgments (Lev., ch. 2, p. 10). The relationship between an image and its sign or word, however, is somewhat complex. Hobbes's account of that relationship has been the subject of considerable controversy.

Hobbes maintains that images or ideas are elevated to the level of understanding when they are replaced by "marks" by which images might be recalled. The mark, in other words, is a mnemonic device which is intended to account for the transformation of imagination into memory. If experience is not to blur each experiential moment into the next, like a succession of motion picture frames superimposed on one another, objects of imagination must fade as soon as new ones appear. But the object of each experiential moment cannot disappear altogether; it must endure if we are to possess the capacity of recall.

The marks that serve to signify to ourselves (to recall) our images, Hobbes says, are *names*. However, Hobbes uses *name* to refer to more than the function of recalling images to ourselves. Names, he says, "though standing singly by themselves, are marks because they serve to recall our own thoughts to mind. But they cannot be signs otherwise than by being disposed and ordered in speech as parts of the same" (De Corp., ch. 2, art. 3, p. 15).

Images are subsumed under marks which stand for, or recall to mind, an original image (if it is a singular name) or a group of images "for their similitude is some quality, or other accident" (Lev., ch. 4, p. 21), (if it is a common or universal name). How this mnemonic association of marks and images occurs, Hobbes does not say. That it must suppose a pre-existing similitude—either between one image of an object and another image of the same, or between images of different objects that share some property that is not simply linguistic—is obvious. The property cannot depend upon the function of the mark or name, since it serves to guarantee that the mark has recalled the proper image. A rigorous nominalism cannot make sense out of the most simple mental processes. However, Hobbes does not seem to have concerned himself much with this problem. Had he concerned himself with the problem, it would have taken him to a less immanent, more Platonic, conception of form, since the identity or difference of empirical objects must depend on rational criteria that cannot consistently be products of that identity or difference. This, however, is not the direction that monistically inclined Hobbes wanted to go.

The difference between the name in its function as a *mark* and the name in its function as a *sign* coincides with the difference Hobbes draws between "mental discourse" and discourse in words. Hobbes's distinction anticipates the distinction between propositions and sentences, where any number of different sentences can express or represent the same proposition. We are told by Hobbes that "the general use of speech" is precisely to effect this transformation of mental discourse into verbal discourse (Lev., ch. 4, p. 19). There is a difficulty in this unaddressed by Hobbes which is closely related to the difficulty previously mentioned, that of determining how the mark that we arbitrarily select to stand for an image can properly select the same image every time it is called upon to do so without having recourse to some separate standard or measure of comparison. Here the problem arises in the relationship between mental discourse and verbal discourse. Insofar as verbal discourse is distinct from mental discourse, it cannot, in itself, be the agent by which the two are related. If a series of words in speech represents a series of images in thought it is not sufficient to say that the one is a mnemonic device which recalls the other without explaining how it can do so correctly. The best that Hobbes has to offer is to suggest, in effect, that verbal discourse and mental discourse are not different except in our designation of the functions that discourse performs, one to oneself, and another to others for the sake of communication, but both verbal. Hobbes does say that there is no reason without speech:[5] "Children therefore are not endued with reason at all, till they have attained the use of speech... " (Lev., ch. 5, pp. 35–6); "understanding being nothing else but conception caused by speech" (Lev., ch. 4, p. 28); "it appears that reason is... attained by industry; first in apt imposing of names... " (Lev., ch. 5, p. 35); "The faculty of reasoning being consequent to the use of speech... " (Lev., ch. 46, p. 665), though there may be understanding, for example, the ability of the beast to understand. Such a solution generates as many problems as it resolves, however. It does not account for the "identity in difference" of sentences occurring in different languages, the fact that what "sounds" different can express the same thought.

A brief controversy arose some years ago between J.W.N. Watkins, R.S. Peters and J.M. Brown, revolving around Hobbes's distinction between the mark as mental discourse and the mark as verbal discourse. The issue concerned whether, for Hobbes, all words name conceptions. Might a word name a thing? Watkins claimed to have been convinced by Brown's critique of Peters' book that "Hobbes admits a name-thing relation as well as a sign-conception relation," in spite of the fact that Hobbes says almost nothing about the name-thing relation."[6] Watkins attributed Hobbes's silence on the name-thing relation to the fact that "his materialism and causal psychology did not allow him to describe it." The assumption is that Hobbes has a causal psychology and that his materialism is the sort that precludes description of features that it nonetheless permits. Both these assumptions, I believe, are illicit. Watkins argued that there is "a large difference between what a name signifies and what it names."[7] He explained that "a name cannot be taken as a *sign* of the thing-itself." It must signify the presence in one's mind of an idea. This is due to the fact that Hobbes "identified a name with the physical expression of itself." Each expression of a name is a new name; it is not an instance of a common name,"i.e., an abstract entity immanent in, but not identical with, its various physical expressions," The two words "red" and "red" are not instances of one abstract word for Watkins' Hobbes but, rather, two distinct words. This is a difficulty for any nominalist. Resolving the dilemmas that the distinction causes is not at all easy.

The name-thing relationship is not compatible with a subjectivist psychology for reasons that are obvious. The assumption is that there are things external to, or independent of, their relationships to man's perception of them. On the contrary, Hobbes argues that the thing-itself, by which he means "fancy-itself," that is, the imagined or determinate object (Lev., ch. 2, p. 5), is inseparable from its phenomenal appearance. Things are phenomenal. A thing-itself may be referred to but not characterized regarding its qualities and other attributes because in-itself it has nothing to show. Everything knowable and delimitable about a thing-itself is exposed only in its phenomenal situation as an object of study for man, relative to his well-being.

In *De Corpore*, Hobbes tells us that "names ordered in speech . . . are signs of conception . . . [and] not signs of the things themselves" (De Corp., ch. 2, art. 5, p. 17). As an example, he refers to the sound of a particular word which causes the hearer to "collect what he that pronounces it thinks" of the referent intended (De Corp., ch. 2, art. 5, p. 17). Signs, then, are exclusively the phenomena of communication, and the communicants must take signs as signifying certain images or "marks" about which the other speaks.

In contradistinction to its function as a sign, the name as a *mark* refers to our individual images. It facilitates mental discourse with oneself. In *De Corpore* we are told that not every name need be the name of something, that is, of some determinate object that is part of our waking experience. Some names, for example, "a *man*, a *tree*, a *stone*, are the names of the things themselves, so the images of a man, of a tree, and of a stone, which are represented to men sleeping, have their names also, though they be not things, but only fictions and phantasms of things" (De Corp., ch. 2,

art. 6, p. 17). The important distinction that Hobbes appeals to is not between a perceived object and an unperceived thing in-itself but, rather, between an object of experience *in sleep* and an object which is part of our
waking experience. Hobbes's problem is not whether our significations
signify what our names name (i.e., the concept-object relationship) but,
rather, the sense in which a name can be said to refer to a thing itself, that
is, an object of waking experience, rather than an image produced in sleep
or an hallucination, since both the waking and sleeping experiences are
phenomenal. It is this problem that he undertakes to resolve. This problem
is not part of an epistemological controversy over the psychological isolation of man from objects, that is, from bodies independent of thought, but
rather the problem of distinguishing those images which are distorted and
confused because of blending and mixing from those which are precise and
dependable.

Hobbes's concern, then, is not with the problem of images that lack an
existential referent but, rather, with images that are incoherent, that fit
into no lucid train of thought, and also (we shall soon see) with names, or
signs, that add to the confusion because they lack clarity, or because they
exclude images which properly belong with that mark or include images
that don't. Any image that is coherent, that conveys a distinct purpose or
organizing endeavour, is self-evidently a waking experience:

> For my part, when I consider that in dreams I do not often nor con-
> stantly think of the same persons, places, objects, and actions, that I
> do waking; nor remember so long a train of coherent thoughts,
> dreaming, as at other times; and because waking I often observe the
> absurdity of dreams, but never dream of the absurdities of my waking
> thoughts; I am well satisfied, that being awake, I know I dream not,
> though when I dream I think myself awake. (Lev., ch. 2, p. 7)

All naming is of conceptions or images, according to Hobbes. This does
not mean that names are not names of things themselves. By thing-itself
Hobbes means a phenomenal object, an object of waking, that is, lucid experience, as distinct from the objects of dreams, hallucinations and other
confusions, as happens when memory fails. Hobbes is, in this sense, a
phenomenologist.

According to Hobbes, we "register to ourselves" (Lev., ch. 45, p. 673;
ch. 5, p. 30) the images or ideas of experience by attaching a word or mark
to them in order to recall them at a later time. This procedure is limited by
the fact that it involves no assurance that it will not be "inconstant." The
possibility always exists that men will "register their thoughts wrong, by
the inconstancy of signification of their words; by which they register for

their conception, that which they never conceived, and so deceive themselves" (Lev., ch. 4, p. 20; cf. El. of Law, ch. 5, art. 8).

The problem of inconstancy of signification is bound up with the very nature of the procedure by which man has conscious experience, that is, the personal or perspectival character of experiences. Language, and even the names which, when combined, constitute language, are no less subjective and coloured by the passions than are our most immediate experiences. Hobbes writes:

> The names of such things as *affect* us, that is, which please and displease us, because all men be not alike affected with the same thing, nor the same man at all times, are in the common discourses of men *inconstant* signification. For seeing all names are imposed to signify our conceptions, and all our affections are but conceptions, when we conceive the same things differently, we can hardly avoid different naming of them. For though the nature of that we conceive, be the same; yet the diversity of our reception of it, in respect of different constitutions of body, and prejudices of opinion, gives everything a tincture of our different passions. And therefore in reasoning man must take heed of words; which besides the signification of what we imagine of their nature, have a signification also of the nature, disposition, and interest of the speaker; such as are the names of virtues and vices; for one man calleth *wisdom* what another calleth *fear*; and one *cruelty*, what another *justice*; one *prodigality*, what another *magnanimity*; and one *gravity*, what another *stupidity*, etc. And therefore such names can never be true grounds of any ratiocination. (Lev., ch. 4, pp. 28–9)

There is, then, a two-dimensional possibility of error: inconstant marking, or naming, of ideas or objects of experience, and inconstant signification of those ideas to others with whom we are in discourse. Ideas or images, it seems, always carry the *tincture of our own passions*, and names reflect that tincture. We always run the risk, therefore, of self-deception, and with that the chance of deluding others. When words are rigidified by custom, or when we agree upon stipulated definitions, it becomes possible to reckon or deduce in mathematical fashion consequences that are consistent and non-deceiving. Such deductions, Hobbes says, constitute "science" (Lev., ch. 5, pp. 37–8).

Inconstancy in scientific deductions, when it happens, is not to be called error. It is absurdity (Lev., ch. 5, p. 32). Many animals besides man are liable to err, but only man enjoys the "privilege of absurdity" (Lev., ch. 5, p. 33), since only he is capable of separating his ideas from himself through the agency of naming, and is capable of "adding and subtracting" those names "scientifically" and then recommending his reasonings and conclusions to others. He alone is capable of becoming "excellently wise," but also "excellently foolish" (Lev., ch. 4, p. 25), for there is neither reason nor absurdity without speech. Speech or language, then, is a principal cause of the absurdities in which man tends to entangle himself. "[A]s all the ornaments of his philosophy proceed only from man so from man also is derived the ugly absurdity of false opinions. For speech has something in it like to a spider's web, (as it was said of old Solon's laws) for by contexture of words tender and delicate wits are ensnared and stopped; but strong wits break easily through them" (De Corp., ch. 3, art. 8, p. 36).

Well-ordered, systematically coherent language can be the medium of great wisdom, but also of great absurdity. What, then, is the principle difference between the two possibilities? Clearly important is "a good and orderly method in proceeding from the elements, which are names, to assertions made by connexion of one of them to another; and so to syllogisms... " (Lev., ch. 5, p. 35). But systematic methodology is a necessary cause of both wisdom and absurdity. Hobbes adds that an "apt imposing of names" (Lev., ch. 5, p. 35) is also a prerequisite. What constitutes an apt imposing of names is not for Hobbes merely a matter of consistently selecting the same name to represent the same idea or image every time. Such naming can be consistent yet insignificant. Significance in language occurs only when speech is guided by the desires and affections of men who speak. Significant language, in short, has its origins in "need." In chapter 4 of Leviathan, Hobbes gives an elaborate account of the biblical explanation of language and its origin. We are told that Adam was instructed by God regarding names, but that God's instruction was narrowly limited to assigning names to "such creatures as he presented to [Adam's] sight" (Lev., ch. 4, p. 18). Adam added other names entirely on his own, names that he found useful, such as "names of all figures, numbers, measures, colors, sounds, fancies, relations" (Lev., ch. 4, p. 19). All the ingredients of mathematical rationality, in short, were human in origin. The efforts of both God and man were negated, however, at the Tower of Babel, "when, by the hand of God, every man was stricken, for his rebellion, with an oblivion of his former language." Men were reduced to silence. They were rescued from that silence, however, by the gradual generation of the "diversity of tongues" that are spoken today, a generation that was produced by "need, the mother of all inventions... " (Lev., ch. 4, p. 19). Presumably, man reacquired all that he had obtained by his own efforts earlier, that is, mathematical reason. Hobbes's exegesis tells us that there is no Divine sanction for the words we choose, and no guarantee that arbitrarily chosen words do not mislead us. Our only warrant of accuracy is in the fact that words and their organization into language are a product of the use they have in fulfilling needs.

This is corroborated in *Leviathan*, chapter 3, where Hobbes distinguishes two sorts of mental discourse: unguided and regulated. Unguided thoughts are those which are "without design, and inconstant; wherein there is no passionate thought, to govern and direct those that follow, to itself, as the end and scope of some desire or other passion: in which case the thoughts are said to wander, and seem impertinent one to another, as in a dream" (Lev., ch. 3, p. 12). Unguided thoughts are like those of a man in sleep. Regulated thoughts, on the other hand, are "regulated by some desire, and design" (Lev., ch. 3, p. 13; cf. ch. 8, p. 60). That is to say, they are regulated by some concern for that which we need.

The point of this is that imagination, language, and method are not the only, or even the primary, components of human nature and reason. Imagination, language, and method are the mediating devices for something still more primary—the *conatus* or endeavour that characterizes human nature. Hobbes, though he is a rationalist, is not a rationalist in the reductive sense that he wants to equate reason with speech, or philosophy with discourse, even logical discourse. To identify philosophy with logical discourse per se is to obscure the relationship which Hobbes perceives between reason and nature. It ignores the *conatus*, or dynamic and dialectical, nature of man, the world, and their interrelationship in human experience. This is precisely what Hobbes wanted to avoid.

Hobbes's distinction between a *mark*, which is a name for ideas or images which one recalls to oneself, and a *sign*, which is a name designated to permit communication with others, is not the same as—nor does it imply—the contemporary distinction between *signifying* a meaning or concept and *referring* to a thing (body) independent of experience. This is indicated even more by Hobbes's suggestion that things have a sign-character. They appear to man as signs, though as signs which might easily be misread. The sign-character of things is implied by Hobbes's statement that nature is an "inference, made from the passions" (Lev., ch. 13, p. 114). It is part of the reciprocally determinate relationship of man and nature. An indication of this reciprocally determinate sign-character of natural things is given in a passage in *De Corpore*, where Hobbes writes:

> For example, a thick cloud is a sign of rain to follow, and rain a sign that a cloud has gone before, for this reason only, that we seldom see clouds without the consequence of rain, nor rain at any time but when a cloud has gone before. And of signs, some are *natural*, whereof I have already given an example, others are *arbitrary*, namely, those

we make choice of at our own pleasure, as a bush hung up, signifies that wine is to be sold there; a stone set in the ground signifies the bound of a field; and words so and so connected, signify the cogitations and motions of our mind. (De Corp., ch. 2, art. 2, pp. 14–15)

Whatever else Hobbes may intend by this example, he means at least this, that nature exhibits signs which reveal her underlying inclinations. His statement in *Leviathan*, that "the nature of foul weather lies not in a shower or two of rain but in an inclination thereto of many days together... " (Lev., ch. 13, p. 113) indicates this feature of nature. Hobbes does not intend to maintain that the possibility of rain is a mere matter of empirical inference from past occurrences, though experience is important. The nature of foul weather is reflected in the inclination to rain because the inclination to rain is a sign of nature's not having been designed exclusively for, nor inclined towards, man's welfare. Reading that sign requires more than an accumulation of data. It requires living in a damp, rainy, health-jeopardizing climate, perhaps, or in some other equally unsuitable situation. The validity of the inference is lost without this underlying interrelationship.

Both man and nature exhibit *natural* signs which may be misread, perhaps for lack of suitable relationship which permits the natural signs to appear as signs, but which are generally reliable. Only man imposes *arbitrary* signs, signs which, because of their arbitrariness, are more frequently misleading. Men's words are like the bushes hung up on doors to signify that wine is sold there. Men who have no wine to sell may hang up bushes anyway. And, men who do have wine to sell may not hang up bushes to signify the fact, for example, if the sale of wine were to be declared illegal by a sovereign's edict. It is better, then, to rely upon natural signs which, if we are sufficiently aware, are more reliable indicators of things. A person is sufficiently aware only if he has used himself, that is, his own need, his well-being, and his special concern for it, as an index of the signs he sees. In *Leviathan*, Hobbes declares:

> *nosce teipsum, read thyself,* which was... meant... to teach us, that for the similitude of the thoughts and passions of one man, to the thoughts and passions of another, whosoever looketh into himself, and considereth what he doth, when he does *think, opine, reason, hope, fear,* etc., and upon what grounds; he shall thereby read and know, what are the thoughts and passions of all other men upon the like occasions. (Lev., Intro., p. xi)

Hobbes's unusual translation of the inscription in the above passage, "read thyself," rather than "know thyself," is not a blunder on his part. He means to say that one can understand the actions of others by reading oneself, that is, by taking one's own thoughts and passions, the motives of one's actions, as indexes of the same in others. This self-inspection is not, as many would have it, a mode of intuition, introspection, or even speculation. In *De Corpore*, we are told that all observation, sense itself, has its beginning in difference (De Corp., ch. 25, art. 1, p. 389) that is visible to man as opposition, and not in any intellective or intuitive capacity to see intrinsic similitude and designate it with selected names. All sense of difference is a reading of signs. We have no special access to inward or private being, according to Hobbes. Not even our own. We must take our bearings by the signs we manifest. We read the "language of the passions" (Lev., ch. 6, p. 50). The best signs of the passions are not what we say, because, the "characters of man's heart, blotted and confounded as they are with dissembling, lying, counterfeiting, and erroneous doctrines, are legible only to him that searcheth hearts" (Lev., Intro., pp. xi-xii).

The dependability of what men say as an index of what they mean or intend is qualified by the arbitrary character of language and also by the fact that what men mean always bears the "tincture of our different passions" (Lev., ch. 4, p. 28). Language has a twofold deceptiveness about it. According to Hobbes, one can best discern another's intentions by reading his passions; and one can most reliably do that by reading *natural* rather than *arbitrary* signs. "The best signs of passions present, are either in the countenance, motions of the body, actions, and ends, or aims, which we otherwise know the man to have" (Lev., ch. 6, p. 50). By reading ourselves and using ourselves as a key to the intentions of others, we can know the meaning of the behaviour of others. This is true because of the "similitude of the passions" which all men exhibit. Men have the same passions. This is not to say, however, that all men are the same, that they have passions for the same objects. "I say the similitude of *passions,* which are the same in all men, *desire, fear, hope,* etc; not the similitude of the *objects* of the passions, which are the things *desired, feared, hoped,* etc." (Lev., Intro., p. xi).

Men with similar passions nevertheless have their own private designs and secret thoughts. All men desire, but not all men desire wisdom, nor can they. Hobbes adds, "though by men's actions we do discover their design sometimes; yet to do it without comparing them with our own, and distinguishing all circumstances, by which the case may come to be altered, is to decipher without a key, and be for the most part deceived, by too much trust, or by too much diffidence; as he that reads, is himself a good or evil man" (Lev., Intro., p. xii).

One comes to know human nature, then, by reading the signs which communicate the passions, first by reading them in oneself in the context of others, accurately acknowledging what they represent, and then observing them in others in relationship to oneself. Such reading of signs is no mere matter of passively perceiving. Signs do not reveal themselves self-evidently to be signs. They reveal themselves only to one who has intentions or objectives that are aided or hindered by that which the sign represents. Of course, the room for self-deception is enormous. This is especially the case with political men who place principles—honour and glory—above all else. We shall see in subsequent chapters that the love of glory is taken by Hobbes to be a self-destructive impulse that appears to him who is so motivated to be an interest which will augment his well-being. Hobbes's opinion of what is partly required of a competent sovereign is reflected in his statement that "naturally, the best men are the least suspicious of fraudulent purposes" (Lev., ch. 46, p. 687). The point here is that experience and understanding are not adequately described by the mechanics of perceiving, knowing and speaking. These several phenomena are functions of human endeavour or desire, which is determinate and, therefore, observable only in a dynamic encounter with others. Hobbes's infamous remark, *homo homini lupus*, man to man is a wolf, follows from the *conative* character of human nature, which implies how any man will act with others. It is an insight that can easily be obscured by (especially by) the best of men, who fail to "read" the wolf in themselves and therefore are terrible measures of the wolf-like intentions of others. They tend naïvely to think good thoughts of others. They are inclined to be trusting. Reading mankind in oneself is not an easy task, Hobbes says; it is "hard to do, harder than to learn any language or science" (Lev., Intro., p. xii). It requires, first of all, a self-knowledge that the best of men are least able to achieve, because they depreciate the *conative* (desiderative and egoistic) inertia in human nature. Language, coated with the sediment of customs and coloured by the passions, cloaks our own thoughts, and even conceals its very concealment from us, leaving us unacquainted with our own most fundamental intentions and desires.

To summarize the point of this chapter, man's liberation from natural necessity is not the product of spontaneous will, nor the result of intellective intuition. Rather, man is free, according to Hobbes, to the extent that his own most natural desire, his desire for self-preservation and well-being, transcends the immediacy of natural relations, and thereby escapes their transient character. Since man is unquestionably a natural being, there can be no actual escape from determinacy or causal necessity. Freedom not only does not require it; it is incompatible with indeterminacy. Human purposiveness is rooted in the natural desire for self-preservation over which man has no control.

Sense, imagination, memory, and understanding mediate human desire and are comprehended by Hobbes only in relationship to this function. Hobbes expresses no systematic concern over an epistemological gap between mind and exterior bodies. The function of understanding is not to relay to man an independent exteriority, but rather to mediate human desire. It is always intentional, an "outward endeavour." Language is the vehicle of both understanding and discourse with others. It assists in man's liberation from natural necessity, that is, more effectively permits the expression of human purposiveness and self-concern by withdrawing itself and the images to which it is attached from the otherwise transient flow of images and thoughts characteristic of animals. Language and understanding liberate, then, to the extent that they consistently signify, that is, make determinate, the *conatus* that is basic to human nature, the first beginning of all voluntary motion. They simultaneously convey the nature of reality to man only because reality is dynamic rather than static, determined only in the dialectical encounter of *conatus* with *conatus*, man with nature.

4

The
Passions

Hobbes's infamous claim that men are naturally alienated from one another and that they will invade each other with impunity if they see profit in it, did not originate in observations he made of men living in society, though it was certainly confirmed by those observations. By his own statement, it was an "inference made from the passions" (Lev., ch. 13, p. 144). While it is a claim that may be confirmed *by* experience, it is not an inference *from* experience. For Hobbes, man is a creature of passion. This is not to say anything about the disposition of any man, but only about the ultimate origins of thought and action. Every thought and opinion, and therefore every action, carries the tincture of the passions.

Hobbes's claim is intended to say something about the nature of man, that man is pre-eminently a natural being. He is not the product of his social environment. Man's needs are not generated by life in civil society, though they are certainly qualified by it. Appetite and aversion, the twin components of passion, are ontologically prior to civil association. They are the first endeavours of all animal motion, found "even in the embryo." They are, in fact, the human manifestations of the *conatus* that animates all things. Because they are natural, not civil, human appetite and aversion have no merely social terminus. That is, their satisfaction is never fully obtained through the benefits gained by living in a commonwealth. Neither peace nor the commodities provided by a market society can fully satisfy the infinite desire of Hobbesian man. Hence, he cannot help but find himself at war with others as unsatisfiable desire comes into conflict with unsatisfiable desire.

Recent interpretations of Hobbes's philosophy have abandoned this view. The argument has been made that Hobbes's concept of human nature was the result of a "moral insight," the result, for example, of his empirical observations of men living in modern society. C.B. Macpherson, to cite just one Hobbes scholar, has maintained that "the nature of man is thus got primarily from observation of contemporary society, and incidentally confirmed by examining definitions."[1] The difficulty with this approach and its variants is that it takes some of the implications that follow from Hobbes's theory, particularly those regarding what a man will do in a given situation, for the theory itself. It exaggerates Hobbes's belief in the potential for the political or moral satisfaction of human desire, and even worse, it tends to identify reason with the effort to transcend or escape the domain of desire. Reason is reduced to logical discourse. The man of reason is reduced to the positivist whose behaviour is grounded in logical computation.

The resulting bifurcation of reason and desire has led to an interpretive dismissal of Hobbes's notorious "egoism" by many recent Hobbes scholars. This generates more confusion than it resolves. Hobbes is clear about the matter. "Life itself is but motion and can never be without desire, nor without fear, no more than without sense" (Lev., ch. 6, p. 51). He says, "Nor can a man any more live, whose desires are at an end, than he, whose senses and imagination are at a stand" (Lev., ch. 11, p. 85). There is, in short, no legitimate question whether man, in Hobbes's estimation, is egoistically bound or not. Desire and life are co-terminous. The fundamental question for any interpretation of Hobbes is the origin of this claim. Is it an empirical hypothesis, the implication of some moral or socio-economic (but not philosophic) backdrop, or something else?

Hobbes's theory, as it has been developed in the preceding chapters, is that there is a typical structure to all relations whatsoever, and that this structure is the product of the interrelation of motions, understood as *conatus*, where *conatus* is itself comprehended as a dynamic principle, visible only in (or delimited as) the dialectical interplay of opposing forces in nature. As a determinant of human actions, *conatus* is referred to by Hobbes as endeavour. Endeavour is accounted for in the two dialectically related intentions—endeavour *toward* and endeavour *from*, which Hobbes refers to with the more emotive names, "appetite" and "aversion" (Lev., ch. 6, p. 39). All human behaviour is the product of the interplay between these two mutually implicating moments in what is, for Hobbes, the reciprocal determination of *conatus*.

What will be seen in the present chapter is that felicity, the abstract "summum bonum" for man, is the infinite extension and unending satisfaction of his passionate concern for preservation and augmentation of life. The backdrop against which Hobbes develops this idea is political. In his pursuit of felicity, man alienates himself from the natural condition. He liberates himself from nature's malevolent indifference by contracting with others to form civil society. Unfortunately for him, however, civil association cannot provide a basis for satisfying the infinite desire that is latent in all human endeavour. The alienation of man from the natural condition is at the same time an alienation of his right to seek an unqualified acquisition of his own good. Political association is a self-imposed coercive measure intended to prevent physical war between individuals. It provides no guarantees against abuses of sovereign authority; sovereign authority is the precondition of civil society, and cannot be limited without creating a crisis of authority. Neither does it provide assurances against threats to man's well-being that are not political in nature or in their point of origin, for example, threats against one's mental and physical health, or the dangers of natural catastrophes. Because of the unlimited character of human desire, Hobbes maintained that there is no *summum bonum*. Felicity, in other words, is not a condition one might find oneself in for once and for all, but is the sense of success enjoyed by one who has successfully mastered all obstacles so far, and who perceives no end to his success. Felicity arises not merely because man has insulated himself politically from the natural condition. If felicity is to be possible, once his political relationships are stabilized, man must turn back to nature in an attempt to "imitate the creation" (De Corp., Epistle to the Reader, p. xii), to reshape nature according to an image of his own will. The alienation of man from man is ultimately only an expression of man's alienation from nature per se. Only by engaging with his problems scientifically and philosophically as well as politically can man make himself the measure, and therefore the "master," of nature. The possibility that man might enjoy what Hobbes calls "the great and master delight" (El. of Law, ch. 10, art. 6, p. 56) is proportionate to his having successfully undertaken this pursuit of mastery.

The centrality of the passions in Hobbes's account of the human situation makes a very careful examination of his treatment of them fundamental. Oddly enough, this is precisely what is lacking in most studies of Hobbes. It has not been generally observed by students of Hobbes's philosophy that his account of the passions underwent a complex development that influenced his entire philosophical system. Failure to appreciate this development has led to the dismissal of much of what Hobbes says in his later works as inconsistent, and has tended to promote the thought that, "What he (Hobbes) wrote in his youth, and thus before he was influenced by mathematics and natural science, expresses his most original thoughts better than the work of his maturity."[2] As interesting as this idea is, it is wrong.

SELF-PRESERVATION

Because of the *conative* character of every human act—cognitive, perceptual, and emotional as well as merely locomotive—all human behaviour whatsoever is necessarily reflexive. There is no action that does not somehow express the endeavour of man to preserve his own life or to augment his own well-being, that is to say, to preserve and augment those motions which in human beings we call "life." Man's endeavour to preserve himself necessarily takes him beyond the satisfaction of his immediate needs, since beings endowed with foresight tend to be interested in the conditions necessary for assuring their well-being even in the distant future, and even in an "imaginable" future that may never actually come to pass. Unfortunately, the effort spent to "assure the power and means to live well" (Lev., ch. 11, p. 86) unavoidably jeopardizes the life of him who seeks such power because it arouses the suspicion and envy of others who, concerned for their own safety, will also be concerned about actions undertaken by others that hint at possibly hostile intentions. Thus, Hobbes writes, "Competition of riches, honor, command, or other power inclines to contention, enmity, and war, because the way of one competitor to the attaining of his desires is to kill, subdue, supplant or repel the other" (Lev., ch. 11, p. 87).

In this competitive interplay of man with man, no man acts intelligently without taking "himself" as the key to rational behaviour (Lev., Intro., p. xii; ch. 46, p. 681). What this implies is that rational behaviour (reason itself) is the precondition of war in the state of nature. Because felicity is unobtainable in the state of nature, the rational pursuit of felicity in that condition mirrors the inexhaustible restlessness of nature, "a general inclination of all mankind," which Hobbes describes as "a perpetual and restless desire of power after power that ceases only in death" (Lev., ch. 11, pp. 85–6).

Man's restlessness is an extension of the restlessness of nature itself. And the necessity of this in human nature is nothing other than the dialectical character of human endeavour. Man cannot but desire his own preservation if he is a rational being, and cannot but jeopardize his preservation in the very process of successfully acquiring those powers which would assure it. Preservation and augmentation, if pursued as finite objectives, are simultaneously self-affirming and self-destructive modes of the objective implicit in the endeavour of every natural body. As we have already heard Hobbes say, they are objectives "found even in the embryo; which while it is in the womb, moveth its limbs with voluntary motion, for the avoiding of whatsoever troubleth it, or for the pursuing of what pleaseth it" (De Corp., ch. 25, art. 12, p. 407).

To say that human endeavour is found even in the embryo is to say that it is inherent in the nature of man. It is not an historically acquired, or learned, trait. The endeavour varies in amplitude among men, perhaps as their individual bodily constitutions differ and as experience and education vary (Lev., Intro., p. xi; ch. 6, p. 40; Ele. of Law, ch. 10, art. 1, p. 54; De Corp., ch. 25, art. 12, p. 407). Because of these variations, men differ in the objects of their desires. Some prefer sensuous pleasures while others prefer wealth, political office, social prestige, and so on. Of all the possible objects of desire, Hobbes says, only the desire for knowledge does not culminate necessarily in grief. Knowledge as an object of desire permits limitless progress and, therefore, can promote felicity and joy. All other pursuits presuppose an "utmost degree" of achievement, at which point, Hobbes says, "men justly complain of a great grief, that they know not what to do" (El. of Law, ch. 7, art. 6, p. 33). Success, not failure, is the great nemesis of man, since it deprives the one who is successful of the prerequisite of continued success, that is, other obstacles to overcome.

Traditionally, Hobbes has been thought to have grounded man's concern for knowledge on his fear of violent death. This observation is correct, insofar as fear propels men into philosophical inquiries, the object of which is to remove the source of fear. The criticism made of Hobbes's claim is that fear cannot be the origin of philosophical inquiry because it cannot provide a sense of the "whole." Fear needs an object, and so is inherently finite. A philosophical quest founded on, or motivated by, fear would culminate in no complete account. It would cease once the fear-generating object were mastered or removed. The rationality that fear would generate would be pragmatic, not philosophical.

This criticism neglects the infinite character of fear and desire in Hobbes's account of the genesis of philosophy in the passions. The pursuit of knowledge is, for Hobbes, a dialectical engagement of man with nature itself. It is a pursuit in which the passions of fear and desire are radically extended. Properly understood, this pursuit is not irredeemably finite. Part of the claim that Hobbes's conception of the philosophical pursuit is finite is a result of understanding the passions of fear and desire to be conceptual opposites, but not to take that opposition dialectically. Leo Strauss, for example, has argued that the dichotomy of fear and desire is, in fact, a dichotomy of fear and vanity. And that, in turn, is nothing less than a dichotomy of reason and passion, since fear is the passion which promotes reason, and vanity is clearly associated by Hobbes with unreason.

Strauss's argument, however compelling it may be, is incorrect. Desire and fear function together for Hobbes in the promotion of felicity, the restless modern counterpart to the ancient philosophical ideal of contemplative happiness. Independently of desire, fear does not promote philosophical inquiry. To see why this is the case, one must examine the distinction Hobbes makes between desire and fear (or aversion). He writes: "of things we know not at all, or believe not to be, we can have no further desire, than to taste and try. But aversion we have for things not only which we know have hurt us, but also that we do not know whether they will hurt us, or not" (Lev., ch. 6, p. 40).

Fear, admittedly, needs an object and is, therefore, unavoidably finite. This is to say that fear carries with it the conviction that there is a cause of fear. It is also true that the source of fear is not always locatable. In such situations, Hobbes writes, men "are inclined to suppose and feign unto themselves, several kinds of powers invisible; and to stand in awe of their own imaginations; and in time of distress to invoke them" (Lev., ch. 11, p. 93). In short, finite fear exhibits an inner infinitude, a sense of the "whole," insofar as one may fear any object, known or unknown. Any object can conceivably become the cause of a man's "death, poverty, or other calamity" (Lev., ch. 12, p. 95). And, insofar as *any* object can be the object of fear (i.e., whether there is actual reason to fear it or not) *every* object becomes the possible object of fear. In fear, man exposes the limitless possibility of the hostility of nature. One need acknowledge only that man's well-being is not nature's sole guiding purpose, an acknowledgment that is an almost unavoidable accompaniment of misfortune. Fear can lead man to see the *absence* of purpose or benevolence in nature. Leo Strauss has fittingly quoted in this regard Pascal's *Pensées:* "The eternal silence of these infinite spaces frightens man."[3]

Unlike fear, appetite is not the consequence of one's experience of misfortune, which comes only with an experiential entry into the world, but is, instead, spontaneous,[4] restless, unceasing striving for power after power. At its utmost degree, however, all desire is a desire, or love, of self. It is reflexive. In this way, infinite desire exhibits an essentially finite and intelligible structure, insofar as man is understood to take himself as the measure of all things.

We have, then, a dialectic of fear and desire in Hobbes's account that incorporates a dialectic of finite and infinite. Fear is finite insofar as it is directed toward, and delimited by, a multitude of external objects, but is also infinite since it is directed indifferently toward *any*, and therefore toward *every*, natural object. Desire, on the other hand, is finite insofar as its object is only the self, but it is infinite in that the meaning and significance of all external objects whatsoever, either desired or feared, are found in reference to self.

For Hobbes, reason does not emerge in proportion to man's liberation from the illusions of self-love, leaving fear as the sole remaining ground of reason, as many have maintained. Rather, man's inexhaustible fear of his natural environment, itself an expression of his unlimited self-concern, exposes the absence of external purposiveness in nature, its unresponsiveness to human need and desire. Man has good reason for his infinite fear. For the very same reason, however, there exists the possibility of limitless self-assertion. The possibility that man might impose the image of his own will on nature, making himself the true measure of all things, gives direction to desire. Hobbes recommends that men strive to imitate the creation (Lev., Intro., p. ix; De Corp., Epistle to the Reader). We are told that "to know this [i.e., any] truth is nothing else but to acknowledge that it is made by ourselves" (De Cive, ch. 18, p. 303). The limitless indifference of the universe opens the way to an "indefatigable generation of knowledge" (Lev., ch. 6, p. 45). At its zenith, this passion is represented by what Hobbes calls the "spirit of gravity," and its objective "the great and master delight" (El. of Law, ch. 10, art. 6, p. 56).

THE DEVELOPMENT OF HOBBES'S ACCOUNT

The evolution of Hobbes's account of the passions becomes especially visible through a contrasting examination of the respective accounts given in the earlier *Elements of Law* and in the later *Leviathan*. The two accounts differ significantly. As has been suggested already, the idea fundamental to his mature account of human nature is the dialectical character of *conatus* represented in the dichotomy of appetite and aversion. This dichotomy, when perceived according to its different temporal manifestations, is responsible for all the simple passions and their pairing with counterpassions. In *The Elements of Law*, Hobbes first prepared the foundation for this discrimination of appetite and aversion temporally into the different passions. He wrote:

> I have therefore obliged myself, as far forth as I am able, to search out and declare from what conception proceedeth every one of these passions which we commonly take notice of: for seeing the things that please and displease, are innumerable, and work in innumerable ways, men have not taken notice but of a very few, which also are many of them without name. And first, we are to consider that of conceptions there are three sorts, whereof one is of that which is present, which is sense; another, of that which is past, which is remembrance; and the third, of that which is future, which we call expectation... and in every of these conceptions is pleasure or pain present. (El. of Law, ch. 7, art. 1, pp. 34–5; cf. Lev., ch. 6, pp. 42–3)

Hobbes separates the passions into kinds by subordinating them to these three temporal modes of cognition. These forms of cognition represent an *a priori* that does not vary from man to man. The passions, then, must share this *a priori* form. Hobbes's statement in *Leviathan* that there is a "similitude of the thoughts and passions of one man to the thoughts and passions of another" (Lev., Intro., p. xi) has been frequently and mistakenly taken to represent Hobbes's declaration of the natural equality of all men. The *a priori* similitude of the forms of passion in men does not imply a "similitude of the *objects* of the passions, which are the things, *desired, feared, hoped,* etc.: for these the constitution individual, and particular education, do so vary... " (Lev., Intro, p. xi).

Hobbes, of course, must not be taken to mean here by "objects" merely corporeal things. In the Latin *Leviathan*, he uses the word *objectum*, which can mean *res*, but which can also mean *finis*. And in *The Elements*, he maintains "that *bonum* and *finis* are different names, but for different considerations of the same thing" (El. of Law, ch. 7, art. 4, p. 32). The objects of the passions are not, then, merely sensual objects but, rather, various conceptions of the good life. This difference in the objects, that is, objectives, of human passion is partly due to the difference of education among men, and so is in part historical, but is also due to differences in individual constitution, and so is more primarily natural. That is, there are natural differences among men; some men naturally gravitate toward sensual satisfaction, some toward the acquisition of wealth or political office and honours, and some few toward the acquisition of knowledge.

The Elements of Law differs significantly from *Leviathan* insofar as it places the primary human objective in the acquisition of honours, an objective associated with Hobbes's early conception of life, referred to in *The Elements of Law* as a kind of race. The analogy of life and a race would suggest that the differences among men are social and historical rather than natural. The analogy is abandoned by Hobbes in *Leviathan*. There the primacy of honour is replaced by seven simple passions. The tendency among Hobbes's commentators to use the analogy found in *The Elements of Law* as a model for understanding his philosophy per se, *Leviathan* included, represents a failure to have recognized the substantial change from the former work to the latter.

THE ELEMENTS OF LAW: LIFE AS A RACE

The peculiar character of Hobbes's treatment of the passions in *The Elements of Law* is a product of the view of life, or human existence, that he adopts there. Life is like a race (although Hobbes admits that the comparison is not entirely valid). Predictably, the goal of a race-like life is being foremost (El. of Law, ch. 9, art. 21, p. 53). Since winning is the very meaning of life, life is perceived by Hobbes to be incurably competitive. Of course, the passion for winning depends on there being competition against which one can race. Passions, in other words, are social; they are acquired responses to the recognition given or withheld by others. "In the pleasure men have, or displeasure from the signs of honour or dishonour done unto them, consisteth the *nature* of the passions" (El. of Law, ch. 8, art. 8, p. 40).

The competitive view of life provided in *The Elements of Law* is retained in *Leviathan*. Nonetheless, the account found in *The Elements* is inadequate, mainly because its image of life as a race is not compatible with all the objectives, or forms of human desire, Hobbes attributes to man, and because the image itself fosters an idea of life which conflicts with the preconditions of life. It is not only abandoned by Hobbes later on; it is implicitly condemned. We will examine these two criticisms more carefully.

If the object of a race is to win, it is by definition contentious. As Hobbes sees it, however, the objective of life is felicity, and felicity requires a degree of peace if it is to be enjoyed. But peace is a goal which, if it is to be obtained by men, requires their admission of natural equality. To admit equality is to terminate one's efforts to be foremost (Lev., ch. 11, p. 86). In the language of *The Elements of Law*, this would be to forsake the race and, therefore, to die! In short, there is a tension between Hobbes's conception of life, or human nature, and the image of life as a race.

A comparison of the list of passions that precedes Hobbes's analogy of life as a race with the list given in *Leviathan* would show that the list in *The Elements of Law* is abbreviated. It omits many passions that are present in the *Leviathan* account. It has been observed, for example, that *fear* is absent from the earlier account. The reasons given for its absence have been various. I believe that fear is not a passion treated by the earlier account simply because, as Hobbes defines it, fear is incompatible with the image of a race. That is, fear is a negative passion that would encourage one to give up the race, much as it forces men in the natural condition to admit their mutual equality and abandon their separate efforts to be "foremost." It generates a desire in them to contract with one another to form a civil community. This is not to say that, for Hobbes, fear is never a cause of desire, for example, the desire to win, but only that, where the prospect for winning cannot be sustained indefinitely and the prospect of losing can be fairly well eradicated (as is the case in social situations), fear will encourage men to be prudent, to compromise.

Also absent—and significant in their absence—are the passions of curiosity, admiration, religion, contempt, joy, grief, and magnanimity (the latter only as Hobbes defines it in *Leviathan*, as a mode of contempt).

Curiosity and *admiration* might be said to be more spectator's passions, their proper end not involving the running of a race. One might exhibit curiosity as to why a race is or is not run, and also curiosity regarding who won and why. Likewise, one might admire the winner, the sportsmanship of the loser, and even the whole spectacle of the race itself. But as a runner, one never exhibits any special curiosity about, nor admiration for the finish line, the final objective of the race. In a real sense, if you have seen one finish line, you have seen them all.

Religion Hobbes includes as a passion in *Leviathan*. That seems somewhat odd. It is identified there as a form of fear which is, in turn, a form of aversion. It involves a submission or "giving over" that is not at all characteristic of a racer. Religion is characterized by faith, which implies an admission of one's limitations. An obstinate endeavour to be foremost would be the equivalent of hubris, or pride. In a religious context, it would represent the negation of faith. Consequently, religion is absent from *The Elements of Law* account.

Contempt, too, is a passion (albeit a curious one) which fails to fit into Hobbes's analogy. Contempt is a disregard of little and therefore contemptible, helps and hindrances. The contemptuous (or magnanimous) one—as Aristotle indicated in his *Nicomachean Ethics*—sets himself above the race, apparently because he would not want to risk the embarrassment of losing to an inferior.

Finally, *joy* and *grief* are conspicuous in their absence. They, too, are in a sense the passions of spectators. Hobbes's discussion of joy and grief in *The Elements* recalls ancient Lucretius' admonition of those who, fearing death immoderately, can welcome a brother's death with heartless glee. Hobbes echoes Lucretius' observation, omitting the admonition, when he writes:

> from what passion proceedeth it, that men take *pleasure* to *behold* from the shore the danger of them that are at sea in a tempest, or in fight, or from a safe castle to behold two armies charge one another in the field? It is certainly, in the whole sum, *joy*; else men would never flock to see such a spectacle. Nevertheless there is in it both joy and *grief*: for as there is novelty and remembrance of our own security present, which is delight; so there is also pity, which is grief; but the delight is so far predominant, that men usually are content in such a case to be spectators of the misery of their friends.[5] (El. of Law, ch. 9, art. 19, pp. 51–2)

Understandably, Hobbes does not attempt to incorporate this pair of passions into his analogy. One might recall Lucretius' claim that life is most complete when one liberates oneself from the travails of having to run the race, to compete for contingent goods. In competing, one is always living for tomorrow's pleasures, always immersed in the conscious realization of one's present needs, never enjoying those pleasures that are available to be enjoyed today.

Hobbes does not, of course, incorporate into his philosophy Lucretius' contemplative ideal, since that ideal calls for contemplative passivity. Hobbes's spectator virtues are passions more proper to the director-producer of a theatrical spectacle who is rapturously engaged in developing the scene that unfolds before him, neither a spectator nor entirely an actor, yet partially both, and entirely responsible for all that happens.

The account of the passions in *The Elements of Law*, then, is only partial—whether intentionally or not may be disputed—and demands completion. The complete account requires that Hobbes abandon the analogy of life as a race. The analogy suggests the incurably competitive character of human nature, and to that extent it is instructive. However, it does not show the self-destructive implications of "being foremost" in a social context, the fact that the successful satisfaction of the desire for glory and honour is a prelude to one's downfall. Neither does the analogy illuminate the philosophical and scientific dimensions of human endeavour, where man's competitiveness is directed against nature itself.

THE LEVIATHAN ACCOUNT OF THE PASSIONS

As has already been suggested, in *Leviathan* Hobbes corrected his account of the passions. It is a rather orthodox opinion among the majority of commentators on Hobbes that the *Leviathan* analysis of the passions is little more than a piecemeal regurgitation of Aristotle's list of the passions in the *Rhetoric*,[6] disorganized and rambling, not the coherent account that we find in *The Elements of Law*. To be sure, the analogy of life with a race which unifies *The Elements* account has been dropped and not replaced by any other organizing image. But images can be deceiving. The *Leviathan* account, when patiently examined, reveals a geometrically structured treatment of the passions which—and this is most important—no longer makes glory, honours, or "being foremost," the principal end of all human endeavour. In *The Elements*, nothing intrinsically natural was implied by the differentiation of passions because no end other than glory, being foremost, was fundamental. If the various passions are modes of the pursuit of glory, then they are irreducibly social. Glory, honour, and being foremost are not the concerns of a man in isolation from others with whom he might compete. They arise only in social situations as products of social and educational antecedents. Variations of the concern for honour are learned, or acquired, rather than natural. Hobbes's *Leviathan* account abandons this social derivation of the passions and replaces it with a geometrical account, grounded upon several simple, axiomatic passions.

In chapter six of *Leviathan*, after a preliminary account of the derivation of the simple passions from the two modes of human endeavour (endeavour toward and endeavour from), Hobbes provides us with a list of the simple passions: "appetite, desire, love, aversion, hate, joy and grief... " (Lev., ch. 6, p. 43). The evidence for the different passions, he says, are those "signs" that men exhibit, that is, those which we can observe, "in the countenance, motions of the body, actions, and ends or aims which we otherwise know the men to have" (Lev., ch. 6, p. 50).

The important point to Hobbes's statement is that such movements are "signs" of the passions, not an account of their nature or derivation. In this, *Leviathan* differs from *The Elements of Law*. Hobbes presents us with three pairs of contrasting passions in *Leviathan*: desire and aversion, love and hate, joy and grief. The three pairs are distinguished, first, on the basis of the temporal character of the passion, that is, whether its object is absent (in the past or the future) or present (that is, present to sense), and second, on the basis of whether the passion involves a sense of expectation. Love and hate are passions concerned with an object that is present; desire and aversion, joy and grief are passions concerned with objects absent, that is, in the past (remembered) or in the future (imagined).[7] When desire and aversion for objects that are absent (remembered from the past and considered as part of a possible future) are accompanied by expectation, those passions take the form of joy and grief. These are the different ways in which the human endeavour or *conatus* individuates itself:

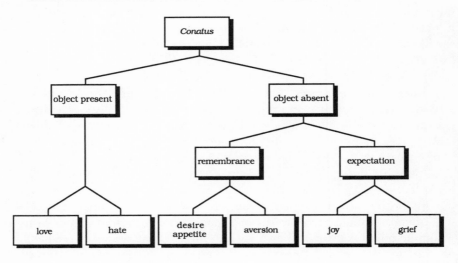

Desire and Aversion

The first of Hobbes's contrary pairs of passions, desire and aversion, is obscured by a distinction he appears to make between desire and "appetite." If appetite, which appears as the first passion in the list of simple passions, is indeed one of the simple passions, the grouping of the passions into three pairs would, of course, no longer be possible. Hobbes makes it clear, however, that appetite is not a passion distinct from desire. Desire, he says, is more general. Appetite refers only to those desires, for example, hunger and thirst, that are concerned with the satisfaction of our immediate needs; that are easily satisfiable, at least in comparison with other desires that are capable of being extended infinitely; and the satisfaction of which cannot serve as the end or good of life. The distinction, I believe, is meant more to exclude the natural appetites from Hobbes's treatment of desire than it is meant to include appetite as a primitive passion. After drawing a distinction between appetite and desire, Hobbes tends to use the two terms, in effect, as synonyms, when he is abstracting from bodily, that is, satisfiable, need. The same distinction is apparent in the treatment of aversion, but Hobbes does not make it thematic by supplying two different terms for the different usages.

The distinction between appetite and desire (and whatever the counterpart of this distinction would be in regard to aversion) certainly does not represent a contrast between voluntary and involuntary passions. Hobbes clearly maintains that there are no voluntary passions per se, because there is no will per se: "Appetite, fear, hope, and the rest of the passions are not called voluntary; for they proceed not from, but *are* the will; and the will is not voluntary: for, a man can no more say he will will, than he will will will, and so make an infinite repetition of the word; which is absurd and insignificant" (El. of Law., ch. 12, art. 5, p. 69).

The distinction between appetite and desire is of no interest to Hobbes from this point on, that is, in those aspects of human nature in which human beings are different from mere animals. Desire and aversion are nothing more than the "endeavour toward" and the "endeavour from" some object desired or disliked. In *The Elements of Law*, Hobbes defines them as the will to do and the will to omit. In *Leviathan*, Hobbes further identifies desire and aversion by contrasting them with the passions of love and hate. He writes, "So that desire and love are the same thing, save that by desire we always signify the absence of the object, by love most commonly the presence of the same. So also by aversion we signify the absence, and by hate the presence of the object" (Lev., ch. 6, p. 40).

Desire and aversion involve a remembrance of what is past and a concern for what lies in the future, the two possible temporal senses of "absent," with this proviso, that concern for the future is not accompanied by an anticipation of success or failure. For that joy and grief will be more appropriate.

Hobbes's account further shows that these two primitive passions (desire and aversion) are the source of numerous derivative passions. Hope, despair, confidence, diffidence, charity, good nature, covetousness, ambition, revengefulness, and curiosity are all identified as forms of *desire*, while fear, courage and anger, indignation, wretchedness, religion, superstition, true religion and panic terror are all listed as different modes or determinations of *aversion*, ways that aversion manifests itself. Some derivative passions such as pusillanimity are listed as modes of both desire and aversion, reflecting the reciprocal character of the two more primitive passions.

Joy and Grief

Hobbes defines the passions of joy and grief as "the *expectation* that proceeds from *foresight* of the end or consequence of things, whether those things in the sense please or displease" (Lev., ch. 6, p. 43). Included as subpassions of *joy* are admiration, glorying (or confidence), vainglory, and sudden glory. As determinations of *grief* Hobbes lists dejection, sudden dejection, shame, pity (or compassion), emulation, and envy.

The passions of joy and grief differ from passions of desire and aversion in that the latter are passions the emphasis of which is on objects absent, that is, in the past or in the future, in which *remembrance* is the dominant intellective function. In joy and grief, on the other hand, the emphasis is placed on the *expectation* of fulfilling the needs which are represented by one's desires, and therefore on *knowledge* (foresight) of what the future is likely to hold.

Love and Hate

Love and hate differ from desire and aversion, as well as from joy and grief, insofar as they represent an endeavour toward or endeavour from an object which is *present* (Lev., ch. 6, p. 40). That is, they are passions whose proper object is immediate, and so are properly referred to as *the sensuous passions*. Their object is the pleasures of sense rather than the pleasures of mind, with recognition of the fact that mind (imagination, memory, and understanding) differs from sense for Hobbes only by being sense that is retained or recalled. There is in Hobbes's account only a functional difference between sense and understanding; they are not different faculties. Hobbes lists, as subspecies of *love*, kindness, natural lust, luxury, passion of love, and jealousy. Interestingly, he does not list any subspecies for *hatred*.

The reason for the absence of subspecies of hate may be found in the fact that those subspecies are given, instead, to another quasi-passion, "contempt." In the preliminary discussion of simple passions in chapter 6 of *Leviathan*, Hobbes discusses and defines "contempt," but fails to include it in the summary list of simple passions that follows his discussion. It is not clear, therefore, whether contempt is meant to be taken as a simple passion or not.

Later, contempt reappears as the genus of several derivative passions, so we can conclude that it must be a passion, one of the simple passions, even though it is not included in Hobbes's list. It is obviously not derived from the six simple passions listed by Hobbes. It is defined by Hobbes in such a way that it can be neither an endeavour toward nor an endeavour from anything. Contempt is defined as an insensitivity. Ultimately, Hobbes will discuss contempt as the insensitivity some men show toward the preconditions of social existence, "an immobility, or contumacy of the heart, in resisting the action of certain things; and proceeding from that the heart is *already moved* otherwise, by other more potent objects; or from want of experience of them" (Lev., ch. 6, p. 40).

Contempt is implied by the mutually exclusive character of some desires. For example, to a businessman art may mean nothing, just as to an artist, business affairs may mean nothing. The contemptuous neither desire nor hate (Lev., ch. 6, p. 40) but simply disregard things that are of little importance. And, of course, within Hobbes's conception of the nature and origin of human sensibility, where sensibility is directly proportionate to one's concern for one's own survival, a thing is of little importance only to him who senses his own invulnerability or lack of need. This is especially the case with "magnanimity," a passion which Hobbes defines as a subspecies of contempt! Magnanimity, he says, is "a contempt of little helps and hindrances" (Lev., ch. 6, p. 44). This represents a correction of Hobbes's earlier account of magnanimity in *The Elements of Law*, where it is identified as a subspecies of glorying, the "internal gloriation or triumph of the mind... which proceedeth from the imagination or conception of our own power above the power of him that contendeth with us" (El. of Law, ch. 9, art. 1, p. 40).

In *The Elements of Law*, we have seen, contempt is treated as a subdivision of glory. Glory, in turn, is not distinguished from magnanimity. In *Leviathan*, on the other hand, glory is listed as a subdivision of the passion "joy" and magnanimity is listed as a subspecies of "contempt." Hobbes's intention here is not so much to make a firm distinction between glory and magnanimity as it is to make a statement regarding the reciprocal nature of the passions "joy" and "contempt." Contempt is an outward manifestation of the self-esteem, or joy, in imagining one's own powers. And joy in imagining one's own powers is inseparably associated with a disregard of, or contempt for, the powers of others. The contemptuous cannot properly be said to hate, according to the definition Hobbes gives for contempt, because hatred would involve an acknowledgment of the potentially threatening powers of others and, by implication, a sense of one's own vulnerability or defective power. That is precisely what contempt is not. Hatred for an object that is present would, then, be either a form of fear (i.e., endeavour from) or contempt, that is, a self-esteem of such magnitude as to make hatred (in the sense of fear) inconceivable. And, therefore, it is contempt, not hatred, that is given all the various sub-passions that one might think belong to hatred as a simple passion. Hatred, it was noted, is distinct among the six simple passions in that Hobbes attributes to it no subspecies.

The subspecies of contempt are magnanimity and valour. Valour, Hobbes says, is a contempt for the prospect of death and wounds (Lev., ch. 6, p. 44; El. of Law, ch. 4, art. 4, p. 42). Hobbes also says that such contemptuousness toward the prospect of death and wounds "enclineth men to private revenges, and sometimes to endeavour the unsettling of the public peace" (Lev., Rev. & Concl., p. 701). That is, contempt represents an insensitivity to the preconditions of civil existence insofar as it is an insensitivity to those fears which moderate political behaviour. It suggests that there is not really a distinction between glory (a form of joy) and magnanimity (a form of contempt). They represent two reciprocal aspects of the same passion. The significance of this for Hobbes's more mature political theory in *Leviathan* will be substantial.

Other subspecies of contempt are liberality (a contempt for wealth), impudence (contempt for one's good reputation), and cruelty (contempt for the calamities that befall others). With these passions now clarified, we have systematically exhausted all the passions treated in *Leviathan*. Hobbes's account in *Leviathan* is, then, less disorganized than his readers would have us believe. More importantly, it is evident that, in its most important aspects, it owes no debt whatsoever to Aristotle as has frequently been suggested.

THE INFLUENCE OF DESCARTES

It is far more useful to examine Hobbes's account of the passions in relation to the writings of his contemporaries, especially Descartes, than it is to associate it haphazardly with Aristotle's account. There can be little doubt, in fact, that Hobbes drew upon, or at least was influenced by, Descartes' famous treatment of the passions, *The Passions of the Soul*. Leo Strauss goes so far as to say that Descartes' influence led Hobbes to incorporate in *Leviathan* Cartesian ideas entirely inconsistent with the principles of his political philosophy. Strauss overstated his case. His argument overlooks substantial differences between their respective accounts of the passions and, therefore, neglects the criticism of Descartes that is implicit in Hobbes. The issue turns on the origin and nature of what Descartes called "generosity," and what Hobbes called "magnanimity," the highest of all human virtues (which is the same as to say the greatest of all human passions). The importance of the distinction is in what it implies for Hobbes's political theory and especially for his conception of the philosophical quest per se.

Even so, the influence of Descartes on Hobbes tends to explain the development of Hobbes's account of the passions from the time of *The Elements of Law* to the time of *Leviathan*. Descartes' *Passions of the Soul* was published in 1649, just prior to *Leviathan* (1651), during Hobbes's prolonged stay in Paris during the English Civil War. Hobbes can hardly be considered to have been a pupil of Descartes'; more correctly, they were antagonists. In a real sense, philosophy for Hobbes is war, the paradigm case of man's fundamental and inescapable concern for mastery. The mutual antagonism that existed between Hobbes and Descartes was initially a result of the intolerability of their agreements and Hobbes's desire to establish himself as the philosophical authority of his time.

A comparative study of their respective accounts of the simple passions is especially instructive. Their basic agreement makes the disagreements more revealing of the peculiarity of Hobbes's psychology and its role in his political philosophy. Hobbes wrote a political philosophy while Descartes, the paradigmatic rationalist, did not. The differences found in their treatments of the passions suggests why.

In his *Passions of the Soul*, Descartes maintained that the simple or primitive passions "are but six which are such, i.e., wonder, love, hatred, desire, joy, and sadness; and that all the others are composed of some of these six, or are species of them."[8]

Superficially, there seems to be mostly agreement between Hobbes and Descartes regarding their respective lists of simple passions. Hobbes's seven simple passions and one distinctly non-passion (contempt) reduce to six upon careful inspection, since appetite is indistinguishable from desire. All the subsequent passions are either subspecies of the simples or combinations of them, as is the case with Descartes. In fact, the differences between their respective accounts are substantial.

Descartes	Hobbes
wonder	contempt
love	love
hatred	hate
desire	desire
	aversion
joy	joy
sadness	grief

To begin with, two of Descartes' six simple passions (wonder and desire) have no opposites, no correlative passion, and only one passion (desire) leads, Descartes says, directly to action. These facets of Descartes' theory will be more fully discussed shortly. Sufficient for now to say that Hobbes disagrees with Descartes on each of the above points. For Hobbes, passion is always a form of action, an endeavour toward or endeavour from, and not simply the unmoved cause of action. These differences reflect deep-seated disagreements between Hobbes and Descartes in their respective accounts of human nature (e.g., of the nature of "soul").

The first of the simple passions for Descartes is *wonder.* Wonder, he says, is a "first encounter with some object [which] surprises us, and we judge it to be new or very different from what we formerly knew."[9] Descartes' notion of wonder obviously has its philosophical antecedent in Aristotle. It differs from the latter's classic account, however, in that it is not (as it is for Aristotle) an encounter with intellectual perplexities, or *aporeia.* It is a passion, not a faculty of intellect. However, wonder is unique among the simple passions that Descartes enumerates in that it moves man "without our in any way perceiving if the object which causes [it] is good or evil."[10] Wonder is neutral to questions of good and bad. But, because good and bad, for Descartes as for Hobbes, are terms designating things agreeable or hurtful (i.e., subjective designations of things as good because we desire them, and not desirable because they are good, as the ancients maintained), wonder involves a partial liberation of man from the passions, and, to that extent, from the limitation of human subjectivity. It is not an expression of a subjectively generated preference or value.

Descartes refers to wonder physiologically as a phenomenon of the brain; its effects do not extend to the heart.[11] The objects of wonder are only those that are "rare, and... consequently *worthy* of much considera-tion."[12] But the motive power of wonder cannot lie in self-interest or in desire. Rather, its "strength depends on two things, i.e., on the novelty, and on the fact that the movement which it causes possesses its entire strength from its commencement."[13]

Wonder is the spontaneous but efficacious passion which guarantees the possibility that philosophy can take the form of disinterested knowing. It provides for the liberation of man's philosophical proclivities from their natural or subjective limitations: "These two passions (esteem and disdain) are thus only species of wonder; for when we do not wonder at the greatness or smallness of an object, we do not make more or less of it than reason tells us that we ought to do in its regard, so that we then esteem or disdain it without passion."[14] It is the means by which man is open to nature, without the burden of human subjectivity, or "egoism." It is a passion that has no contrary. Descartes says, "if the object which presents itself has nothing in it that surprises us, we are in nowise moved regarding it, and we consider it without passion."[15]

Significantly, there is no counterpart to wonder in Hobbes's treatment of the passions. The neutrality of Cartesian wonder, its disregard for good and evil, is found, if anywhere, only in Hobbes's treatment of "contempt" (contempt involves an insensitivity to goodness and badness in those things that are inferior) and "admiration" (which involves appreciation for what is novel, albeit without Cartesian disinterestedness).

For Descartes, wonder is divisible into two subspecies, "esteem" and "disdain" (i.e., contempt). The most eminent of all Cartesian virtues, magnanimity (generosity) is, in turn, a subspecies of esteem for self. Because it is the subspecies of esteem rather than disdain (contempt), Cartesian magnanimity (generosity) does not possess the properties associated with contempt. In Hobbes's *Leviathan* account, to recall what we have already observed, magnanimity is identified as a subspecies of contempt. Hobbes, in short, contradicts Descartes' analysis of that virtue. One could hardly interpret this disagreement to represent anything other than an attempt on Hobbes's part to indicate something defective in Descartes' account. Self-esteem, however magnanimous it may make one seem, implies a contempt for those people and those qualities that the self-esteeming person considers to be inferior. This contempt carries with it further deleterious implications for social and civil relationships. I will turn to this political implication in subsequent chapters.

Hobbes's criticism of the Cartesian analysis of wonder is echoed in Spinoza's discussion of Descartes in his *Ethics*. We can make use of that discussion here. Spinoza makes no clear distinction between wonder and astonishment, the latter of which is for Descartes an excess of wonder.[16] Spinoza does not regard astonishment as an "affect" or passion at all, because it is an *"abstraction* of the mind [which] arises from no positive cause by which it is abstracted from other things, but merely from the absence of any cause by which from the contemplation of one thing the mind is determined to think other things."[17] That is, astonishment, or wonder, because it is impassionate, can have no consequences. Spinoza adds, "On the other hand, if we suppose ourselves to imagine in an object something peculiar which we have never seen before, it is the same as saying that the mind, while it contemplates that object, holds nothing else in itself to the contemplation of which it can pass, turning away from the contemplation of the object, and therefore it is determined to the contemplation solely of the object."[18]

Wonder, according to Spinoza, "arises from no positive cause." It is spontaneous. It is merely the attention of imagination directed to novel images. In this it differs from passion. It leads to no philosophical consequences. It is inadequately identified by Descartes as the origin of philosophical curiosity. Furthermore, to attribute to wonder the spontaneous efficacy of presenting for man rare and novel objects worthy of thought, thereby provoking this thought, is to make the wondering soul a cause of motion, that is, of the motions implicit in reflection, and therefore to presume the antiquated doctrine of the soul as the mover of the body, abandoning the effort to account for the movements of man entirely by reference to the passions, or naturally.

The philosophical validity of Spinoza's criticism of Descartes is not to be raised here. The criticism is included here only to make more obvious the difference between Descartes and Hobbes. Hobbes rejects altogether the disinterested character of wonder or intellectual delight. All thought is, for Hobbes, mediated by self-interest because it is always an expression of the human *conatus.* Nonetheless, man is not necessarily isolated psychologically from external nature for that reason. Fear reveals to man the infinitude of nature and desire the infinitude of man himself, according to Hobbes. The reciprocal dependency of fear and desire, where one is the opposite of, and indeterminate without, the other leaves Hobbes with a conception of the passions, of human nature in general, and of the nature of the philosophical undertaking distinct from anything encountered in Descartes' writings.

Besides "wonder," Descartes identifies five other passions as simple or primary, four of which he treats as correlatives: love and hatred, joy and sadness. Hobbes does not disagree with Descartes regarding his pairing, or with the general description of each pair. However, he does disagree with Descartes' claim that none of these four primitive passions is, in itself, the immediate cause of action.

According to Descartes, *love* and *hatred* are the passions with which man responds to matters which appear to him to be good (i.e., agreeable) or evil (i.e., hurtful).[19] But love and hate, as also joy and sadness, are passive, insofar as "when they are considered precisely in themselves, [they] do not incite us to any action."[20] "In so far" as they excite in us *desire* by means of which they regulate our habits,[21] we are led to act. Love and hatred, joy and sadness, all incite in man desire, and through the mediating effect of desire, one is encouraged to act. For that reason, Descartes maintains, "it is this *desire* particularly which we should be careful to regulate, and it is in this that the principal use of morality consists."[22]

Morality, understood in the light of Descartes' conception of desire, must take the form of a prescriptive regulation of desire. We shall see in the final chapter that this is, for Hobbes, the principal characteristic of traditional morality. It is also politically ineffective, since it holds that what regulates desire is reason or some moral axiom rather than, say, another desire.

Joy and *sadness* are for Descartes those passions which mediate love and desire, insofar as they implicate oneself as the primary referent. We are told that love "is necessarily followed by joy, because it [joy] represents to us what we love as a good which *pertains to us*."[23]

Joy proceeds from the belief that we have of possessing some good, and sadness from the belief that we have of possessing some evil or defect:[24] "Things loved become things of joy as we sense *in* ourselves *the power to procure them* plus the willingness or intent to do so. Without the requisite *strength* and *disposition* for obtaining the object of our love, there is no basis for joy."[25]

The problem with this, according to Descartes, lies in the fact that the objects about which man can feel joy and grief are innumerable; and so he tends to desire either too much or too little. That is to say, he tends to desire too many things and, therefore, to lack sufficient desire for any one object to establish within himself the *resolution* to obtain it. To this dilemma Descartes responds:

> For as to those [goods] which only depend on us, i.e., on our free will, it is sufficient to know that they are good, not to have in our power to desire them with too much ardour, because it is following after virtue to perform good actions which depend on ourselves, and it is certain that we cannot have a too ardent desire for virtue. Besides which, since that which we in this way desire is incapable of failing to succeed with us, as it is on ourselves alone that it depends, we shall always receive from it all the satisfaction that we have expected from it. But the fault

which is usually committed in this is never in desiring too much, but only in desiring too little; and the sovereign remedy against that is to free the mind as much as possible from all kinds of other less useful desires, and then to try to know very clearly and to consider with attention the goodness of that which is to be desired.[26]

The problem that besets man, then, is his failure to desire enough, that is, to have sufficiently firm resolution behind his desire. One thinks in this case of the scientist who, because of many and various distractions, fails to accomplish what he might have. For Hobbes, the difficulty with Descartes' thought is not the remark that too many desires for too many different things distract a man and weaken his resolve to act. With that Hobbes would agree. But Hobbes would argue that all these competing desires are, in fact, different expressions of the one desire which every man has, the desire for power that expresses the natural, or embryonic, *conatus* fundamental to human nature. Man is characterized primarily by a "perpetual and restless desire of power after power that ceases only in death" (Lev., ch. 11, pp. 85–6). Desire for knowledge, wealth, honour, public office, and so on are all forms of man's desire for power, which is the means by which he might preserve his life and augment his well-being. Polymorphous pursuit of different objects of desire is attributable to ignorance rather than to desire itself. And, Hobbes maintains, ignorance is a product of insensitivity to the reason-inducing effects of fear. Fear reduces and aligns man's desires by motivating self-knowledge. That is what renders a man resolute.

We have, then, a major disagreement between Descartes and Hobbes regarding desire, the last of Descartes' six primitive passions. For Descartes, desire is like wonder, a passion that has no opposite, no counter-passion.[27] It lacks an opposite because "it is but one passion which brings about both the one and the other"[28] (i.e., both seeking good and avoiding evil). Desire represents the resolution to act, and so encompasses all modes of action. Even fear is a mode of desire, a "kind of desire which we commonly call avoidance and aversion."[29]

The dispute with Hobbes arises because of the entirely negative function which Descartes gives to fear. Fear is not only not associated with any mode of virtue in Descartes' account. It is, in fact, the very origin of cowardice and irresolution.[30] Insofar as desire represents the resolution to act, and the fault in men lies in desiring too little, fear represents irresolution, and so is the very fault—or the origin of the fault—in men who lack resolution.[31]

Descartes, then, disagrees with Hobbes's claim that fear works to focus desire and make it resolute. Insofar as it is associated with irresolution, fear becomes the antithesis of the final, highest passion in Descartes' analysis—generosity (magnanimity)—which is the perception in oneself of extraordinary resolution, "firm and constant resolution to use it well [the free disposition of one's will], that is to say, never to fail of his own will to undertake and execute all things which he judges to be the best— which is to follow perfectly after virtue."[32]

Such resolution, Descartes says, is "the key of all other virtues, and a general remedy for all the disorders of the passions."[33] Generosity (magnanimity), for Descartes, is resolute desire mediated by wonder, love (self-esteem), and joy. It is a subspecies of wonder in the sense that it is an esteem for what is extraordinary in oneself and, therefore, takes the form of extraordinary disposition (resolve) never to neglect to act on one's best judgment. This, Descartes says, is perfect virtue. Its perfection is a result of its being a judgment derived from the disinterestedness of wonder rather than from the biased nature of self-interest. It is capable, therefore, of representing a "just estimate" of one's worth.

Magnanimity, then, is not only for Descartes an index of personal, philosophical excellence; it is also a generosity, the foundation of true moral excellence. The just self-estimate of the magnanimous man makes him morally superior. Magnanimity is a generosity because the things that make men magnanimous, the great accomplishments in science, politics, or other fields are the things that benefit mankind most. The man who gives mankind modern mechanics is simultaneously the benefactor of mankind and, because of the supreme self-confidence required to produce a new science, a magnanimous being. By contrast, the moral concerns that are typical of the ordinary good man are not a "generosity" in any interesting sense. Descartes writes:

> Those who are generous in this way are naturally impelled to do great things and at the same time to undertake nothing of which they do not feel themselves capable. And because they do not hold anything more important than to do good to other men and to disdain their individual interests, they are for this reason always perfectly courteous, affable, and obliging towards everyone. And along with that, they are entirely masters of their passions, particularly of the desires, of jealousy and envy, because there is nothing the acquisition of which does not depend on them, which they think of sufficient worth to merit being much sought after; they are likewise free of hatred to other men because they hold all in esteem; and of fear, because the confidence which they have in their virtue assures them; and finally of anger, be-

cause, esteeming very little all those things that depend on others, they never give so much advantage to their enemies as to recognize that they are hurt by them.[34]

The Cartesian generous few are, then, perfectly virtuous in every way. The sciences they construct are benefactions to mankind, and the "resolve" required of such scientific and philosophical benefactors precludes their being distracted by or competing for lesser desires, honours, and offices. "They never despise anyone."[35] And, because their philosophical resolve redirects their interests away from the ordinary pleasures of men and from acquiring reputations with the ordinary sort of men, Descartes says, "the most high-minded are thus usually the most humble."[36]

Hobbes rejects Descartes' analysis on two grounds. In the first place, fear is not only incorrectly associated with irresolution, but is rather the impetus to virtuous resolute action, insofar as, by taking their bearings by their fears, men become prudent and act to contract with others in order to live in peace. In Hobbes's view, Descartes' claim that the generous few are both free of hatred because they hold all in esteem, and free of anger because they esteem very little that which belongs to others, is contradictory. Men esteem others only out of respect for their powers (e.g., political office, wealth, reputation, wisdom), and that respect is a consequence of the desire men have to make the same their own. Descartes, it would seem, has confused the contempt or disregard that superiors have for their lessers with good-will toward men in general, as if the two were the same. Contempt is like good-will, of course, insofar as it involves no envy, and so is not the source of malicious intentions. However, Descartes' esteem does not imply a benevolent intent to assist others either. It results in indifference, not charity.

That the most high are also the most humble is, from Hobbes's viewpoint, entirely incredible. Hobbes indicates his disagreement with Descartes by emphasizing the negative aspects of magnanimity, that is, by identifying it in *Leviathan* as a subspecies of contempt, rather than following Descartes' lead and identifying it with esteem. Love of one's own interests, and especially love of one's own self, implies a contempt for the interests of another, and so for the other himself. There is no reason for such *amour propre* to culminate in humility and every reason why it would not.

Hobbes's harsh and radically contentious characterization of Cartesian magnanimity (including Christian generosity) arises from his scepticism of moral or political virtue unalloyed to fear. An indication of this is to be found in his comments on glory. Glory is the passion identified by Hobbes as the counterpart to magnanimity. They differ only in that glory is a mode of joy, whereas magnanimity is identified as a mode of contempt. They can (and usually do) coincide. Hobbes explains that if all men have glory or magnanimity, then none has it (El. of Law. p. 40). Equal glory "cancels out" (El. of Law, p. 38). Above all, glory can be acquired only in the context of battle of one form or another (Lev., ch. 14, p. 129). Hobbes's observations show us, then, what he thinks of the highest Cartesian virtue. It is inescapably contentious.

Descartes seems to acknowledge this at certain places. He writes, "sadness... by providing restraint and fear, disposes in certain degree to prudence, while the other [i.e., joy] makes those who abandon themselves to it rash and imprudent."[37] Rashness and imprudence are more than forms of joy; they are also evidence of contempt or disregard for those who would be injured by such rashness.

Furthermore, Descartes admits that the irresolution he attributes to fear is "truly of certain value" insofar as it gives one "time for choosing before deciding. . . . "[38] But for Descartes fear itself never leads to virtuous action. Its sole value is the pause it promotes, and only on certain occasions. Fear is not the mediator of desire as it is for Hobbes.

Descartes, consequently, does not build upon this acknowledgment of the value of fear, apparently leaving it to the individual to decide whether the actions which emerge from the esteem he has for his own extraordinary resolve are prudent or rash. One may want to augment Descartes' account to say that perpetual irresolution is a virtue in truly inferior men since they are already incapable of great and virtuous designs. But Descartes provides no means by which inferiors and superiors can be distinguished aside from their generous self-esteem and self-assertion which, unfortunately, can be exhibited or feigned by both inferiors and superiors.

Hobbes also disputes the possibility that Cartesian self-esteem can, or does in fact, provide the foundations for philosophical curiosity. He reintroduces fear, not only as a primary passion to be relied upon in political matters, in order to make men sensitive to prudent, peace-inducing avenues of action, but also as the inducement to philosophical curiosity. After all, the social alienation of man from man is ultimately an expression of man's alienation from nature, beginning with the self-destructive aspect of all behaviour that follows from unmediated human desire. The mastery of the contentious and bestial characteristics of human nature is the first step in man's mastery and possession of nature per se.

We can now take up Leo Strauss's argument once again. According to Strauss, Hobbes's references in *Leviathan* to certain rare people who have a natural generosity and who are naturally just were the result of borrowings from Descartes' *Passions of the Soul*. The result, Strauss says, was disastrous for the internal consistency of *Leviathan*.[39] If Strauss is right, and Hobbes's account is a duplicate of Descartes' account of generosity (or magnanimity), rather than an implicit criticism of that account, then Strauss's conclusions are also correct.

According to Strauss's analysis, Hobbes's dichotomy of fear and desire is the basis of another dichotomy between reason and vanity and, as a result, a dichotomy between rationality and irrationality.[40] Where fear is the origin of reasonableness, magnanimity—associated with vanity—is the origin of unreasonableness, representing the inclination toward an uncompromising self-concern. The praise of magnanimity runs counter to this doctrine of the roots of reasonable political and moral action. Therefore, Strauss concludes, Hobbes's earlier writings, in which this praise of magnanimity never occurs, are more accurate indexes of his actual political thought.[41]

Hobbes clearly does praise a rarely found generosity that some men do possess. The issue is whether his references to this generosity, or "relish of justice" as he also calls it, are references to what we have referred to as Cartesian magnanimity (generosity) or to something different. The passages in *Leviathan* in which Hobbes makes this praise state:

> That which gives to human actions the relish of justice is a certain nobleness or gallantness of courage, rarely found, by which a man scorns to be beholden for the contentment of his life to fraud or breach of promise (Lev., ch. 15, p. 136). The force of words being... too weak to hold men to the performance of their covenants, there are in man's nature but two imaginable helps to strengthen it. And those are either a fear of the consequence of breaking their word, or a glory or pride in appearing not to need to break it. This latter is a *generosity* too rarely found to be presumed on, especially in the pursuers of wealth, command, or sensual pleasure—which are the greatest part of mankind. The passion to be reckoned upon is fear. . . . (Lev., ch. 14, pp. 128–9)

Hobbes's statements lend themselves to an interpretation which elevates aristocratic virtue. He calls generosity a "nobleness," a "gallantness of courage," "glory" and "pride"—all aristocratic virtues. Nonetheless, he also notes that it does not belong to those whose goals are wealth, command or sensual pleasure. Command is the goal of those such as the English nobility, who seek honour as the primary goal of life. The frequently made suggestion that Hobbes's referent for this adulation is the English aristocracy is, therefore, at least questionable. Their virtue is an ambition that inclines them to "stir up trouble and sedition." Their ambition reflects a refusal to admit their natural equality and shows them to be undaunted by prospects of the future which ought to generate fear and, therefore, the moderation that fear induces. In the next chapter, I will examine Hobbes's argument for natural equality and see how, in fact, it is intended to address this problem. For the moment, it is sufficient to say that one would not expect Hobbes to make this criticism of aristocratic virtue too explicit, insofar as his own patrons were themselves representatives of the English aristocracy. His doctrine of the generosity of the philosophical few, because of its critical implications, required a twofold dissimulation which disguises his conflicts with (and therefore his criticism of) both theological and aristocratic virtue.

If it were simply the case that Hobbes momentarily adopted Descartes' notion of magnanimity while writing *Leviathan,* ignorant of the destructive implications that is has for the *Leviathan* doctrine of the origins of civil association in fear, as Leo Strauss has maintained, then it would be impossible to make sense out of Hobbes's analysis of magnanimity, that is, his association of magnanimity with valor, liberality, imprudence and cruelty as forms of *contempt.*[42] Rather, one might suspect that Hobbes is attempting to indicate something about the civil implications of Cartesian magnanimity—that it is not a "generosity" at all. As an unqualified self-esteem, it seems to imply an insensitivity to the presence of others, insofar as its origins are to be found, Hobbes says, in "observing the imperfections of other men" (Lev., ch. 6, p. 46). Unlike philosophical curiosity, the contemptuous characteristics of Cartesian magnanimity tend to promote contention and war. The contemptuous man who feels magnanimous is not Hobbes's "rare soul." And therefore it is not the virtue peculiar to Hobbes's naturally just and noble individual. Strauss is wrong when he equates them, and identifies Cartesian "generosity" with Hobbesian "magnanimity."

The difference between the two concepts is that, for Hobbes, magnanimity is mediated in some men by a curiosity which, as we have seen, is a self-concern deriving from fear (Lev., ch. 12, p. 94). That is, there is a dialectical interplay between fear and desire that makes magnanimity both moderate and just in political matters in those men in whom the dialectic is well developed. Descartes, on the other hand, writes: "I do not see that it (fear) can ever be praiseworthy or useful; it likewise is not a special passion, but merely an excess of cowardice, astonishment and fear, which is always vicious, just as bravery is an excess of courage which is always good, provided that the end proposed is good."[43]

Hobbes and Descartes would agree, I believe, that self-esteem is often sought in the acquisition of political power, which must be exercised authoritatively—often abusively—in order to be retained. That is, it must be exercised with "magnanimity" in its Cartesian form. The only way to mitigate the contemptuous and socially disruptive implications of such magnanimity is to emphasize the self-concern, or fear for one's own safety from which it originally emerged. It is in the fearful concern for one's own safety that the assured way to peace and justice is to be found.

Where Hobbes and Descartes disagree is on the nature of that magnanimous self-esteem in some men that is satisfied only by great scientific or philosophical achievements. This, too, Hobbes would maintain, is grounded in fear as well as desire. Hobbes's "generous few" are those in whom desire and fear interact as an inner infinite, a motivation not limited by any finite or worldly objects, but governed by a concern for preservation of self against the malevolent indifference of nature itself. This inner infinite is a natural obsession that directs man's illimitable lust for power to the pursuit of knowledge and the felicity that that pursuit brings, thereby removing them from the political domain per se. Fear exposes something of the nature of the universe, the unavoidable alienation of man from nature and the need for mastery over nature if man is truly to be able to esteem himself.

We shall soon see that it is only philosophical curiosity that breeds Hobbesian "generosity." Such curiosity is the consequence of natural inclinations and abilities, and so cannot be taught to, or cultivated by, man in general. Generosity, that is to say, is not a virtue (passion) characteristic of the common run of men. On this Hobbes and Descartes agree. And it seems that Descartes appreciates Hobbes's argument that political moderation and justice must, therefore, find their source in fear, that is, in fear of a sovereign whose authority derives as much from his power to dominate as it does from the consent of the governed. Such fear exists in all men to some degree, and can be cultivated in those who, because of their magnanimous concern for the acquisition of honor and glory, that is, for the recognition by others of their power, are inclined toward seditious undertakings. Hobbes and Descartes disagree only with regard to the function of fear at the philosophical level of desire. In Hobbes's view it is the dialectical correlative of self-esteem. Since Descartes associates self-esteem with disinterested and objective "wonder," to him fear would suggest irresolution and cowardice. In philosophical matters, irresolution and cowardice would most likely take the form of conformity with orthodox ideas. Ultimately, Descartes' dissociation of fear and desire, his identifying them, respectively, with cowardice and resolution, is the result of his dissociation of reason and passion, where reason is rational, meaning by that identical with logical discourse. With this, Hobbes takes issue.

THE DIALECTIC OF DESIRE

We are now in a position to bring together the strands of Hobbes's philosophy, to show how they are woven together according to the dialectical character of *conatus*, and how that dialectic becomes extended in man as a dialectic of desire, culminating in the philosophical project to make man master and possessor of nature. Once this is shown, it will be possible to re-examine his political theory and those doctrines, for example, his doctrine of natural equality, that are inseparably associated with it.

We have already seen that Hobbes's thought is philosophically preceded by the specific character of his rejection of classical metaphysics. His well-known denial that there is anything in nature other than *bodies* is, in effect, a claim that nature is radically determinate or particular. His statement is not a claim for the existence of Lucretian-type atoms or material bodies but, rather, a denial of the objective status of metaphysical objects of "universal essences" that have no spatio-temporal location. Metaphysical objects are phenomena of neither mind nor nature; they exist in language alone. They are empty abstractions.

What is interesting about Hobbes's concept of nature is the idea implicit in his concept of *conatus*, that difference or determinate particularity implies opposition. Bodies are individuated, he says, solely by their peculiar motions. And motions are relationally distinct, their specific differences determinable only as one motion comes into opposition or conflict with another resisting motion. All motion is both inertia and resistance, determined relative to the motions to which it is opposed. Difference, then, is simultaneous with, or a function of, opposition and contradiction (De Corp., ch. 11, art. 2–3, p. 133). Nature, therefore, is characterized by opposition and contradiction.

It was shown in chapter three how Hobbes's conception of human nature develops from his own notion of nature. Life is but motion. By this, of course, Hobbes does not mean that life is mechanical motion. Rather, life is characterized by an endeavour, or "inertia" (Lev., ch. 2, p. 4), to overcome all that resists or opposes it. The genesis of human nature is a division and opposition within nature itself. Will, the embodiment of human fear and desire, is man's natural response to the resistance of nature, his desire to endure in spite of those natural forces that would confound his greatest efforts.

"Life itself is but motion and can never be without desire, nor without fear, no more than without sense" (Lev., ch. 6, p. 51). The dynamic character of human nature is comprehended in the dialectical interplay of these two moments of endeavour, fear and desire, "the first unperceived beginnings of our actions" (El. of Law, ch. 12, art. 1, p. 67). In the same sense that there is no natural desire for rest in material bodies, no "appetite to rest and to conserve their nature in that place which is most proper for them" (Lev., ch. 2, p. 4), so there is no natural repose for man. Insofar as life is motion, the good life is to be found in the accentuation of that motion. Man's proper end is the "felicity" which accompanies continually prospering. There is, Hobbes says, no *finis ultimus*, no *summum bonum*, for man, precisely because he is a natural being.

Hobbes admits that his dynamic conception of human nature "is not easily assented to" (Lev., ch. 2, p. 4), because men tend to misinterpret their own intentions. Nonetheless, he maintains the mind cannot always deny what reason may dispute. "For nature itself does often press upon men those truths which afterwards, when they look for somewhat beyond nature, they stumble at" (Lev., ch. 6, p. 39).

Hobbes does not deny that many will reject his conception of man. Men will want to argue that the contentiousness and opposition are not necessary ingredients in all human relationships and that men are, in fact, capable of sincere, honorable, selfless compassion for other men. What Hobbes maintains is that the very actions and behaviour of his doubters "disavow what their discourses approve of" (De Cive, Pref., p. xv). The natures of men, their natural inclinations, are revealed in their various actions. The locks with which they decorate their doors and the swords which they keep to accompany them on their travels testify to their actual, albeit subconscious, beliefs. Even the contentious disavowals they make of Hobbes's conception of man's nature are themselves evidence of that natural proclivity for opposition and contention characteristic of man.

Human good is entirely natural good, the felicitous accentuation of natural motions. The success of man's endeavours to accentuate his motions and thereby obtain the good life, "felicity," depends upon successfully grounding philosophy (the pursuit concerned most clearly with the acquisition of that good) on principles of natural science, making philosophy a natural, rather than a metaphysical, enterprise. For Hobbes, this did not mean grounding the philosophy of man (psychology and politics) on a science of mechanical motion, but rather grounding both a philosophy of man and a science of mechanical motion on a concept common to both, that is, *conatus*.

The natural axiom of human behaviour is nothing more than that man, by natural necessity, desires his own good and shuns whatever is destructive of his well-being. All behaviour is egoistic, necessarily self-interested. However, the self-interested nature of his actions thrusts man into relations with others. By nature, "solitude is an enemy" of man (De Cive, ch. 1, art. 2, p. 2). Man is born a social animal, but only in the sense that his needs are satisfied in concert with others. This does not mean that man is naturally sociable. The very needs that make him a social animal also render him unfit for the society of others, since the satisfaction of his needs ordinarily must be obtained at the expense of the others whose society he seeks. Every man seeks the society of others for his own benefit, not theirs.

Fear of the insecurity he suffers in the natural condition and desire to escape it lead man to abandon the natural condition and enter into a contractual relationship with others. This is no more than to say that at times of crisis creatures that are otherwise irreconcilably hostile to one another—natural enemies—may share the same sanctuary. The contractual relationship is intended to mitigate nature's hostility which, in the case of social relations, is the mutual hostility of men's own unmediated self-interests. But, when man undertakes to abandon the state of nature it is not his own free will at work, resisting nature's opposition; it is nature itself, in the form of human nature, that compels him to liberate himself from the misery of his natural condition. To fail to act in response to this demand of nature is to oppose and contradict one's own best interests (De Cive, ch. 1, art. 13, p. 12; ch. 3, art. 3, p. 31). "[T]he state of men without civil society, which state we may properly call the state of nature, is nothing else but a mere war of all against all; and in that war all men have equal right unto all things. Next, that all men as soon as they arrive to understanding of this hateful condition, do desire, *even nature itself compelling them, to be free* from this misery" (De Cive, Pref., p. xvii).

Man is a sociable animal (not merely "social") only by virtue of the self-imposed, i.e. political, limitations he places on his natural right to pursue his own well-being without consideration for the welfare of others. Commonwealth is a necessary condition of human felicity, to be sure. Without political order no life can be truly felicitous. But political order is not sufficient by itself to provide man with felicity either. The civil satisfaction of desire by the acquisition of wealth, political power, fame, and peace is obtainable too readily in an utmost and therefore unnatural degree. It is unsatisfying. Satisfaction itself is unsatisfying; it represents a kind of repose. The satisfied man, Hobbes says, is left with nothing to do but to grieve over the fact that he has nothing more to do. Wealth, political power, and fame are not productive of what Hobbes has referred to as human felicity, the "continual progress of the desire, from one object to another. . . " (Lev., ch. 11, p. 85).

Human felicity, in short, cannot be acquired politically. Consequently, if to be a political philosopher one must take political action and order as the fulfillment of, or the highest expression of, human potentiality, then by these rigid standards Hobbes is not a political philosopher at all.

The argument being developed here is not to be found—at least not consistently or thematically found—in either *De Cive* or *The Elements of Law*. One might suspect that this distinction (between the civil and natural satisfaction of desire) was incidental to the objectives of those earlier works, written as they were in the context of the Civil War. Nonetheless, Hobbes's mature treatment of human well-being differs dramatically from those earlier accounts, and the development of the account in *Leviathan* required that he abandon the image of life as a race that he had used in his earlier writings. The image of life as a race is exclusively "social;" it presupposes competition among men for social goods and honours. Even success in competing for those goods and honours, does not guarantee anyone against the natural calamities that can befall any man. Hobbes's analogy of life and a race, in short, is incapable of conveying all that is contained in his mature conception of human felicity.

Man's escape from the awful misery of the natural condition cannot be achieved once and for all, and certainly not by mere political action. This thought is an integral part of the fabric of both *Leviathan* and *De Corpore*. Furthermore, while it is possible that misery can be overcome, the path one is required to take in order to escape the natural condition is not a path that all men can travel. All men are equal, of course, since they are all mortal. And all men are equal, too, insofar as they reveal in their actions a "similitude of the passions" (Lev., Intro., p. xi). But they are not equal in every manner. Hobbes explains that men do not exhibit a "similitude of the *objects* of the passions" (Lev., Intro., p. xi). In the remainder of this chapter I will examine Hobbes's diplomatically worded claim that some few men, the naturally superior, have as their objective that "master delight" that accompanies only the indefatigable generation of knowledge. While this philosophical or scientific character may be qualified by, and even liberated by, educational and social contingencies, it cannot be generated in a man by those contingencies. That is, only a magnanimous, philosophical few, inspired by their "great designs," and in pursuit of what Hobbes calls "the great and master delight," can obtain the freedom and felicity that fully satisfies the human desire for the good life.

CURIOSITY: THE INDEFATIGABILITY OF DESIRE

Fear is, according to Hobbes, philosophically inseparable from the desire to overcome. The indefatigable extension of this complex passion Hobbes identifies with "curiosity." He explains: "It is peculiar to the nature of man, to be inquisitive into the causes of the events they see; some more, some less; but all men so much, as to be curious in the search of the causes of their own good and evil fortune" (Lev., ch. 12, p. 94).

All men respond to the events that take place about them with a curiosity that is generated out of, and so is qualified by, self-concern. Natural inquisitiveness is not an expression of disinterested wonder, but of anxiety. "Anxiety for the future time, disposeth men to inquire into the causes of things: because the knowledge of them, maketh men the better able to order the present to their best advantage" (Lev., ch. 11, p. 92).

Curiosity is not spontaneous wonder but, rather, prudent foresightful self-interest. A problem arises, however, in that we cannot foresee the future. The uncertainty of his future turns man toward the past. Hobbes maintains: "No man can have in his mind a conception of the *future*, for the future is *not yet*: but of our conceptions of the past, we make a *future*; or rather, call *past*, *future* relatively" (El. of Law, art. 7, p. 16).

Man solicits his future from the past; he makes "remembrance to be the *prevision* of things to come, or *expectation* or presumption of the future" (El. of Law, art. 7, p. 17). Man's concern for his future evokes a recollection of causes in an endeavour to overcome the fortuitous character of his future by soliciting it from himself as its cause, by making himself its measure. The difficulty is that men are "very seldom... able to see the end" of the chains of consequences (Lev., ch. 6, p. 50). Solicitation is itself paradoxical. "The solicitude" of one's future "both inclines to fear, and hinders them from the search of the causes of other things; and thereby gives occasion of feigning of as many gods, as there be men that feign them" (Lev., ch. 12, p. 96).

The problem is that the desire to know the causes of things promotes even more anxiety in man. Fear without a corresponding object of fear is intolerable. It is this, clearly, that Hobbes has in mind when he writes that "fear of things invisible is the natural seed of that, which everyone in himself calleth religion" (Lev., ch. 11, p. 93). Religion, he says, arises from the fact that fear "must needs have for object something" (Lev., ch. 12, p. 95). Hobbes does not, of course, make this claim without prudently sidestepping any incriminating references to Christianity. Nonetheless, that Christianity is not exempt from the logic of his analysis of religion in general is transparently obvious. He writes: "And therefore when there is nothing to be seen there is nothing to accuse, either of their good or evil fortune, but some power or agent invisible; in which sense perhaps it was that some of the old poets said that the gods were at first created by human fear; which, spoken of the gods—that is to say, of the many gods of the Gentiles—is very true" (Lev., ch. 12, p. 95).

One might, with justification, refer to Hobbesian religion as a contract that religious men make with the incomprehensibility of nature which, like the civil contract between men, serves to inoculate them against (but also to blind them to) the calamities brought on by an un-cooperative environment. By "contract" I mean a reconciliation in thought of interests that are, in fact, alienated. Religious faith, to Hobbes, represents the self-vitiating tendency of curiosity, where the fear that men exhibit in their ignorance of natural causes is not accompanied by a serious desire to overcome. This results from man's sense of the finitude of his own power to comprehend. Hobbes writes:

> And they that make little, or no inquiry into the natural causes of things, yet from the fear that proceeds from the ignorance itself, of what it is that hath the power to do them much good or harm, are inclined to suppose, and feign unto themselves, several kinds of powers invisible; and to stand in awe of their own imaginations; and in time of distress to invoke them; as also in the time of an unexpected good success, to give them thanks; making the creatures of their own fancy their gods. (Lev., ch. 11, p. 93)

Man is inclined to read natural calamities as Divine intervention, as Providence, or acts of God's Will. By virtue of his convention-bound reactions to the calamities that befall him, he reads himself to be a child of God, obligated, by virtue of his God-given nature, to obey, to submit graciously to the fate which Divine Providence has chosen for him. As the social contract represents man's reconciliation with the inability of reason to legislate to the passions, so his religions represent a reconciliation with the inability of reason to grasp rationally and legislate to the infinite extension and unresponsiveness of the natural universe.

Thus it is that man's curiosity becomes the "seed of religion." That is to say, it is impossible to make a profound inquiry into the human condition and the natural causes of human misery without an accompanying inclination to believe in a creator God (Lev., ch. 11, p. 92). All men, therefore, are inclined to believe in God. However, a mere inclination to believe is in no way a demonstration of God's existence. In *Leviathan* we are told that curiosity leads one of necessity to this thought, that there is a first cause which is preceded by no other. This, presumably, is Hobbes's version of the proof for God's existence. In *De Corpore* Hobbes goes into greater detail in explaining the nature of this necessity. He tells us that all men are inclined to *weary* of the search for an invisible and incomprehensible first cause. It is inevitable that, wearying of the unending effort necessarily required by the search for a first cause, men will "at last give over, without knowing whether it were possible... to proceed to an end or not" (De Corp., ch. 26, art. 1, p. 412). The necessity in Hobbes's argument for

God's existence as a first cause is grounded, then, upon the inevitability that the limited powers of man will not be able to sustain an infinite endeavour. That is, Hobbes's proof of God's existence rests on the finitude of man and the exhaustibility of human curiosity.

Hobbes does say that ignorance of remote causes "disposeth men to attribute all events, to the causes immediate and instrumental: for these are all the causes they perceive" (Lev., ch. 11, pp. 91–2). Nonetheless, this does not mean that man's prudential concern for the present makes him any less religious. Without knowledge of the natural causes of present events, men are inclined to read into those events causes that are not really there. "Ignorance of natural causes, disposeth a man to credulity, so as to believe many times impossibilities: for such know nothing to the contrary, but that they may be true; being unable to detect the impossibility" (Lev., ch. 11, p. 92).

All men are not equally willing to "give over" to this inclination to posit causes for events present, or to "give over" and posit an arbitrary terminus to thought, that is, a remote cause, or God. This point Hobbes does not make without considerable caution. One must read him with some care and some sensitivity to the problems accompanying the theological inspection of doctrines that were characteristic of Hobbes's times.

In *Leviathan*, Hobbes illustrates the emergence of religion from curiosity with an example of curiosity at its extremes. One ought to be alerted by the fact that the example is utterly incompatible with the conclusion he draws from it. The example is that of Prometheus, the Titan who sided with Zeus and the Olympians in their war with the Titans, and who later still rebelled against Zeus, placing himself in the service of man. Hobbes writes:

> For being assured that there be causes of all things that have arrived hitherto or shall arrive hereafter, it is impossible for a man who continually endeavours to secure himself against the evil he fears and procure the good he desires not to be in a *perpetual solicitude* of the time to come, so that every man, *especially those that are over provident*, are in a state like that of Prometheus. For as Prometheus—which interpreted is the prudent man—was bound to the hill Caucasus, a place of large prospect, where an eagle feeding on his liver devoured in the day as much as was repaired in the night, so that man which looks too far before him in the care of future time has his heart all the day long gnawed on by fear of death, poverty, or other calamity, and has no repose nor pause of his anxiety but in sleep. (Lev., ch. 12, p. 95)

Hobbes's choice of image could hardly be more inaptly representative of the termination of curiosity in man's belief in God. Prometheus was the one Titan, wiser than all the Olympian Gods, who tricked Zeus out of man's sacrifices to him, and who stole fire, that is, the arts, from the Olympian, for man's use. He is the very symbol of rebellion against the authority of Divine power. The symbol is incongruent with that which it is to symbolize. It certainly cannot represent the submission of curiosity to Divine Omniscience (ontological omnipotence).

One could conclude that there is no duplicity intended in Hobbes's argument, but that he is merely not expressing himself with rigorous precision. However, the duplicity (or possible duplicity) occurs again and again, taxing one's ingenuity to interpret it out of his thought. Later, in the same chapter of *Leviathan*, Hobbes explains that the seeds of religion are cultivated by "two sorts of men" (Lev., ch. 12, p. 98). One sort cultivates the seeds of curiosity according to God's commandment, the other sort "according to their own invention." We are told that the religion of the former is "divine politics" which "containeth precepts to those that have yielded themselves subjects in the kingdom of God" (Lev., ch. 12, p. 99). The un-Promethean representatives of divine politics that Hobbes selects are Abraham, Moses, and Christ. The religion of the latter, those who cultivate curiosity according to their own invention rather than by yielding, is "human politics" which teaches duty to earthly kings, and has as its symbol "the founders of commonwealths and the lawgivers of the gentiles" (Lev., ch. 12, p. 99).

We know, then, the religion of the two sorts of men, but not the science. One could speculate that if the counterpart to divine politics in knowledge were School metaphysics, then the counterpart to human politics would be mathematical science. While man can conceal from himself the frightening, almost intolerable discovery of the indifference of nature by appealing to the creative capacity of his own imagination to posit a benevolent Divine ordering power where there is none, it is not necessary, according to Hobbes, that he do so. Man can take heart from the prospect of an empty universe. The way is thereby opened for him to impress upon nature the image of his own desires, to recreate nature in his own image. Man's endeavour to secure his own future and promote his own well-being, coupled with the invisibility, or at least the indeterminate nature, of the future, culminates in an effort to solicit the future from the past, "making remembrance a prevision of the future" (El. of Law, ch. 4, art. 7, pp. 16–17; cf. Lev., ch. 3, p. 15). Curiosity need not culminate in that "weariness" that is the seed of religion. Philosophical curiosity in particular, Hobbes says, is "the care of knowing causes, which is a lust of the mind that, by a *perseverance* of delight in the *indefatigable* generation of knowledge, exceeds the short vehemence of any carnal pleasure" (Lev., ch. 6, p. 45).

In the indefatigability of the effort to generate knowledge, and in the delight which accompanies this creativity, man finds a liberation not from the passions, but rather from the finitude which the omnipresence of fear initially imposes on man. Hobbes invokes a Lucretian image to explain this liberation. He writes:

> from what passion proceedeth it, that men take pleasure to behold from the shore the danger of them that are at sea in a tempest, or in fight, or from a safe castle to behold two armies charge one another in the field? It is certainly, in the whole sum, joy; else men would never flock to such a spectacle. Nevertheless there is in it both joy and grief; for as there is novelty and remembrance of our own security present, which is delight; so there is also pity, which is grief; but the delight is so far predominant, that men usually are content in such a case to be spectators of the misery of their friends. (El. of Law., ch. 9, art. 19, pp. 51–2)

In *The Elements of Law*, from which this passage was taken, Hobbes already had the idea of the essence of the felicity and liberation that serve as the highest objects of life. However, he had not at that point reconciled his ideas with the image of life, represented by the metaphor of the race, that then guided much of his thought.

Men who combine a native curiosity with a "quick ranging mind" delight themselves "either with finding unexpected similitude of things, otherwise much unlike... or else in discerning suddenly dissimilitude in thigns that otherwise appear the same" (El. of Law, ch. 10, art. 4, p. 55). The sudden and unexpected discoveries men make recommend the excellence of their own discernment to themselves. Hobbes explains that "novelty causeth admiration, and admiration curiosity, which is a delightful appetite of knowledge."[44] Novelty promotes admiration not simply for the novel, but more significantly, for the discerning power of him who has discovered that novelty. The taste of such power of discernment promotes a desire for more. Like the gambler who is excited by the taste of winning to gamble more, in the prospect of *great* success, profitable curiosity about causes encourages curiosity still more. "Because curiosity is delight, therefore also novelty is so, but especially that novelty from which a man conceiveth an opinion true or false of bettering his own estate; for, in such a case, they stand affected with the hope that all gamesters have while the cards are shuffling" (El. of Law, ch. 9, art. 18, p. 51).

Curiosity alone does not provide for man's liberation. We are told that when curiosity involves "too much equality and indifference" it suffers that defect of mind called levity; "for when all things make equal impression and delight, they equally throng to be expressed" (El. of Law, ch. 10, art. 5, p. 56). Hobbes adds: "The virtue opposite to this defect is gravity, or steadiness; in which the end being *the great and master-delight*, directeth and keepeth in the way thereto all other thoughts" (El. of Law, ch. 10, art. 6, p. 56).

Curiosity that is resolute, that is, which exhibits gravity in undertaking great designs, generates the "great and master delight" which Hobbes understands philosophy to be, that is, philosophy that has become scientific rather than speculative. He writes: "And from this passion of admiration and curiosity, have arisen not only the invention of names, but also supposition of such causes of all things as they thought might produce them. And from this beginning is derived all *philosophy*" (El. of Law, ch. 9, art. 18, p. 51).

The nature of the great designs of the over-provident and solicitous few whose curiosity is never abated is revealed in Hobbes's advice that men "imitate the creation" (De Corp., Epist. to the Reader). Through their creativity, men are able to attain "exact and perfect knowledge" (El. of Law, ch. 10, art. 4, p. 56). "To know... truth," we are told, "is nothing else but to acknowledge that it is made by ourselves" (De Cive, ch. 18, art. 5, p. 303).

To say this, of course, is to say that felicity, the great and master delight, is ultimately a private rather than a public pursuit. By private pursuit is meant, of course, not political ambition but, rather, philosophical and scientific desire. It is only with philosophical science that the pursuit of felicity leads, not to self-negation, but to the "great and master delight" that accompanies the "continual and indefatigable generation of knowledge." The philosophical pursuit is felicitous, however, only when man is able to transcend the limits of nature, liberating himself by learning the principles of natural intelligibility which so long as they are inaccessible keep man's fate out of his own hands. And that liberation is possible only when man has realized that the principles of order are to be found not in a world that is external to human thinking but in himself. Subtly, the claim that we know only what we make transforms itself into the conviction that knowing is making, that intelligibility and order are the products of human creativity and, finally, that knowledge is power.

With this in mind, Hobbes recommends to men that they endeavour to "imitate the creation." To do that, however, is no less than to legislate the criteria to which one must appeal in order to determine the intelligibility of things and, therefore, to make possible the acquisition of knowledge.

It goes without saying that there are difficulties in Hobbes's theory. The philosophical or scientific form of the infinite prospect of prospering, the indefatigable generation of knowledge, presupposes an abandonment of metaphysical boundaries (i.e., forms or essences) which limit the extent of human knowledge at the very time that they make knowledge possible, since to know is to be able to define or delimit one thing from another by appeal to some non-arbitrary criterion, form, or essence. If the claim "we know only what we make" implies that knowing is making, then philosophy and science become inescapably historical. Philosophy is reduced to a form of poetry, *poiesis*. Hobbes's conclusions, in short, contain a presentiment of the problems of creativity and the paradoxes of historicism that occupy much of the philosophical concern of our own time.

The revolutionary transformation of philosophy into the project to make man himself the measure, and so the master, of all things implies abandoning the ancient conception of philosophy as the pursuit of wisdom or absolute knowledge. Hobbes, of course, is aware of this implication. He maintains that men can never acquire absolute or final knowlege. There is no such thing as a systematic account of all things; all science, he says, is conditional. This includes his own. Consequently, it is inaccurate to treat Hobbes as a naive, textbook rationalist. He writes: "No discourse whatsoever, can end in absolute knowledge of fact, past, or to come. For, as for the knowledge of fact, it is originally sense; and ever after, memory. And for the knowledge of consequence, which I have said before is called science, it is not absolute, but conditional" (Lev., ch. 7, p. 52).

Hobbes has no illusions even about his own philosophical efforts. He concludes *De Corpore*, in fact, with the realistic admission that his work may well be superseded one day by another. "[I]f any other man from other hypotheses shall demonstrate the same or greater things, there will be greater praise and thanks due to him than I demand for myself, provided his hypotheses be such as are conceivable" (De Corp., ch. 30, art. 15, p. 531).

This concession does not diminish the delight that accompanies philosophical and scientific pursuits. For since those pursuits are initially generated by man's natural fears, fear can never entirely be allayed, and neither, therefore, can the delight that accompanies satisfying the need for reducing one's fears, even though that need is inexhaustible.

However, Hobbes never lost sight of the fact that the "great and master delight" enjoyed by the philosophical and scientific few can, without the pacifying influence of fear, lead to contention, illusion, and abstraction from human realities. He was acutely aware of the potential for social and political insensitivity in the scientist and the natural philosopher. The magnanimity of the philosopher-scientist is a form of glory, the product of his admiration for the image of his power (Lev., ch. 6, p. 45). Glory is

born of comparison with lessers; it is generated by "comparison with another man's infirmity or absurdity" (El. of Law, ch. 9, art. 13, p. 46; cf.
Lev., ch. 6, p. 45). Hobbes explains that "glory is like honor, if all men
have it, no man hath it, for they consist in comparison and precellence"
(De Cive, ch. 1, art. 2, p. 5). The association of one's own glory with the
fate of the hypotheses and theories one proposes in science, religion, or
politics does not inspire great "generosity" if, that is, men are moved to do
what they do primarily from self-love. This recalls one aspect of Hobbes's
dispute with Descartes on the status of fear as a precondition of the philosophical pursuit. Fear reveals not only the limitless character of nature
and, therefore, the limitless possibility of philosophical mastery. It also
mitigates the contentious tendency of the philosophical pursuit. If philosophy is war, as it clearly is for Hobbes, war against the malevolent dimensions of nature (including human nature), it ought to be prevented from
spilling over into daily politics and religion, since the disputes it would
generate there would be destructive. It would destroy the social and political preconditions of philosophy itself.

In word, if not in deed, Hobbes rejected glory as the motivating impulse
of philosophical desire. In *De Corpore* he writes:

> The *end* or *scope* of Philosophy is, that we may make use to our bene-
> fit of effects formerly seen; or that, by application of bodies to one an-
> other, we may produce the like effects of those we conceive in our
> minds, as far forth as matter, strength, and industry, will permit, for
> the commodity of human life. For the inward glory and triumph of
> mind that a man may have for the mastering of some difficult and
> doubtful matter, or for the discovery of some hidden truth, is not
> worth so much pains as the study of philosophy requires; nor need
> any man care much to teach another what he knows, if he thinks that
> it will be the only benefit of his labour. (De Corp., ch. 1, art. 6, p. 7)

Hobbes's "great and master delight" is not reducible to mere "inward
glory and triumph of mind." All glory is comparative, or competitive. It is
a magnanimity, an objective of self-love that implies contempt for lessers
(as we saw earlier in this chapter), the total absence of fear and therefore
respect for their powers. In such attitudes there is no "sociability."
Hobbes's great and master delight carries instead an accompanying sense
of gravity that is intimately appropriate to human need, whose origins are
in fear as well as in self-love, in recognition of the precarious character of
existence. It is the objective of desire that is directed toward nature itself
rather than to other men. Its objective is not glory, inward or outward, but
mastery of nature. Consequently, its natural accompaniment is not con-

tempt for other men but fear of the consequences that may follow from man's ignorance of natural causes.

Hobbes, in short, has a high estimate of the political or social (not moral) generosity of philosophy properly conceived. Purely philosophical delight is not dependent on the infirmities of others because it is not competitive with others in any social sense. In his Preface to Davenant's *Gondibert* (1650), in the middle of a discussion of the relationship of epic poetry, comedy, and satire, Hobbes explained what it is in great men that causes them to have "great designs." "*Great persons*, that have their minds employed on *great designs*, have not leisure enough to laugh, and are pleased with the contemplation of their own power and virtues, so as they need not the infirmities and vices of other men to recommend themselves to their own favour by comparison as all men do when they laugh" (El. of Law, "The Answer of Mr. Hobbes. . . ," pp. 454–5).

There is no gravity, no seriousness, in the efforts of those who are not concerned with the generation of knowledge, meaning by that those who are interested only in the glory associated with the production of socially impressive hypotheses. Such persons lack the "generosity" that is found in truly great minds. In *Leviathan*, Hobbes writes:

> *Sudden glory*, is the passion which makes those *grimaces* called LAUGHTER; and is caused either by some sudden act of their own, that pleases them; or by the apprehension of some deformed thing in another, by comparison whereof they suddenly applaud themselves. And it is incident most to them, that are conscious of the fewest abilities in themselves; who are forced to keep themselves in their own favor, by observing the imperfections of other men. And therefore much laughter at the defects of others, is a sign of pusillanimity. For of great minds, one of the proper works is to help and free others from scorn (in the Latin, "contemptu"); and compare themselves only with the most able. (Lev., ch. 6, p. 46)

Because fear of the limitlessness of nature and the finitude of man is integral to the foundations of philosophical desire (even though a liberation from the immediacy of fear may have been achieved) the master delight is a kind of gravity, or resoluteness, which does not culminate in laughter or contempt for others. Among the tasks of the great mind, as Hobbes understands greatness, is the liberation of others from the scorn or contempt which hinders their ability to direct their philosophical efforts to truly great designs.

The scorn, or contempt, of the greatest number of people, both the common people and the aristocratic, is usually directed against philosophy because it appears to have little public use. Because it is not eminent, that is, not acknowledged by many to have any use, it has little power. Liberating people from their contemptuousness would certainly involve, then, a raising of the public estimate of philosophy. Hobbes's great mind is certainly not selfless in its interests and objectives.

To liberate a person from contemptuousness would be to cause him to compare himself not with inferiors (which would make *glory* his primary concern), but rather "only with the most able" (Lev., ch. 6, p. 46). Comparing himself only with the most able, the liberated person would be better enabled to see himself reflected in their estimates of him, better able to "read" himself more perfectly. Among those who seek only glory, as the greatest good in life, one can only be known for the glory he has won. And, in "reading" one's self in others, in the acknowledgements made by others regardless of who they are, one can only know oneself from others' opinions. The intent of one who comprehends his purposes solely in terms of the competition for honours has to be an entirely social or political intent. That which passes for philsophy in such contexts is little more than fashionable rhetoric. This was Hobbes's opinion of the School philosophy of his time.

Because of the foundation of the philosophical quest on fear, initially on the fear of others, the truly philosophical mind, according to Hobbes, is eternally conscious of the political environment as a precondition of philosophy. Because of his enlightened concern for political peace and order, and his realization that the moral interests of men are, more often than not, concealed expressions of their passions (Lev., ch. 46, p. 669), the Hobbesian philosopher possesses a "nobleness or gallantness of courage, rarely found" (Lev., ch. 15, p. 136), a "generosity too rarely found to be presumed on" (Lev., ch. 15, p. 128). It is the philosopher who is, for Hobbes, pre-eminently just, because only he is fully aware of, and therefore considerate of, the fragile nature of civil society, that is, morality, without the conspicuous presence of sovereign power to encourage him, and is aware, too, of the necessity for mitigating the bestial tendencies of human nature if anybody is to be able to enjoy the leisure necessary for undertaking the project of conquering the brutish character of nature per se. In the Hobbesian philosopher-scientist, one discovers the identity of scientific and moral wisdom.

Hobbes's remarkable confidence in the social generosity and the political sensitivity of the philosopher as he conceives him has certainly not been justified by subsequent developments in philosophy. The historicist character of the philosophical project, as Hobbes implicitly conceives it, leaves philosophy free of transrational limitations on thought and, therefore, on action, since thought is conceived as a form of action, knowing as making, theory as *praxis*. In our own times this view of theory has tended to cul-minate in a self-certifying paternalism, where the benefits derived from theory or from science, have become inseparable from submission to an engineered way of life over which individual men have no control.

Whether Hobbes could have been expected to see the social and political implications of his notion of philosophy as a project to make man the mea-sure and the master, of nature, is not of special interest to us at the mo-ment. However, because mastery of human nature is the practical (albeit not the philosophical) precondition to his conception of man's mastery of nature per se, our comprehension of the latter aspect of the philosophical project directs us, now, to the former—his political theory.

The general tendency of Hobbes's interpreters has been to take his polit-ical theory as the clue to his physics, rather than vice versa. For example, the axiomatic status given to Hobbes's doctrine of the natural equality of all men has led to the location of conceptual antecedents of this doctrine in his physics and his psychology, and to the location of the source of the doctrine in Hobbes's own social, economic, and cultural background. The result has been to superimpose interpretations on his philosophy in gen-eral, interpretations that Hobbes's writings resist, but interpretations that bolster the political "axioms" that gave them their original impetus. Con-sequently, my interest now is to re-examine Hobbes's political theory be-ginning with the doctrine of natural equality. It is important to realize that the doctrine of natural equality, unqualified and unexplained, is not altogether compatible with the notion of a naturally generous (because philosophically superior) few. My next task is to examine the doctrine of natural equality to see how it is, in fact, compatible with the notion of a naturally superior philosophical few and what function a doctrine of natu-ral equality compatible with that notion of the philosophical few would have in Hobbes's political philosophy. Eventually, this will take us to an examination of Hobbes's political philosophy as a whole.

5

Hobbes's Doctrine of Natural Equality

In spite of the conspicuously inconsistent manner in which Hobbes proclaimed the natural equality of all men, there is very little suspicion expressed by his present-day readers that he was not on this point completely sincere. On the contrary, the doctrine of natural equality has been considered an indispensable precept of his philosophy. The doctrine appears to emerge from Hobbes's conception of the state of nature, a state in which men find—or at least ought to find—that life is agonizingly insecure and that all men are vulnerable to capricious fate. The most frequently given justification of Hobbes's doctrine is that it is needed to show why the struggle for power in a state of nature could never end.[1] Were men by nature unequal, the stronger would eventually assert themselves and dominate the weaker. Competition would wither and society, under the domination of the stronger, would become rigidly stratified. Without the threat of war which the competition of equals would generate, there would be no universal desire for peace. Only the weak would desire peace, whereas the strong would desire power and glory. If the prospect of acquiring power seemed realistic, those who entertained that prospect would never voluntarily commit themselves to a contract which, in the process of establishing a political association, would obligate them to abandon their pursuit of power. Unending war, conquest and domination would be unavoidable.

This is the orthodox interpretation of the nature and function of Hobbes's doctrine of equality.[2] In what would appear to be his own corroboration of this interpretation, he elevates equality to the status of a natural law. He writes: "and, therefore, for the nineth law of nature, I put

129

this: that every man acknowledge another for his equal by nature" (Lev., ch. 15, p. 141; De Cive, ch. 3, p. 39; El. of Law, p. 103). We shall see in this chapter that this interpretation is neither compelling nor supported by a more careful reading of the text. What we shall see is that the doctrine of equality is the result of arguments that are prudential in their intent.

There are other reasons Hobbes scholars have found for maintaining the fundamental character of Hobbes's doctrine of equality. It has been argued that Hobbes's doctrine is implied by his mechanistic metaphysics,[3] his subjectivist epistemology,[4] and his nominalism.[5] However, if the present analysis of Hobbes's philosophy is correct that all relations and events must be understood in terms of a dialectic of forces which manifests itself in man as endeavour or desire, then the orthodox interpretation of his equality doctrine will have to be revised. The issue in this chapter is the status of Hobbes's claim and the function of the arguments for equality in his political philosophy. Of special importance will be the much disputed issue of what Hobbes meant by "natural law."

Clearly, his theory of the natural equality of all men is, at the very least, a rejection of the classical Aristotelian distinction between the few and the many. In *Leviathan*, for example, Hobbes writes:

> I know that Aristotle in the first book of his *Politics*, for a foundation of his doctrine, maketh men by nature, some more worthy to command, meaning the wiser sort, such as he thought himself to be for his philosophy; others to serve, meaning those that had strong bodies, but were not philosophers as he, as if master and servant were not introduced by consent of men, but by difference of wit, which is not only against reason; but also against experience. (Lev. ch. 15, p. 141)

It is Hobbes's judgment that Aristotle's teaching is inimical to the political reconciliation of men. The fact that men have a greater regard for their own opinions than for those of others suggests to them their greater worthiness, for instance, their worthiness to command. Unfortunately, self-esteem is often inversely proportionate to one's ability to comprehend issues and resolve problems effectively. When, as often happens, men differ in their opinions regarding an appropriate course of action in political matters, different claims to the right to rule are advanced. Obviously, those who are right ought to have the authority to rule. The problem is that often there is no way short of war to decide who is right. Seventeenth-century England suffered endlessly from just such a confusion of rule.

To Hobbes, the pursuit of political power is an extension of the human desire for glory, a desire which is latent in all men. However, the ability to acquire political power does not imply an equal ability to maintain that power and rule effectively. In fact, the desire for glory which promotes the pursuit of political power presupposes a contempt for the power and authority of others. That unavoidably lays the groundwork for further enmity and disaffection. In short, the desire for glory is an inescapably contentious desire.

The modern revolution in science disclosed the absence of natural standards for determining who ought to rule. The neutrality of nature served to emphasize the problem of political hegemony. In the absence of natural standards, political rule, or the right to rule, must be artificially decided.

Hobbes's intent is to show us that those who "arrogate to themselves" (El. of Law, p. 103) the right to command do so without justification. The reasons are both more complex and simpler than the reasons cited by those who look upon Hobbes's doctrine of natural equality as the conceptual antecedent of his political theory. The corrective to the incendiary arrogance of those who pursue political power and glory is enlightenment. Hobbes recommends education and the dissemination of the sciences in the unequivocable belief that such enlightenment will have a salutary effect upon civil society, ultimately promoting political moderation. The doctrine of natural equality is, indeed, central to his argument. Its function in that argument, however, is not so obvious as many would have it.

HOBBES'S ARGUMENTS FOR NATURAL EQUALITY AND THEIR FUNCTION

Re-examination of Hobbes's political philosophy in recent years, as we have seen, have tended to focus on the centrality—even the "axiomatic" character—of the doctrine of natural equality. One result has been the emergence of a radically new and unconventional conception of Hobbes as "the philosopher of the bourgeoisie,"[6] a view which clashes with the traditional identification of Hobbes as an absolutist, as the apologist for English royalty. The credibility of either view is compromised by the fact that neither is unequivocally stated by Hobbes himself. Though he clearly sympathized with royalty, the right by which royalty rules is so equivocally stated in his works as to support popular rule with equal credibility. In fact, certain of Hobbes's contemporaries suggested that he wrote Leviathan during his French exile because he wanted to return, in 1652, to an anti-royalist, parliamentary England[7] in spite of having fled with the English royalists during the Civil War.

Nevertheless, Leviathan's emphasis on power, rather than honour, as the primary ingredient in political behaviour is not sufficient evidence to indicate that it is a bourgeois rather than, say, a royalist apology. Its theoretical demonstrations of the necessity of indivisible, or absolute authority are entirely neutral to the particular character of authority, that is, of who rules. All this is to say that Hobbes's writings do not clearly reveal either bourgeois or royalist sentiments, and so the suggestion that Hobbes was either a defender of royalty or the philosopher of the bourgeoisie cannot be used to interpret or illuminate the meaning of his philosophical statements. His arguments will have to stand by themselves.

The arguments that Hobbes provides to convince us of the natural equality of all men have been praised time and again for their clarity and their persuasiveness. I would suspect that the persuasiveness of the arguments has derived from a predisposition to accept the conclusions of those arguments as reasonable. The arguments themselves could hardly be considered paradigms of logical perfection. The logical structure of each of the arguments compromises the apparent conclusions in such a way that the careful reader is obliged to draw altogether different conclusions. Even the less careful reader cannot deny that Hobbes's demonstrations are incredibly, even conspicuously, unsound. The historical development through which the argument went from *De Corpore Politico* and *De Cive* to *Leviathan* is a significant measure of the argument itself. Questionably valid arguments in his earlier writings are augmented by incredibly bad arguments in his later writings. The worse the argument, the more, it seems, Hobbes praises it.

De Corpore Politico

The first instance of Hobbes's argument for natural equality appeared in *De Corpore Politico*, the second part of a work originally distributed to Hobbes's close friends in 1640 with the title *The Elements of Law*. The work went unpublished until 1650, and then only as two distinct works, part one of which was entitled *Human Nature*. In *De Corpore Politico*, Hobbes writes:

> If we consider how little odds there is of strength or knowledge between men of mature age, and with how great facility he that is the weaker in strength or wit, or in both, may utterly destroy the power of the stronger; since there needeth but little force to the taking away of a man's life, we may conclude, that men considered in mere nature, ought to admit amongst themselves equality; and that he that claimeth no more, may be esteemed moderate. (El. of Law, pp. 81–2, 103)

Here we are told of the ease with which the weaker in both strength and wit, or knowledge, may dispose of the power of the stronger and, presumably, the more intelligent. From the point of view of strength, the argument is that little is necessary to enable a man to take another's life. We are asked to accept, as the latent implication of this observation, that men *ought* to admit that they are equals in strength.

Hobbes would appear to be claiming, as well, the equality of men regarding their irrational faculties. Men are given no insurmountable edge in battle because of their superior minds. In fact, Hobbes will argue that men who are wiser are more often the losers in battle (De Cive, ch. 3, p. 39; El. of Law, ch. 4, p. 103). Men are equally adept, it seems, at destroying both the physical and mental powers of one another.

Destroying physical power, of course, amounts to the taking of a man's life. Every man, we are told, has the ability to kill every other man. However, we are not told that all men have an *equal* ability to kill all others. And, though Hobbes will later maintain that men can compensate by enlisting the aid of others to subdue an opponent, he does not say that men are of equal ability in persuasively enlisting that aid. The substance of their equality, in other words, is somewhat suspect. Hobbes *seems* to be making a claim greater than the one the argument contains.

Hobbes argues that the equality of men is found in both strength and knowledge. Presumably, equality of knowledge comes about in somewhat the same way that equality of strength is achieved, that is, through the ability to destroy the other. But, what is the rational counterpart of killing? That is, how might one destroy another rationally? There are two possibilities: refutation and censorship. Refutation cannot be what Hobbes had in mind because it depends on greater strength of mind, or greater powers of debate. Those who lack such powers will not be much of a threat to their superiors. More likely, the equalizing annihilation of an opponent's rational power takes the form of censorship. By means of censorship wise men are disarmed, made equal with their intellectual inferiors.

In the state of nature, however, where there is no agency for such legal actions, silencing an opponent would have to take the simpler form of not listening to him or, even more simply, being too ignorant to understand. The rational and persuasive power of an opponent in the state of nature is nullified by mere ignorance, or by one's simply refusing to listen. And this, like the taking of life, involves little power of one's own. In fact, those who find themselves in the natural condition are in a state of perpetual fear. We might suspect that they would lack the patience required to endure and appreciate the rigours of logical argumentation. Reason, in short, is not an effective tool in the natural condition. Consequently, the fact that the weaker have the ability to nullify the arguments of the stronger is not sufficient to prove that they are not, in fact, still the weaker!

It would be difficult to believe that Hobbes was not aware of the limitations of his proof or the exaggerated character of its conclusions. Its invalidity is emphasized by the otherwise odd fact that the conclusion he draws is *prescriptive*. He infers not that men are equal by nature, but only that they ought to admit their equality. His conclusion is both more and less than the argument warrants. It is less in that it does not state that men are, in fact, equal by nature. It is more insofar as it categorically states what men ought to admit. Hobbes's conclusion is the persuasive, not the logical, consequent of his argument.

The argument supports only the conclusion that no man is eternally immune to the threats to which he is exposed, that is, no man is immortal, and that no man is so persuasive as to be able to convince those who will not listen. One might think, in this case, of the professors of Padua who refused Galileo's offer to look through his telescope to observe the nature of heavenly bodies. By their inaction they made themselves his equals. It is only the privilege of historical perspective that enables us to see it otherwise.

With regard to strength of body, Hobbes's argument tells us that those men are moderate who are not blinded by convictions of invincibility. The royalist who might otherwise consider with disdain the outrage of the common man can learn that there is power in numbers. He can know that he is vulnerable and must consider the threat the common man poses. This is, of course, politically relevant, but it leaves palpably unsupported the natural equality that we usually take to be the argument's conclusion.

Hobbes would seem to be arguing that equality produces danger (El. of Law, p. 85) and that from danger proceeds the natural right one has to protect himself. This would leave us with a logically sound syllogism entailing the conclusion "if men are equal, then they equally possess right." And, indeed, it is Hobbes's persuasive intent to show this. It enables him to say that men may eliminate the danger they represent for one another by eliminating equality, that is, by selecting a sovereign to rule absolutely over them all. That is, the argument seems to contain the structural core of Hobbes's political philosophy. Nevertheless, right is not a function of danger for Hobbes. Men do not have a right to self-preservation only when danger exists. Perhaps the presence of danger entails the translation of right into action, and the suspicion of danger entails the translation of right into "anticipation." But natural right itself remains prior to man's historical vulnerability. Natural right is the juridical designation for the defining characteristic of man, the *conatus*, or, more simply, desire.

Furthermore, it is clear that, for Hobbes, danger and war are not consequences of equality but, rather, consequences of the diversity of human desires[8] without which equality would be no motive. Hobbes explains:

considering the great difference there is in men, from the diversity of their passions, how some are vainly glorious, and hope for precedence and superiority above their fellows, not only when they are equal in power, but also when they are inferior; we must needs acknowledge that it must necessarily follow, that those men who are moderate, and look for no more but equality of nature, shall be obnoxious to the force of others that will attempt to subdue them. And from hence shall proceed a general diffidence in mankind, and mutual fear of one another. (El. of Law, p. 82)

What we learn here is that men are naturally contentious, even those who are inferior in power. Great desires cause men to disregard their situation, for instance, their inferiority, and to undertake seemingly impossible things. Even the possibility of death will, on occasion, be no deterrent (El. of Law, p. 43). The result is that no man can easily predict the behaviour of another, and therefore must distrust him. The inability of each to know the intentions of the other generates a need to compensate, or to "anticipate" whatever needs might arise in the future. This gives man a right to *everything* in principle; and that reduces human relations to a state of warfare. Hobbes writes: "Seeing then to the offensiveness of man's nature one to another, there is added a right of every man to every thing, whereby one man invadeth with right, and other man with right resisteth, and men live thereby in perpetual diffidence, and study how to preoccupate each other" (El. of Law, p. 83).

Ignorance of one's future needs and what would satisfy them ignites one's natural passion for preservation of self and augmentation of well-being. One cannot guarantee his future preservation without augmenting his present situation, that is, without acquiring greater power. Paradoxically, the effort spent to augment one's well-being jeopardizes one's future security by arousing suspicion and fear in the minds of others. The unmediated desire for preservation dialectically turns upon itself, forcing its author to a still greater expression of that original concern until, ultimately, he finds himself in the condition of war. He has provoked threats against himself by the simple agency of guaranteeing himself against those threats.

The claim made on behalf of Hobbes by Gauthier and Macpherson that "if men were manifestly unequal, the weaker would recognize their inability to compete in the power-struggle,"[9] does not, then, stand up well. If this is true, then the function of Hobbes's theory of equality in his political theory will have to be re-examined.

De Cive

In *De Cive*, published in 1642, the argument for natural equality reappears. This time, Hobbes augmented his argument for natural equality with the following enthymeme: "They are equals, who can do equal things one against another; but they who can do the greatest things, namely, kill, can do equal things. All men therefore among themselves are by nature equal; the inequality we now discern, hath its spring from the civil law" (De Cive, p. 7).

The death of one's opponent is held here to be the "greatest thing," that is, the extreme case of things one can do to another. Hobbes argues, still further, that whatever is true in the extreme case will be true in every lesser case. We have already learned from Hobbes, albeit indirectly, that killing another person is not much of an accomplishment; anybody can do it! One need not be another's equal in strength to be able to kill him. It can hardly be maintained, then, that the ability of men to kill each other proves their equality. Though one might be able to kill his physical superior, it does not prove that he could induce servility in him or take any "lesser" liberties with him. It is harder to enslave a person than it is to kill him, just as it is harder to refute an opponent than it is to silence him through censorship or, even better, by not listening. In short, Hobbes's argument in *De Cive* does nothing to reestablish the conclusion that men are by nature equal.

Leviathan

Hobbes's argument for natural equality is given its greatest elaboration in *Leviathan* in 1651. There for the first time Hobbes provides separate proofs for the equality of men in body and mind.

The argument for natural equality of man in physical strength is much the same as it was presented in *De Corpore Politico* and *De Cive*. Nature has made men so equal that the differences in strength are insignificant. The weakest in body is able to kill the strongest. A qualification is introduced, however, which appears aimed at strengthening the argument, but which, in fact, affirms the argument's inadequacies. Any man can kill another, if in no other way, then by secrecy and confederation with others whose lives are also jeopardized by another's superior strength.

That such agencies are required to establish the vulnerability of every man in the state of nature affirms rather than refutes the fact that there is a difference between men in strength. The argument proves no more than the fact that men are mortal and, therefore, vulnerable. Men can be killed. From this Hobbes infers that they are all equal (Lev., ch. 13, p. 110).

Furthermore, since man is by nature a solitary brute, if his natural equality with others is a function of associations or confederations, then natural equality, paradoxically, cannot be natural. It is a consequence of social or political ingenuity. Implicitly, then, the doctrine of natural equality is a conventional, or prudential, doctrine.

A separate argument for equality of mind also appears in *Leviathan* for the first time. The circumstances under which it appears are rather odd. The argument is substantially the same as that found in Descartes' *Discourse on Method*, published in 1637.[10] *The Discourse on Method* was at Hobbes's disposal in 1637, but its argument did not appear in *De Corpore Politico* (1640)[11] or in *De Cive* (1642).

Indeed, Hobbes does not appear to use the argument until one year after Descartes' death in 1650. We can suspect that Hobbes was indebted to Descartes for the argument, and further, that Hobbes's use of the argument is possibly as deceptive as Descartes' was acknowledged to be. In *Leviathan* he says:

> As to the faculties of the mind, setting aside the arts grounded upon words, and especially that skill of proceeding upon general, and infallible rules, called science; which very few have, and but in few things; as being not a native faculty, born with us; nor attained, as prudence, while we look after somewhat else, I find yet *a greater equality* amongst men, than that of strength. For prudence is but experience; which equal time, equally bestows on all men, in those things they equally apply themselves unto (Lev., ch. 13, p. 110).

This measure of man's equality, Hobbes tells us here, is even more conclusive than the previous arguments. Paradoxically, it is worse. The very form of the argument affirms its opposite. Hobbes begins, incredibly, by abstracting from the inequalities of mind, that is, from the inequality of imagination and reason that he elsewhere says is as natural to man as are the passions (El. of Law, p. 87).

Hobbes supports his proof with another observation for which he is again indebted to Descartes' *Discourse on Method*. He admits that the idea that men are equal in mind seems incredible. Yet he claims to prove the idea of equality by maintaining that the feeling of incredibility "is but a vain conceit of one's own wisdom, which almost all men think they have in a greater degree, than the vulgar" (Lev., ch. 13, p. 110). Men are of such a nature that, regardless of the wit and eloquence they observe in others, they refuse to believe that anybody else is wiser. This, says Hobbes, is proof of their equality rather than their inequality. "For there is not ordinarily a greater sign of the equal distribution of any thing, than that every men is contented with his share" (Lev., ch. 13, p. 111).

The fact that men appear to be contented with their own wisdom is utilized here by Hobbes as proof that they are equally wise or prudent. What it shows, in fact, is that many men are vain and are not sufficiently prudent to be able to recognize wisdom greater than their own.

The initial argument Hobbes gives for equality of mind is subject to this same criticism. He says that men who apply themselves equally for equal amounts of time to a subject will be equal in their experience or prudence. But this is hardly obvious. History is dotted with the mistakes of those who were unable to learn from their experiences and, in spite of their ages, were painfully deficient in prudence. Hobbes devoted much of his writings to the education and enlightenment of such fools in the hope that they might awaken to see their actions for what they are, misguided actions which tend to thrust men back into the natural condition and all that that entails.

There is a sense in which equality of time and experience implies equality of prudence. But we must be careful to avoid reading into this thought the depreciation of experience it would appear to imply. Experience is not merely a quantitative accumulation of images and ideas. Rather, Hobbes tells us, it is a product of those faculties of intellect that are unequally distributed among men: "Men of quick imagination, *caeteris paribus*, are more prudent than those whose imaginations are slow; *for they observe more in less time*. Prudence is nothing but conjecture from experience, or taking of signs from experience warily, that is, that the experiments from which he taketh such signs be all remembered; for else the cases are not alike that seem so" (El. of Law, p. 18).

Hobbes affirms that experience is a function of man's rational capacity to discriminate like from unlike. It is a product of his capacity for classifying correctly the "kinds" to which things and events belong. Men begin to experience when they first imaginatively recognize that the event or situation before them is like certain events of the past. Where imagination and judgment vary in quickness and acuteness, experience, too, must vary. Those who are more quick and more acute in their observations experience more in less time. Inequality of prudence, then, results from the unequal ability of men to observe and judge discriminately. Since the difference in men's capacities to observe and make judgments is natural, inequality, too, is natural. No other conclusion can be drawn consistently from Hobbes's analysis.

Hobbes is not hesitant in maintaining the natural dissimilarity, that is, inequality, of men in intellectual virtue or natural wit when he is not making an argument for their natural equality. He writes:

This natural wit consists principally in two things: celerity of imagining—that is, swift succession of one thought to another—and steady direction to some approved end. And this difference of quickness is caused by the difference of men's passions that love and dislike, some one thing, some another; and therefore some men's thoughts run one way, some another, and are held to and observe differently the things that pass through their imagination. (Lev., ch. 8, p. 56)

The great difference among men in natural wit or reason is a consequence, according to Hobbes, of a natural difference of passion. Specifically, some men possess great curiosity and have great designs which, when accompanied by a sense of resolution or gravity and a "steady direction," promote a quick imagination and an acute sense of judgment. Most important, however, this dissimilarity of men has an ineradicable basis in nature; it is not the arbitrary result of different education, though education certainly makes its own differences:

The causes of this difference of wits, are in the passions; and the difference of passions proceedeth, partly from the different constitution of the body, and partly from different education... The passions that most of all cause the difference of wit, are principally, the more or less desire of power, of riches, of knowledge, and of honour. All which may be reduced to the first, that is, desire for power. For riches, knowledge, and honour, are but several sorts of power. And therefore, a man who has no great passion for any of these things; but is, as men term it, indifferent; though he may be so far a good man, as to be free from giving offense; yet he cannot possibly have either a great fancy, nor much judgment. For the thoughts are to the desires, as scouts, and spies, to range abroad, and find the way to the things desired. (Lev., ch. 8, p. 61)

I do not claim to have shown in the foregoing that Hobbes's theory of equality is not a serious part of his teaching; indeed, it is in a sense a serious part of his teaching. What I hope to have shown is only that its credibility as a straightforward and candid teaching is seriously compromised by the arguments with which it is stated. Hobbes's proofs for natural equality are deceptively ambiguous. Time and again his reasoning involves equivocation plus gratuitous, and often contradictory, assumptions regarding the nature of human action. Inevitably, his logic is qualified by conditional conclusions which suggest still more the possibility that his argument is not what it seems. Hobbes terminates his argument with the observation that it does not matter whether men are equal or not, because the preservation of civil order demands it in either case: "If nature therefore have made men equal, that equality is to be acknowledged: or if nature have made man unequal; yet because men that think themselves equal; will not enter into conditions of peace, but upon equal terms, such equality must be admitted."[12]

In each case, Hobbes's justification for equality is political necessity. The demands of civil order, not reason or nature, declare the equality of men.

THE FUNCTION OF THE DOCTRINE OF EQUALITY

More specifically, Hobbes's arguments are intended to neutralize certain tendencies of human nature which promote civil war, notably, the tendency to base one's actions on the desire for glory and honour. The arguments are meant to be enlightening to rulers and pretenders to rule, men who are most tempted by the seductive character of glory. This is suggested by the carefully designed formal structure of chapter 13 of *Leviathan*, the chapter in which Hobbes makes his most famous and eloquent plea for natural equality.

The chapter consists of fourteen paragraphs divided into two equal parts. It begins with a statement of man's natural equality, explaining that equality is the natural, that is, proximate, cause of strife. This claim is corrected, however, in the culmination of the first part, in paragraph seven, where Hobbes discloses that the immediate, as opposed to the proximate, causes of strife are the three kinds of motives that lie behind all men's actions, "first, competition, secondly diffidence; thirdly, glory. The first makes men invade for gain, the second for safety; and the third for reputation" (Lev., p. 112). In sum, desire, fear, and glory are the war-promoting impulses in human nature.

With paragraph eight the second part begins. We have been told that equality is the cause of war, but also that concern for augmentation of one's well-being, that is, for gain, safety, and glory, is the cause of war. The mulitiplicity of causes is as yet unexplained. The second part of the chapter, beginning with paragraph eight, is a counterpart to the first, which began with equality and ended with war. This half of the chapter commences with a discussion of the state of war and concludes in paragraph fourteen with the state of peace or, more specifically, with Hobbes's explanation of the passions that incline men to peace, "fear of death, desire of such things as are necessary to commodious living, and a hope by their industry to obtain them" (Lev., p. 116). This list of peace-inducing passions overlaps in all but one instance the initial list of passions which, in paragraph seven, were observed to lead men to war. Glory, the desire for reputation, is replaced by hope, which Hobbes associates with equality, at least in the sense that only those who are able to perceive themselves as the equals of others can have a hope to compete with them. When they do hope, however, it is for success, that is, for the inequality that competing successfully brings. To that extent, hope easily gives over to glory. Either way, glory is dramatically isolated and emphasized as the cause of war. One might say that, while glory inclines men to war, it does not in any way incline them toward peace. In fact, the inclination toward the acquisition of glory and honour magnifies the possibility of war by emphasizing just that solitary and radically self-directed aspect of human nature that makes war inevitable in the first place. It is also of interest to note that Hobbes not only drops glory as a cause when discussing the cause of peace, but also reverses the order of priority of the other two causes, with gain placed prior to safety among the causes of war, and safety (i.e., fear of death) put prior to gain among the cause of peace. Concern for gain would, perhaps, be more akin to glory for Hobbes, and concern for safety more like a practical concern for equality. The two motives are not entirely unrelated, however, insofar as hope encourages a willingness to attempt those things that promote glory.

The structure of chapter 13 reflects the dialectic that moves through Hobbes's thought. The motives behind men's actions, that is, fear of death (desire for self-preservation) and desire to augment life (to provide for commodious well-being) dialectically turn back upon themselves, promoting both peace and war. Precisely those concerns that instill in men a love of peace also encourage them to engage in war. Engaging in war is no less than a search for peace. Reflection on the cruelties of battle suggests the humbling thought that nobody is a perpetual winner, and in this sense all men are equal; but it also suggests that none need be a perpetual loser, and so holds out the possibility that anybody could be a winner. In this sense, too, it is equalizing.

Unlike the natural fear that man has for his own preservation and the natural desire he has to augment his condition, the concern for glory appears to incline men only to war, never to peace. That seems to be the dramatic message contained comparatively in Hobbes's two lists. The difference between glory and the other two motives can be located in the fact that the passion for glory is exclusively a public desire. Hobbes calls glory an "exultation of the mind"(Lev., ch. 6, p. 45) that occurs when one reflects upon his own power. But there is no necessary correlation between the glory one enjoys and his actual natural power. One sees one's power only in the eyes or opinions of others, that is, in the public manifestation of honour, to which glory is posterior. Honour, Hobbes tells us, "consists *only* in the *opinion* of Power" (Lev., ch. 10, p. 80). And opinions, we all know, are notoriously inaccurate.

Hobbes maintains that honour is known as one's *worth*, and that a man's worth is also his *price* (Lev., ch. 10, p. 76). Furthermore, he says that "not the seller but the buyer determines the price" (Lev., ch. 10, p. 76). Worth, or honour, is exclusively determined by one's market value. Much has recently been made of this way of reading Hobbes's theory. Combined with Hobbes's statement that the differences between men are civil in origin (Lev., pp. 140–1; De Cive, p. 38; El. of Law, p. 103), it seems to suggest a theory of value anticipatory to theories of the "modern competitive market society,"[13] according to which all differences between men are transitory, or historical in origin.

However, Hobbes is rather clear that the public manifestation of glory involves an abstraction from natural inequalities which it cannot make manifest. Worth, he tells us, is not the same as *worthiness* or aptitude (Lev., ch. 10, p. 84). Worth is a product of popularity and reputation, which fails to reflect one's real worthiness. Exemplary of this public inability to make manifest real worthiness is Hobbes's case for science, in which, he says, there is "small power," obviously not because of the nature of science itself, but because of its lack of social eminence, specifically, because of the inability of all but the few to understand and fully appreciate its worthiness (Lev., ch. 10, p. 76). Presumably, there is also small power, or little glory, in being scientific. The public cannot appreciate what cannot be made publically manifest. Hobbes's claim, then, that the differences in men are civil in origin is not, for Hobbes, an admission that beneath the exclusively civil differences there are not real, or natural, differences that do not necessarily coincide with those civil differences.

Glory tends to obscure real, non-illusory determinations of power. It involves no dialectic and so represents a defective or incomplete expression of desire. The dialectic involved in the determination of physical power, which at once seems to expose both physical superiority and physical equality, would lead to the annihilation of glory altogether. Hobbes tells us that if all men have glory, then none have it (De Cive, ch. 1, p. 5)! Glory is achieved only at the expense of others who also desire glory.

Men render themselves deaf to praise of the virtue of others through excessive fascination with their own "worth." Excessive self-esteem is indistinguishable from an indifference toward all others, or contempt. This is the characteristic attitude of the aristocrat toward the common man. It is also the source of man's having been left inescapably in a state of perpetual war.

Natural equality is nowhere stated by Hobbes with unequivocal and unqualified conviction. What he does say is that men ought to *admit* their equality because they naturally desire peace. Not admitting one's equality—if it is, in effect, an assertion of one's superiority—is provocative, insofar as others must take it as a challenge. If, on the other hand, it is a latent admission of one's inferiority, it serves to encourage thoughts of impunity in others which, in turn, leads to thoughts of revenge, perhaps through associations with others and subterfuges that negate the natural advantages of the superior few. The inevitable result, either way, is war. More important, the criterion by which superiority is determined will be the lowest, that is, physical superiority. Strengths of mind come to be viewed as subordinate, or inferior, to physical powers and their recognition, that is, to glory. But it is in the powers of the mind, for example, in the capacity for science, that men are most different. Consequently, Hobbes's argument reduces itself to this: if we do not admit our equality, we will all, by the brutishness of our situation, be reduced to equality in those aspects of human nature in which we are least equal.

The suggestion implicit in the structure of Hobbes's argument is that those who indulge in excessive exultation over the public image of their powers can be made to listen by the eloquence of persuasive rhetoric. Hobbes's *Leviathan* will be able to tame the contentious natures of those Englishmen who have been goading their country into war. A provisional correction is provided for the desire for glory through a rhetoric which appeals to self-esteem and which, while showing complementarily that one is not necessarily inferior by nature to his political superiors, teaches incidentally, but not insignificantly, the humbling corollary that one is not necessarily superior to his political inferiors either.

Chapter 13 of *Leviathan*, then, provides us with the provisional solution to the war-producing impulses that some men exhibit. The solution to the problem of the man whose actions are guided exclusively by a concern for glory, and who is thus the perpetual instigator of war, is persuasive rhetoric, a fear-inducing argument which will render him conscious of his own vulnerability. Those who hunger for glory, if they can be persuaded of the truth that all are equal, and so equally vulnerable, can be made self-conscious, aware of the threatening hostility of those who are obviously inferior and insignificant, and so can be encouraged to act with reason, that is, with political prudence. Fear makes men reasonable. The highest manifestation of this reasonableness, Hobbes tells us, is charity (El. of Law, ch. 9, p. 49; Lev., ch. 6, p. 43) (of which Hobbes was, himself, no small recipient). This, however, is for men who will reason from no other ground than a radically defective conception of human well-being, their excessive concern for glory. Irrational men, the predominantly vainglorious, are thus made provisionally rational.

The paramount demand of the commonwealth is that man *admit* his equality with his fellow citizens and, ultimately, his obligation to the sovereign. The peaceful homogeneity of civil society requires that man see himself as a political being, that is, as a being with obligations to the welfare of civil society. This requires that the philosopher-scientist accept with unwavering (albeit, perhaps, simulated) faith the commonwealth's myths and salubrious conventions. The scientist, that is to say, must become politically prudent.

Hobbes's dissembling arguments contain the elements of a political realism that does not depend on natural equality at all. Hobbes is not willing to make obvious his belief that it is only the brutality of the state of nature that makes men equal. On the other hand, the civilizing consequences of the social contract, while perpetuating the idea of the mutual equality of all, liberates the efficacy of natural inequality, that is, the efficacy of that rational and scientific capacity found in only a few. It is only in civil society that man can cultivate the sciences which will make possible the mastery of nature.

Civil existence can provide for man's most immediate needs, but it is not, in itself, capable of satisfying the restructured needs—the liberated needs—of the natural man. There is more that threatens the welfare of man than other men. Civil society has no authority over nature per se, and cannot provide men with security that goes beyond the political. Mastery, in short, is not possible at the level of civil society. The satisfaction of human desire requires the efforts of those—the philosophical and scientific few—who can transcend the authority of the sovereign without disturbing the peaceful, political hegemony of civil society, and redirect their intentions to the "indefatigable generation of knowledge" which Hobbes calls the "great and master delight." It is this latter effort, undertaken by philosopher-scientists, that conceivably may culminate in the establishment of man as the measure of all things. Part of the intent of Hobbes's political philosophy is to insulate the myths and conventions vital to the health of civil society from the potentially destructive implications of this project of philosophical science, that is, from the desire for rational mastery which has not surrendered to sovereign authority. The insulation Hobbes provides includes his proof for the existence of God, his argument for the necessity of sovereign authority and his arguments for the natural equality of all men. This is not to diminish the importance of these arguments. They remain for Hobbes important practical preconditions of the philosophical and scientific enterprise.

6

Political Theory

In the "Epistle Dedicatory" to *De Corpore*, Hobbes remarked that civil philosophy is "no older. . . than my own book *De Cive* (I, Epist. Ded., p. ix). What he meant is evident in his criticisms of ancient and medieval philosophy. The standards and rules of moral life remained, for them, external to actual political life, superimposed from without. Hobbes called the moral principles of the ancients "those hermaphrodite opinions of moral philosophers, partly right and comely, partly brutal and wild; the causes of all contentions and bloodsheds" (De Cive, Pref., p. xiii). Their complex character—partly right, partly brutal—was a product of excessive idealism. The ancients aimed too high. Their principles were too lofty. Most men do not exhibit high aspirations and, especially during times of duress, are not tempted by them. The lives of men are normally governed by more worldly concerns, even on those occasions when they claim to be led by noble aims. Furthermore, both the actions of men and the political institutions they create for themselves, when measured by the lofty principles of ancient morality, look vulgar and contemptible. None measures up against such standards. Hobbes's conclusion was that the great gap between ancient ideals and the worldly human behaviour exaggerated, rather than reduced, the proclivity for contention, and ultimately, war. No government can withstand being judged by principles so high. Such principles are comely and right in themselves, but brutal and wild to the extent that they breed sedition.

Hobbes did not mean to suggest that the ancients were altogether unaware of this disproportion, only that they did not have the modern means to resolve it. Political realism was not for them, as yet, an alternative.

145

Nevertheless, the ancients were able to avoid the seditious implications of judgments grounded in excessive political and moral idealism. The ancients, Hobbes says, "rather chose to have the science of justice wrapped up in fables, than openly exposed to disputations" (De Cive, p. xii). The salutary result of the concealment of noble principles by wrapping them in stories of the gods and noble lies was to insulate them from open criticism and, according to Hobbes, to produce a "golden age," a time of peace. "The simplicity of those times," he says, "was not yet capable of so learned a piece of folly" (De Cive, pp. xii–xiii) as that "doctrine of morality" called upon in Hobbes's own time, "that a prince for some causes may by some certain men be deposed" (De Cive, p. xi).

Whether Hobbes's analysis of the politics of the ancients and the peace he says it generated is accurate or not (or even consistent) is incidental. What is significant for us is his indication of the ineffective character of moral principles in controlling the passions, the need for moral and political authority, and the destructive implications that enlightenment can have for political life when it separates moral principles and political authority. The enlightened distinction between moral principles and political authority is the antecedent to not only the moral condemnation of politics and the principles of political action, but also (as in Hobbes's case) the political condemnation of the seditious principles of morality. Hobbes's corrective to the learned and seditious folly that enlightenment introduced to his times was to ground civil philosophy on "the natural reason of man" (De Corp., Epist. to the Reader) which, he said, is "the child of the world and your own mind... within yourself" (ibid.). Clearly, his intention was to discover the principles of political and moral order within political life rather than to invoke principles outside and above political life. This, Hobbes maintained, was an idea—more accurately, a task—which nobody comprehended adequately prior to his own De Cive.

While civil philosophy as Hobbes conceived it may not have been older than his De Cive (I won't debate the issue), it is nonetheless true that the account given in De Cive was not Hobbes's last. His earliest political writings, De Cive and De Corpore Politico (Part II of The Elements of Law) differ from his later political writings, for example, Leviathan. Unlike his earlier writings, the later writings reflect the substantial changes that took place in his physics and psychology. The result is not a dramatic alteration of the political theory in Hobbes's later writings. In fact, the changes are rather subtle and can be easily ignored without doing great injustice to his political philosophy. The net effect is that his political philosophy becomes more consistent, more exhaustive and better founded, but in such a way as to show the impossibility of political philosophy independent of the philosophical project to make man master of nature per se. The success of the philosophical project depends on man's mastery of what is brutish in human nature. That political project cannot be accomplished without a right philosophical understanding of human nature and, therefore, nature per se. By publishing *De Cive* before he had completed the physics and psychology on which it was to be founded, Hobbes suggested that the success of the project of political philosophy—the mastery of what is brutish in human nature—could be accomplished independent of the larger philosophical project. It's possible, Hobbes says, because the principles of political existence are self-evident to those who are sympathetic to them.

HOBBES'S EARLIER POLITICAL THEORY

We have already seen (in chapter 4) how, in *De Cive* and *The Elements of Law*, Hobbes adopted a conception of life that portrayed it as a kind of "race," the objective of which was to be foremost. By depicting the objective of life this way, Hobbes conceived man as a radically social animal. His greatest desire, and the greatest of all human goods, was exclusively a social objective, glory. Glory is exclusively a product of public recognition; it can be acquired only within society. To the extent that glory is man's greatest desire, man is a social animal. His greatest excellence is a function of association with others. If there are no others with whom he can compete, there will be none to dominate and, even worse, none to recognize his dominance.

While man is, in this philosophical sense, a social animal, Hobbes makes it clear that he is not altogether sociable. Man is not so sociable as to be unable to distinguish his own private welfare from the public good and not to notice that what promotes the public good is not always compatible with his own welfare as an individual. Furthermore, he cannot help but prefer his own private good to that of the public when the two conflict. He is, in short, relentlessly self-interested.

Glory cannot be acquired except at the expense of others. Hobbes writes: "glory is like honor; if all men have it, no man hath it, for they consist in comparison and precellence" (De Cive, ch. 1, art. 2, p. 5). And, he adds, "the benefits of this life... may be better attained to by dominion than by the society [i.e., mutual help] of others" (De Cive, ch. 1, art. 2, p. 5). Consequently, while man is born in need of society, and whereas "solitude is an enemy," he is also, for that same reason, "born unapt for society" (De Cive, ch. 1, art. 2, p. 2). The very principle of his individuation as a human being, his "natural right," is a principle of alienation which indicates the natural and necessary enmity of man and man. "The natural right of preservation," Hobbes writes, "we receive from the uncontrollable dictates of necessity" (De Cive, Epist. Ded., p. ii).

Hobbes blends naturalism with egoism in *De Cive* with his added observation that "profit is the measure of right" (De Cive, ch. 1, art. 10, p. 11). That is, whatever is necessary, (i.e., natural) is, for that reason, right. And whether an action is right (i.e., necessary) is dependent on whether it is profitable. "Profitable" here is a utilitarian term for "reasonable." But if, as Hobbes says, profit is the measure of right, what, then, is the measure of profit? His answer to this question changes somewhat from the time of *De Cive* to the time of *Leviathan*. In *De Cive*, Hobbes's answer to the question is quite clear: the measure of profit is glory! More modestly put, the measure of right is public acknowledgment which always comes at somebody's expense.

The undemocratic character of glory leads us to the conclusion that, while all men have a right to whatever they need, or believe they need, simply by virtue of the fact that they need it (or believe that it is profitable), there is no clearly discernible moral reason why all men should have it.[1] There is no reason why rights should be observed. And, there is a logical reason why all men cannot have all rights observed. Profit, which, here in *De Cive*, is the measure of right, is codeterminate with its public manifestation, glory. Glory is a product of recognition; it is the product of power relations. To share it is to destroy it. It is by logical necessity a "scarce commodity." Civil society, then, so long as it is an association intended to guarantee the natural and inalienable rights of men, is an orderly restatement of the state of nature. Man does not leave nature entirely behind when he enters civil society.

Hobbes maintains "the chiefist of natural evils" is not some misbehaviour on the part of man, but "death" against which it is reasonable and right "for a man to use all his endeavours to preserve and defend his body and the members thereof..." (De Cive, ch. 1, art. 7, p. 9). This is sufficient to show that "right reason" is not a moral demand placed upon men. What is rational need not be morally reasonable. Some scholars have understood Hobbes to have made an appeal to some rational standard of behaviour that transcends historical events. A superficial reading of Hobbes's comments, such as that "right reason" is the measure of what is "done justly, and with right" (De Cive, ch. 1, art. 7, pp. 8–9), might be taken to support this view. I do not believe it is a reading that can be sustained.

The dilemma for man, as it is developed in *De Cive*, is not that there are no moral laws for men to follow (that goes without saying), but rather that it is the nature of unmediated self-interest to be self-contradictory and for the "dictates of true reason" to reflect that. Obeying the law of nature, "the dictate of right reason, conversant about those things which are either to be done or omitted for the constant preservation of life and members, as much as in us lies" (De Cive, ch. 2, art. 1, p. 16), is not in itself a way out of the problem. What right reason, that is, the law of nature dictates, is to a man's benefit and, paradoxically, at the same time threatens his well-being. The preservation of life cannot be accomplished and guaranteed without an effort on the part of a man to augment his condition by anticipating future needs, future dangers and future threats, and by compensating for them by acquiring the powers necessary for resisting the threats and satisfying the needs should they ever actually arise. A right to the end implies a right to the means to that end (De Cive, ch. 1, art. 8, p. 9). The problem is that, whether the powers or means that a man perceives to be necessary to his future preservation are, indeed, necessary to his future preservation cannot "by the right of nature" (De Cive, ch. 1, art. 9, p. 9) be determined by anything other than the fallible, private judgment of the individual. Given the fact that human judgment, especially in matters of life and death, tends toward the excessive, since many conceivable needs and many conceivable threats will never actually arise for most men, right reason itself encourages men to go beyond the boundaries of right reason. Not to anticipate and compensate for those unlikely threats is to leave oneself vulnerable. The Hobbesian result is that men tend to become threats to the well-being of those whom they perceive to be possible threats to themselves. The rational character of this unreasonable tendency is summed up by Hobbes in one terse sentence: "Nature hath given to every one a right to all" (De Cive, ch. 1, art. 10, p. 9).

This is not to say, of course, that man is wicked or sinful. In fact, as John Plamenatz has observed, "the peculiarity of Hobbes is not that he asserted man's natural selfishness—for moralists had been busy asserting and denouncing it for centuries—but that he denied his essential wickedness."[2] The human condition is such that the more rational a man is, the less reasonable he becomes, at least in the natural condition. His natural concern for self-preservation coaxes a man into an effort to augment his power for the sake of guaranteeing his security and well-being. But the acquisition of power only jeopardizes one's life by provoking others to reciprocate, and ultimately eliminate this potential threat to their own safety and well-being. One's security, in short, cannot be guaranteed without at the same time being jeopardized. The natural condition, then, is the natural consequence of natural reason. The more man wants to escape the natural condition and put an end to the uncertainty that it represents, the more he must undertake actions that thrust him inextricably back into the natural condition.

To argue, as some have, that Hobbes believes men will be willing to contract with others to quit the state of nature because "their condition in the state of nature is desperate, and their desire to put an end to that state is urgent and strong,"[3] is to miss the dilemma Hobbes's analysis poses for man. The difficulty is that man's desire to quit the natural condition, urgent as it is, is self-vitiating. Man's natural efforts to quit the natural condition create a situation in which every man is to be distrusted, since one can be expected to escape the natural condition only at the expense of others. Profit, after all, is the measure of right.

Hobbes, we all know, appeals to the enlightening influence of fear to coerce men into obeying the laws of reason. He never recommends that we depend upon exhortations to virtue. Such exhortations will be ineffective, especially during those times of crisis when the private interests of the individual are clearly incompatible with the welfare of others. Hobbes seems to be arguing that, by reflecting on the conflict-generating consequences of his efforts to satisfy his future needs, man can become more prudential, less ready to pursue those ends when they are self-destructive. With his intentions mediated by his fear of the consequences of his actions, a man will be more willing to compromise with others and, ultimately, to contract with them for the sake of mutual defence. In this way man protects himself from the self-destructive implications of his own intentions to preserve his life and augment his well-being.[4]

Man's self-interested intentions, mediated by fear, Hobbes codifies in the first and second laws of nature: "That peace is to be sought after, where it may be found; and where not, there to provide ourselves for helps of war" (De Cive, ch. 2, art. 2, p. 16), and "That the right of all men to all things ought not to be retained; but that some certain things ought to be transferred or relinquished" (De Cive, ch. 2, art. 3, p. 17). One ought to note that the second law of nature derives from—that is, is implied by— only the first half of the first law. The first law is a disjunctive advocacy of peace and, when what appears to be impossible, war. Where peace is not possible (an ever-present possibility according to the first law) the second law will not follow validly. The conscientious character of natural right is still represented in the first law; it is absent in the second. The second law would appear to have ignored the internally self-contradictory character of self-interest. The real problem for students of Hobbes is in determining how he got from the prudential advice of the first law to the more sociable advice of the second.

Indicative of the difficulty confronting anyone who undertakes to understand this transformation of the natural condition into a peaceful civil condition and the function of the natural laws in effecting this transition has been the issue of the status of Hobbes's laws of nature: are they merely prudential counsels or are they Divine Dictates? Hobbes himself tells us that they are dictates of reason, but that these dictates of reason can be considered to be *either* Divine Commands or prudential counsels:

These dictates of reason, men use[d] to call by the name of laws, but improperly: for they are but the conclusions, or theorems concerning what conduceth to the conservation and defense of themselves; whereas law, properly, is the word of him, that by right hath command over others. But yet if we consider the same theorems, as delivered in the word of God, that by right commandeth all things; then they are properly called laws. (Lev., ch. 15, p. 147)[5]

If one interprets Hobbes as saying that natural laws are Divine Commands, and only incidentally prudential counsels, or that they are really prudential counsels, and are Divine Commands only in some lesser sense, one establishes a dichotomy in Hobbes's thought that he has condemned in the ancients and in School philosophy. Clearly it is not Hobbes's intention to do that. If the natural laws are merely prudential advice, then they clearly lack necessity, at least insofar as by prudential advice one means *ad hoc* recommendations regarding how to reach goals one happens to have. There is nothing natural about such laws in that case; they are like prescriptions, "like the doctor's orders,"[6] which may or may not be relevant, depending on whether you have the condition for which he is prescribing.

The principal difficulty with this view of Hobbes's concept of law is that the end which a natural law serves is not an empirically determined or contingent end which men may or may not find is part of their personal persuasion; it is, rather a wholly irresistible end, the motivation for which is found "even in the embryo" (De Corp., ch. 25, p. 407). And, even more, it is the only end of human actions, in the sense that the decision to do or to avoid any particular act ultimately (though perhaps not immediately) turns on the matter of whether it will contribute to my preservation, if not to the augmentation of my well-being.

On the other hand, if the laws are understood to be Divine Commands, paradigms that all men ought to follow all the time, in the interest of "eternal" self-preservation, that is, salvation,[7] then we have the establishment of an other-worldly standard of behaviour, one that is external to political life altogether.

Howard Warrender has attempted to escape this dilemma by appealing to Hobbes's distinction between the *in foro interno* and the *in foro externo* authority of the natural laws.[8] Warrender, in an interesting approach to Hobbes's laws of nature, takes the natural laws to be Divine Commands which always hold *in foro interno*, that is to say, binding on the conscience of every man. If this holds, then Hobbes's moral philosophy no longer has to be thought of as having been founded upon (or "foundering on") a psychological egoism that invalidates any logically valid theory of moral obligation.[9] The obligatory character of moral law extends throughout the state of nature *in foro interno,* that is, in the conscience of every man. However, it is not actually obligatory, that is, *in foro externo,* except when certain "validating conditions,"[10] specifically, "security and belief in God,"[11] exist. In short, we are obliged *in foro externo,* that is, actually obliged, to actually obey the laws of nature only when we as believers in the existence of God (assuming we are believers) find it safe to do so. In the absence of fear of our fellow man, our belief in (and fear of) Divine Power will determine what we will do. It will make us conscientious.

What Warrender's suggestion ignores is Hobbes's persistent claim that in the natural condition it is fear of other men that makes us conscientious, to whatever degree we ever are conscientious. It is not merely a validating condition; it is the agent of rational action. Were it safe to do so, a man would invade other men with impunity. Or, as Hobbes says, "I hope no body will doubt but that men would much more greedily be carried by nature, if all fear were removed, to obtain dominion, than to gain society. We must therefore resolve, that the original of all great and lasting societies consisted not in the mutual good will men had towards each other, but in the mutual fear they had of each other" (De Cive, ch. 1, art. 2, pp. 5–6).

I am not making a case here for the crude egoistic interpretation of Hobbes's theory which would have all actions self-directed and, for that reason, morally condemnable. Rather, I am suggesting that there is contained in Hobbes's theory of self-interest a presentiment of the Hegelian dialectic of self-interest, where the truth of what is one's right is to be discovered in duty or obligation. Self-interest, so long as it remains the crude, unmediated self-interest of the natural condition, is self-vitiating. One's interests cannot be protected without extending one's concern for preservation and protection to others.

It is not at all obvious that the *in foro interno* authority of natural law is moral simply because it is *in foro interno.* The state of nature is a state of war of each against all. But one must not forget that the state of war is not simply a state of actual battle. Rather, Hobbes says, it is a state of will, intent, or desire, where one man's desires are such that they preclude another's satisfaction of his desires. Hobbes writes:

> For WAR, consisteth not in battle only, or the act of fighting; but in a tract of time, wherein the will to contend by battle is sufficiently known: and therefore the notion of *time,* is to be considered in the nature of war; as it is in the nature of weather. For as the nature of foul weather, lieth not in a shower or two of rain; but in an inclination thereto of many days together: so the nature of war consisteth not in actual fighting; but in the known disposition thereto, during all the

time there is no assurance to the contrary. All other time is PEACE. (Lev., ch. 13, p. 113)

War is, in short, an *in foro interno* will to contend with others which is promoted by the condition of distrust and the natural preoccupation with one's own well-being. It is the unmediated *in foro interno* natural right of man.

To define natural law as the *in foro interno* authority of conscience, where conscience is other-directed and altruistic, in distinction from natural right which is self-directed, egoistic, and not an *in foro interno* authority itself, is merely to ignore the complex, dialectical character of Hobbesian self-interest, or *conatus*. The first law of nature, "that every man, ought to endeavour peace, as far as he has hope of obtaining it; and when he cannot obtain it, that he may seek, and use, all helps and advantages of war" (Lev., ch. 14, p. 117), indeed holds *in foro interno*. But it contains the same division that is found in the self-vitiating character of man's unmediated efforts to preserve himself and provide for his well-being. Indicative of this are Hobbes's remarks in explanation of the law. He writes: "The first branch of which rule, containeth the first and fundamental law of nature; which *is to seek peace, and follow it*. The second, the sum of the right of nature; which is, *by all means we can, to defend ourselves*" (Lev., ch. 14, p. 117). The first and most fundamental law of nature, then, sometimes prescribes peace, sometimes war.

Hobbes does say that "the laws of nature... are contrary to our natural passions, that carry us to partiality, pride, revenge and the like" (Lev., ch. 17, pp. 153–4). This might be taken to support the radical separation of natural law and natural right. But it is a statement that holds true only at the most immediate and unreflective level of passion. It is not true at the self-conscious level of desire, where fear of death enlightens one to the fact that his right to preservation cannot be assured without surrendering his natural, that is, infinite, right to everything and everybody whatsoever. Getting to the second fundamental law of nature from the first law depends on mediating the internal division that exists in the first.

Hobbes's difficulty is that the natural *conatus*, the individuating principle in human nature, individuates in such a way as to make mediation impossible. In his earlier political philosophy, in *De Cive*, *conatus* is utilized only to refer to appetite. Its function will be expanded and systematically developed in *Leviathan* and *De Corpore*. However, the dilemma surrounding *conatus* is already apparent. While appetite may be individuated in society according to different social forms, that does not imply that appetite itself is socially acquired or, ultimately, socially satisfiable. That is, the drives and desires that govern a person's behaviour may be peculiarly royalist or, perhaps, conspicuously English. However, desire itself, *conatus*, has a nature that precedes and preconditions its worldly manifestations. In *De Cive*, Hobbes explains the difference by saying that men "are born in infancy" (De Cive, ch. 1, art. 1, p. 2), which is to say that natural appetite or desire is pre-political, not yet ordered by prudential considerations. The desire for glory, the highest form that *conatus* (understood as appetite) takes in *De Cive*, is only a social form of the natural (unsociable) desire for domination. Because he is a materialist, that is, because he denies the reality of anything other than the individual, the unity of individuals can only be political. And no merely political unity will change the fact that "nature dissociates." Political unity will always be, strictly speaking, unsociable. Natural law is the politically reasonable extension of natural right, that is, of desire. It is not a transcendent principle of moral or social unity. To divide natural law and natural right and make the latter answerable to the former is to turn natural law into just another "learned piece of folly" (De Cive, Pref., pp. xi–xiii).

Hobbes's way of getting beyond the impasse created by the mutually antagonistic character of human self-interest is to appeal to the enlightening capacity of fear to induce men to surrender their natural right to all things (De Cive, ch. 2, art. 3, p. 17). The mutual surrender of natural right takes the form of a contract made by every man with every other. How this is supposed to have taken place is a mystery, given the natural suspicions every man will have of the intentions of every other, suspicions generated by the very fear that is supposed to induce men to form civilizing associations. It is as if we are to have only one cause (fear) for two mutually exclusive effects (war and peace). The problem does not seem to have escaped Hobbes. It is implicit in his observation that "words alone are not sufficient tokens to declare the will" (De Cive, ch. 2, art. 7, p. 19).

This particular problem was resolved by John Locke four decades later in his *Second Treatise of Government* simply be reconceiving human nature. Locke portrays man's nature without the internally contradictory character of self-interest[12] and omits the infinite character of human desire, that is, the dialectic of desire one finds in Hobbes's philosophy. He includes no account of man's native concern for glory (the political form that infinite self-love takes). Because of that, he is able to draw a purely juridical distinction between the state of nature and the state of war. In the Lockean state of nature, man is more tractable. He is driven to war by threats to his well-being that originate only in the scarcity of those commodities that are necessary to life. By implication, were there an abundance of commodities for all, there would be peace. Competition would vanish. The need for transforming political association into an ethical association in order to resolve the disunifying tendencies that one finds in Hobbes's citizen would never arise. If there is no scarcity of vital commodities, civil association will be sufficient to resolve man's moral problems. For this reason, it is quite right to understand Locke as the father of democratic liberalism.

Even though Hobbes had not yet drawn out the implications of his conception of human nature in *De Cive*, it remains true, nonetheless, that human nature is depicted in such a way as to preclude the satisfaction of desire with commodities, that is, with material well-being. Already, one can see that there is a dialectic in desire. Man is a creature of infinite desire, an image of the infinitely restless nature from which he was generated. Because desire, *conatus*, is associated only with appetite in *De Cive*, and not yet associated with perception and reason, the concern for the satisfaction of desire does not go beyond a desire for glory or reputation. For men governed by appetite, glory is the highest possible aim. Since, according to Hobbes, there can be no equal enjoyment of glory ("if all have it, none have it"), there will always, by logical necessity, be some who are dissatisfied. Desire itself is socially and politically unsatisfiable.

As a result of this characteristic of human nature, something more necessitating is required of man than good faith and mutual consent if he is to transfer himself from the natural condition to civil society. Hobbes writes, "covenants which are made in contract of mutual trust... are in the state of nature invalid" (De Cive, ch. 2, art. 11, p. 21), since no man can with certitude know the mind of another.

The problem here is nothing more than the problem involved in moving from the dictate of reason as it is expressed in Hobbes's first law of nature to the dictate of reason as it is expressed in the second law, or, stating the problem somewhat differently, mediating the reciprocally related, yet mutually exclusive concerns for peace and safety. Without a power which can compel both parties to respect covenants, the fact remains that "he that first performs, by reason of the wicked disposition of the greatest part of men studying their own advantage either by right or wrong, exposeth himself to the perverse will of him with whom he hath contracted" (De Cive, ch. 2, art. 11, p. 21). There is always reason for some doubt of another's intentions; the absence of doubt and suspicion would be a violation of the dictate of reason! Oddly enough, in *De Cive*, Hobbes's procedure for mediating the twin concerns for peace and safety is to call upon precisely what he has held to be invalid as the foundation of contractual association. He writes, "faith only is the bond of contracts" (De Cive, ch. 1, art. 13, p. 12). By "faith" Hobbes here means nothing other than the mutual trust which he has already rejected as a valid basis for contracting.

Hobbes resolves the problem to his own satisfaction at this time by drawing once again on the principle of enlightened self-interest. He remarks: "Whosoever therefore holds, that it had been best to have continued in that state in which all things were lawful for all men, he contradicts himself" (De Cive., ch. 2, art. 13, p. 12). One contradicts himself when he prefers the state of nature to servitude because the state of nature is a state of war, and in that condition all men are one's enemies. Following the Socratic observation that no man can know the good and not desire it, Hobbes remarks: "of two evils it is impossible not to choose the least" (De Cive, ch. 3, art. 18, p. 26).

If one were to keep a covenant he has made while still in the natural condition (as man must do if he is to escape the state of nature) it would be because keeping faith is a vital part of the credibility of any future covenants one might desire to make. It is conceivable that it would be in one's interest to contract with another person on some future occasion, even if only to take advantage of the other. It would not be in one's interest to discredit his future contractual efforts by acts of bad faith now (De Cive, ch. 3, art. 1–3, pp. 29–31).

The obvious difficulty with this line of thought is that self-interest is not always enlightened. One's interests may be served by adhering to the logic of the above argument, but that may not be apparent to the persons involved. Pre-contractual trust is the pre-condition of contractual association. John Locke had no difficulty with this. He could say, in all candor, that a contract could be entered into safely even "between a Swiss and an Indian in the woods of America . . . though they are perfectly in a state of nature in reference to one another."[13] The problem is in locating a reason to expect men to exhibit trust without some prior guarantee that they will not be betrayed. De Cive still seems to leave us with the paradoxical situation of needing a sovereign authority to guarantee the safety of those who, once confident of their security, will be enabled by that to contract with others in good faith to establish that very sovereign authority. Without such a guarantee, the first step in contracting with others would be a violation of naturally conceived right reason.

Clearly, for Hobbes, sociability is never selfless. The problem is that man's selfishness embodies all the self-destructive tendencies of natural desire. Man cannot leave his natural desire behind. It cannot be, as John Plamenatz would have it, that men must "try to put an end to the state of nature."[14] Rather, they must find a way of providing a reasonable (i.e., sociable) expression of natural (i.e., self-interested) reason.

The nature of man, as it is conceived in De Cive, permits no satisfactory resolution of this difficulty. We are given a theory in which a sovereign power is contractually generated. All rights, excepting the natural right to life (i.e., the natural conatus that individuates any living being) are transferred to the sovereign. The sovereign is the lone person who is not a party to the contract, at least not in his status as a sovereign, though he would be a party to the contract in his status as a natural being. He remains forever in the natural condition, with no civil guarantees for his own safety. He retains, therefore, all the natural rights of the natural man in the natural condition. Natural reason would impel him to establish dominion over all others in order to secure his own safety. In the process, Hobbes explains, he provides an order that is beneficial to the subjects, or, at least, an order that is less "incommodious" than the chaos of the natural condition. Presumably, a symbiotic relationship emerges between the sovereign and his subjects. He is authorized by his subjects. His will is their own. His will cannot substitute for the natural right of the subject, the un-relinquished right to flee or fight if the sovereign should threaten the safety of the subject, or even if he should fail to provide for it adequately. In *De Cive*, the sovereign's self-interest, dependent as it is on both the strength and loyalty of his subjects, is the cause of the civil extension of his subjects' natural rights and the basis for the social augmentation of their well-being.

However impressive *De Cive*'s theory of contractual association may have been to Hobbes's contemporaries or to later philosophers, it still does not explain how the first step in contracting can reasonably have been made, considering the infinite character of desire in natural man. While men in the natural condition may, indeed, conceive their needs pruden-tially, prudence itself—a demand of natural reason—advises against act-ing on mere faith that others will respect contractual agreements. Whether Hobbes will later resolve this problem when he begins in earnest the proj-ect of grounding politics on principles that are not simply self-evident, but that have their foundations in his theory of human nature and his physics, remains to be seen.

LEVIATHAN: THE MEDIATION OF RIGHT AND LAW

It was evident to Hobbes himself, by the time of *Leviathan* at least, that the contract that generates the commonwealth is compromised by the precontractual need for trust. The paradox involved in entering into a first contract is resolved with utter simplicity in *Leviathan*. Civil society can have been generated either by *institution*, that is, through voluntary asso-ciation, or by *acquisition*, that is, by conquest. According to Hobbes, whether society is established by an original contract or by the actions of a William the Conqueror makes little difference. Sovereignty by acquisition differs from sovereignty by institution only in that "men who choose their sovereign, do it for fear of one another, and not of him whom they in-stitute: but in this case, they subject themselves to him they are afraid of. In both cases they do it for fear" (Lev., ch. 20, p. 185). Hobbes adds, "the rights, and consequences of sovereignty are the same in both" (Lev., ch. 20, p. 185). The fact that actions have their origins in fear does not make them any less voluntary. It does not matter whether civil society has its origins in voluntary political association, that is, a contract, or no. Consequently, the need for precontractual faith in others to perform the contract that they have entered into is eliminated. The original contractual unity of the people can be established by conquest without the violation of natural rights. One's submission is always voluntary.

There is a certain amount of reason in Hobbes's argument. It is unlikely that any civil society has ever come about by an original, contractual act of institution. Most likely, the emphasis on sovereignty by institution in *Leviathan* is Hobbes's way of legitimizing sovereignty by acquisition. Every discussion of society originating by institution in a contract voluntarily entered into is reducible to a discussion of society generated by conquest and submission. The consequences and the rights involved are no different. Once this is established, there is no need for Hobbes to draw unnecessary attention to it from those whose liberal sensitivies would be offended.

The identity of acquisition and institution does not resolve the problem of sustaining civil society and keeping men peaceful in their intentions toward one another. That still has to be considered, as does the place of potentially seditious philosophical science in civil society. By the time he wrote *Leviathan*, Hobbes's conception of human nature and nature per se had changed considerably. The alienation of man from man was no longer conceived simply as an observed fact to be dealt with politically. Rather, in *Leviathan*, it is an integral feature of nature itself, understood as *conatus* or endeavour. Hobbes saw, perhaps with greater clarity than before, the truth of Francis Bacon's aphorism that "Nature to be commanded, must be obeyed."[15] Human felicity is not simply the result of one's successfully and uninterruptedly determining one's own social and political fate. Success in civil affairs, for example, the successful acquisition of glory, is precarious precisely because it depends on a civil order that is vulnerable to more than mere civil insurrection. Civil order endures only so long as it ensures the welfare of individuals and satisfies human desire better than the individual believes he can ensure his own welfare and satisfy his own desires in the natural condition. The threat of foreign invasion can cause a man in a Hobbesian civil society to ignore his contractual agreements without violating the dictates of right reason. The threats of famine (Lev., ch. 27, p. 288) or "unforeseen mischances" (Lev., ch. 44, p. 604) are such that no sovereign authority can guarantee a man's natural right to life against them. They, too, are reasonable reasons for violating contracts made.

In *Leviathan*, Hobbes reconceived political philosophy against the backdrop of the newly emerging project of the philosophical science to make man the measure of all things, the master and possessor of nature. Reason was no longer conceived as a kind of deductive sobriety, but rather, as the rational work of the human *conatus* endeavouring to sustain its characteristic motion (cf. Lev., ch. 2). Ultimately, it is philosophical science, not politics, that will produce solutions to the problems presented to man by the un-cooperative brutishness of nature.

However, the political precondition of man's mastery of brute nature is his mastery of what is brutish in human nature. Civil order, the commonwealth, must be securely established since *"Leisure* is the mother of *philosophy;* and *Commonwealth,* the mother of *peace* and *leisure"* (Lev., ch. 46, p. 666). The brutishness of the natural condition effectively silences the voices of those few who, in Hobbes's mind, are capable of undertaking this newly conceived philosophical project. It is the equality of the civil condition that liberates the natural inequalities that exist among men in matters of mind, or intellect. Consequently, the implications of Hobbes's reconceived account of human nature and attempt to ground his theories on his physics, are not all that dramatic for his political theory. The main lines of the political theory of *Leviathan* are precisely what they were in *The Elements of Law* and *De Cive.*

This is not to say that there are no significant differences in the *Leviathan* account of the generation of civil order. Civil order, too, can effectively silence the voices of philosophers and scientists if, within that civil order, life is conceived as a race as it is in *The Elements of Law,* the result of which is "glory" for those who compete successfully. Glory is the aggrandizement of the powers of body or the powers of authority and persuasion, not the powers of mind or intellect, because it is a form of public recognition. It exists in the recognition given by a public for one's public successes. The public cannot recognize and honor what it cannot comprehend and make publicly manifest. This is especially the case with philosophical science, about which Hobbes writes: "The sciences, are small power; because not eminent; and therefore, not acknowledged in any man; nor are at all, but in a few, and in them, but of a few things. For science is of that nature, as none can understand it to be, but such as in a good measure have attained it" (Lev., ch. 10, p. 75)[16]

Civil reasonableness is not the same as scientific rationality. It is submission to authority, to customs, codes and doctrines. It is a submission evoked by one's fear of the bodily harm that others could inflict, all of which serve as the unifying basis of civil society. But the authority of doctrines, grounded as it is in the concern for the physical safety of those who have entered the civil order, emerges as a non-rational standard of rationality. The more that philosophical and scientific ideas depart from accepted doctrines, the less they will be tolerated. Philosophical ideas are not simply judged wrong; they can be heretical, even seditious. One requirement for the success of the philosophical project is that philosophical science make itself look harmless to those who defend the conventions and doctrines at the foundations of civil society.

Implicitly, then, there is a distinction between the natural order and the civil order among men that cannot be made public. One might want to take issue with this observation by pointing to Hobbes's statement that "The *value*, or worth of a man, is a part of all other things, his price: and therefore is not absolute; but a thing dependent on the need and judgment of another" (Lev., p. 76), to show that Hobbes's conception of the nature of man is determined strictly by social considerations. The passage suggests that the philosophical worth of a man or his ideas can be recognized by society. This is, in fact, the faith of liberal political theory. Nevertheless, in the same chapter in *Leviathan* that Hobbes makes this statement, he also writes: "WORTHINESS, is a thing different from the worth, or value of a man; and also from his merit, or desert, and consisteth in a particular power, or ability for that, whereof he is said to be worthy; which particular ability, is usually named FITNESS, or *aptitude*" (Lev., ch. 10, p. 84).

Worth and worthiness do not always coincide, according to Hobbes, which is the same as to say that civil order does not reproduce the natural order among men.[17] Until it does, political authority and philosophical authority will not coincide. There will be no effective civil science, since the mastery of nature, human nature included, is fundamental to the establishing of a secure civil order. The philosophical project to make man the master of nature requires that man "imitate the creation"; it requires that he recreate nature in the image of man's own transient desires. One cannot undertake that project without potentially undermining the accepted doctrines that shore up the peace and leisure on which the philosophical project depends. This is an extremely old philosophical problem. It would appear that Hobbes believes he has found a satisfactory solution to it. It is an extremely old philosophical solution, and the basic lines of that solution are much the same as they were in *De Cive*. However, *Leviathan* permits the problem to emerge in a way that it never emerged in *The Elements of Law* or *De Cive*.

The generation of civil society in *Leviathan* is described much the way it was in *De Cive*. Concern for self-preservation and well-being, even a modest concern, cannot be satisfied without acquiring the means for guaranteeing one's life and well-being over an indefinite period of time. Men need powers that would be useful in responding to future conceivable threats to their preservation and well-being. One cannot provide for self-preservation without being concerned with augmenting one's situation, that is, "without the acquisition of more" (Lev., ch. 11, p. 86), even to the extent of acquiring dominion over others. Hobbes explains, "And by consequence, such augmentation of dominion over men being necessary to a man's conservation, it ought to be allowed him" (Lev., ch. 13, p. 112). The unavoidably contentious character of man's self-concern leads Hobbes to "put for a general inclination of all mankind, a perpetual and restless desire of power after power, that ceaseth only in death" (Lev., ch. 11, pp. 85–6). One could say that, for Hobbes, *whatever is natural is, for that reason, reasonable. And whatever is reasonable is, for the same reason, right.* Right is simply another conception of natural self-interest, exercised naturally by all men. Because of the exaggerated prerequisites of self-interest in the natural condition, the result is the "natural right of every man to everything. . ." (Lev., ch. 14, p. 117). Every man's acting on the basis of his own opinion as to what is needed to provide for his preservation and well-being is a self-vitiating, though compulsory strategy in the state of nature, something akin to a "bad infinite" perhaps, or a Nietzschian "eternal return" in which there is no finality, in which happiness is never more than the final fumes of a swiftly evaporating success. One's utmost desire, Hobbes tells us, is "to assure for ever, the way of his future desire" (Lev., ch. 11, p. 85). The result of his efforts to leave the natural condition, where his future desires are never assured, is that he is thrust back into the natural condition.

Again, as in *De Cive*, Hobbes appeals to the civilizing consequences of fear of violent death to resolve this dilemma and cause men to "seek aid by society" (Lev., ch. 11, p. 88). The enlightenment produced by their fear makes it possible for them to discern those immutable and eternal laws of nature, the dictates of reason, Hobbes says,"by which a man is forbidden to do that, which is destructive of his life, or taketh away the means of preserving the same; and to omit that, by which he thinketh it may be best preserved" (Lev., ch. 14, pp. 116–17). The behaviour of such a man is governed by what Hobbes calls "the morality of natural reason" (Lev., ch. 47, p. 697).

Hobbes's political realism depends on the fact that these natural laws "are easy to be observed" (Lev., ch. 15, p. 145). The difficulty with this is that observing the natural means acting consistently with regard to one's reasonably perceived natural rights. Natural right Hobbes defines as "the liberty each man hath, to use his own power, as he will himself, for the preservation of his own nature; that is to say, of his own life; and consequently, of doing any thing, which in his own judgment, and reason, he shall conceive to be the aptest means thereunto" (Lev., ch. 14, p. 116). What is necessary for the preservation of a man's life can only be decided on the basis of his own judgment and reason. But his judgments and reasons carry with them the contradictory character of the natural condition. As Hobbes has said, man, alone of all animals, enjoys the "privilege of absurdity" (Lev., ch. 5, p. 33). While Hobbes says this as an indictment of the absurdities found in "the books of philosophers," it is an apt phrase to describe those situations in which men prefer to hazard their lives rather than to secure them. Such is the case when men are so obsessed with thoughts of revenge that fear no longer has an enlightening and moderating effect on their actions.[18] Furthermore, an excessive concern for glory,[19] the seditious influence of doctrines, both religious and political,[20] and even an excess of fear itself[21] will incline men toward those actions that are destructive of political order and, therefore, to situations that are not conducive to their own well-being. In short, fear of death is not always an effective inducement to political reasonableness. It is not, as Hobbes seems to suggest, a satisfactory mediation of right and law.

Hobbes was obviously aware of this limitation of his theory. There is ample evidence that he was in *Leviathan*. In both *De Cive* and *Leviathan* he recommends a procedure for neutralizing these excesses of passion that tend to obliterate fear's enlightening and moderating advice. He calls upon the force of religion, which is influential with "the greatest part of mankind," and suggests that religious doctrines preached by the divines be regulated by restructuring the universities from which the divines receive their religious education. Of course, Hobbes takes great care to provide sufficient biblical exegesis in support of his own theories to make them palatable as the basis of a University curriculum. Keep in mind that *Leviathan* is addressed to "He that is to govern a whole nation" (Lev., Intro., p. xii). Part of Hobbes's advice to this adressee runs:

> They whom necessity, or covetousness keepeth attent on their trades, and labour; and they, on the other side, whom superfluity, or sloth carrieth after their sensual pleasures; which two sorts of men take up the greatest part of mankind; being diverted from the deep meditation, which the learning of truth, not only in the matter of natural justice, but also of all other sciences necessarily requireth, receive the notions of their duty, chiefly from divines in the pulpit, and partly from such of their neighbours of familiar acquaintance, as having the faculty of discoursing readily, and plausibly, seem wiser and better learned in cases of law and conscience, than themselves. And the divines, and such others as make show of learning, derive their knowledge from the universities, and from the schools of law, or from the books, which by men, eminent in those schools and universities, have been published. It is therefore manifest, that the instruction of the

people, dependeth wholly, on the right teaching of youth in the universities. But are not, may some man say, the universities of England learned enough already to do that? or is it you, will undertake to teach the universities? Hard questions. (Lev., ch. 30, p. 331)

Hard questions! Hobbes's answer is prudently worded: "[A]ny man that sees what I am doing, may easily perceive what I think" (Lev., ch. 30, p. 332). There is almost a blueprint of Hobbes's suggestion visible in the structure of *Leviathan* itself. The first chapter of *Leviathan* that treats the state of nature thematically is chapter eleven, on "The Difference of Manners." It is part of Hobbes's theory that "the rule of manners, without civil government, is the law of nature" (Lev., ch. 46, p. 669). Obviously, by manners Hobbes means the ways of men exclusive of the civilizing effects of social education; he definitely does not mean the social graces.

The next chapter to treat the state of nature thematically is chapter thirteen, the famous chapter concerning "The Natural Condition of Mankind," which culminates in a list of the causes of peace which reason can codify as "convenient articles of peace," or "Laws of Nature." Between the two chapters on the natural condition is chapter 12, entitled "Of Religion." Why it should be there, sandwiched between the two chapters on nature, is a mystery unless one considers the function religion has to perform in redirecting human desire. In a sense, these three chapters together suggest something of the relationship of the first half of *Leviathan* (Parts I and II, concerned with Man and Commonwealth) to the second half (Parts III and IV, concerned with the Christian Commonwealth and the Kingdom of Darkness).

The advantage of appealing to religion, that is, of utilizing religion for the purposes of generating civil order, is that men have a natural proclivity for religion, unlike all other creatures, because of their "foresight of the time to come" (Lev., ch. 12, p. 94). Hobbes writes: "For being assured that there be causes of all things that have arrived hitherto, or shall arrive hereafter; it is impossible for a man, who continually endeavoreth to secure himself against the evil he fears, and procure the good he desireth, not to be in a perpetual solicitude of the time to come. . . " (Lev., ch. 13, p. 95).

Man is solicitous of the future and, as a result of his ignorance of what the future has in store for him, he is also frightened by the possibilities of death, poverty or other calamities. However "infinite" fear may be, it needs an object capable of serving as the originating source of that fear. Fear without a cause is more frightening than those fears for which a cause is known simply because the absence of a visible cause of imaginable catastrophes leaves man with nothing to do but to invoke his imagination for that cause. Where the cause of fear is known, one can hold out hope that one day it will either be neutralized or eliminated. Man's natural self-interest, then, requires that fear have a cause.

> This perpetual fear, always accompanying mankind in the ignorance of causes, as it were in the dark, must needs have for object something. And therefore when there is nothing to be seen, there is nothing to accuse, either of their good, or evil fortune, but some *power*, or agent *invisible:* in which sense perhaps it was, that some of the old poets said, that if the gods were at first created by human fear: which spoken of the gods, that is to say, of the many gods of the Gentiles, is very true. (Lev., ch. 13, p. 95)

Whether Hobbes is or is not exempting Christianity from this analysis of the generation of gods is open to dispute. I would suggest that his qualifier that this applies only to the many gods of the Gentiles is a prudent dissimulation. The point is, the invisible agents of the greatest imaginable catastrophes and miseries are conceived by "men that know not what it is that we call *causing*—that is, almost all men..." (Lev., ch. 12, p. 97) to be the origins of all fortune, good and bad. And, in their ignorance of the causal antecedents of their good and bad fortune, they attribute the occurrence of one rather than the other to "things that have no part at all in the causing of it," such as "to words spoken, especially if the name of God be amongst them... insomuch as to believe, they have power to turn a stone into bread, bread into a man, or any thing into any thing." (Lev., ch. 12, p. 97). Hobbes's thinly veiled reference to transubstantiation here suggests that he does not intend to differentiate between Moses, Christ, and the shaman priest with his incantations and rituals as spokesmen for the power (or powers) invisible. That is, he intends to cut across religious and quasi-religious divisions, Christianity included, in discussing this tendency in man.

According to Hobbes, it is natural for men to worship such powers invisible (Lev., ch. 12, p. 98). That is, worship has its motive in human fear, desire, and man's concern for self-preservation. Furthermore, worship will take such forms, he says, as "submission of body, considerate addresses, sober behaviour, premeditated words, swearing, that is, assuring one another of their promises, by invoking them" (Lev., ch. 12, p. 98). In short, in the presence of such invisible (i.e., absent) agents, men become more tractable. They are "inclined to suppose, and feign unto themselves, several kinds of powers invisible; and to stand in awe of their own imaginations; and in time of distress to invoke them; as also in the time of an unexpected good success, to give them their thanks; making the creatures of their own fancy, their gods" (Lev., ch. 11, p. 93).

Hobbes's treatment of religion might be thought of as something akin to the social contract, insofar as it serves as a kind of contract men make with the hostile incomprehensibility of natural events, which has the additional effect of making men more tractable in their relationships with one another. The idea of a "contract" here should not be taken literally, of course. But it does suggest something of the function that religion has for Hobbes. This religious behaviour is cultivated by those who would teach men the wisdom of acting on the basis of something more than their most immediate interests. Hobbes tells us that "ignorance of causes, disposeth, or rather constraineth a man to rely on the advice, and the authority of others. For all men whom the truth concerns; if they rely not on their own, must rely on the opinion of some other, whom they think wiser than themselves, and see not why he should deceive them" (Lev., ch. 11, p. 90). The result is that those who cultivate in their subjects a concern for the invisible causes of their imaginable future calamities make them more governable: "And this seed of religion, having been observed by many; some of those that have observed it, have been inclined thereby to nourish, dress, and form it into laws; and to add to it of their own invention, and any opinion of the causes of future events, by which they thought they should be best able to govern others, and make unto themselves the greatest use of their powers" (Lev., ch. 11, p. 93; cf. ch. 12, p. 103; ch. 29, p. 316).

In short, Hobbes subordinates religion to politics at the very same time that he makes spiritual authority appear to be supreme. The political need for religion to augment and redirect natural fear is summarized in chapter 14 of *Leviathan*:

> The force of words, being, as I have formerly noted, too weak to hold men to the performance of their covenants; there are in man's nature, but two imaginable helps to strengthen it. And those are either a fear of the consequence of breaking their word; or a glory, or pride in appearing not to need to break it. This latter is a generosity too rarely found to be presumed on, especially in pursuers of wealth, command, or sensual pleasure; which are the greatest part of mankind. The passion to be reckoned upon, is fear; whereof there be two very general objects: one, the power of spirits invisible; the other, the power of those men they shall therein offend. Of these two, though the former be the greater power, yet the fear of the latter is uncommonly the greater fear. The fear of the former is in every man, his own religion: which hath place in the nature of man before civil society. The latter

hath not so; at least not place enough, to keep men to their promises; because in the condition of mere nature, the inequality of power is not discerned, but by the event of battle. (Lev., ch. 14, pp. 128–9)

In the state of nature, that is, whenever authority rests with every individual and not in any common power, men have two things to fear: invisible powers, the imaginable agents of imaginable future catastrophes, and other men. While the power of the former is greater, Hobbes says, the fear that men have for other men is greater, for the obvious reason that the threats which other men pose in the natural condition are more imminent and more visible. However, a man's fear of other men and the threats that their own needs and desires imply for his welfare are not sufficient to induce men to keep faith for the simple reason that the power of one man is not so much greater than the power of another that the outcome of a battle between them could be determined with certainty before it is fought.

By nourishing the seeds of natural religion in men, Hobbes believes, they might be made more willing to trust one another and to be enabled thereby to enter contractual associations. Religion, then, has a mediating function, intended to induce sobriety, consideration, and submissiveness in those who would not otherwise exhibit such behaviour. In his "Review and Conclusion" of *Leviathan*, Hobbes defends his treatment of Christian doctrines and the use he makes of them on the grounds that, in a time that calls for both peace and truth, to write as he does "is no more, but to offer new wine, to be put in new casks, that both may be preserved together" (Lev., Rev. and Concl. p. 711). The new wine, of course, is the peace that men have not yet enjoyed, and will not enjoy unless it is contained by its new cask, Hobbes's philosophical science. That the mediating function of religion is its primary importance is evidenced by the comments in the "Review and Conclusion." He writes:

To conclude, there is nothing in this whole discourse, nor in that I writ before of the same subject in Latin, as far as I can perceive, contrary either to the Word of God, or to good manners; or to the disturbance of the public tranquillity. Therefore I think it may be profitably printed, and more profitably taught in the Universities, in case they also think so, to whom the judgment of the same belongeth. For seeing the Universities are the fountains of civil and moral doctrine, from which the preachers, and the gentry, drawing such water as they find, use to sprinkle the same (both from the pulpit and in their conversation), upon the people, there ought certainly to be great care taken, to have it pure, both from the venom of heathen politicians, and from the incantation of deceiving spirits. And by that means the most men, knowing their duties, will be the less subject to serve the ambition of a few discontented persons, in their purposes against the state; and be the less grieved with the contributions necessary for their peace, and defense; and the governors themselves have the less cause, to maintain at the common charge any greater army, than is necessary to make good the public liberty, against the invasions and encroachments of foreign enemies. (Lev., Rev. and Concl., pp. 712–13)

Hobbes quite clearly states in this passage that religious doctrines can prevent men from joining seditious causes, and may even discourage sovereigns from maintaining armies of sufficient size and function to threaten their own subjects. Sedition is thereby discouraged even more. Of course, religious doctrines alone cannot maintain civil peace and unity, at least not indefinitely. Since religious authorities do not wield the sword, at least not in their capacity as religious authorities, their authority is bound to fade. When that happens, "the religion which they desire to uphold, must be suspected likewise; and, without the fear of the civil sword, contradicted and rejected" (Lev., ch. 12, p. 106). The obvious need, then, is the unification of religious and civil power. Hobbes says: "and thereby in the kingdom of God, the policy, and the laws civil, are a part of religion; and therefore the distinction of temporal, and spiritual domination, hath there no place" (Lev., ch. 12, p. 105). Enlightenment itself will erode religious conviction and, with it, religion's authority, unless spiritual and political authority are made to coincide.

Hobbes's procedure is to admit the authority of supernatural revelation, but, at the same time, to deny the possibility of knowing whether any claim to supernatural revelation is legitimate, because the claim originates in the inaccessible experiences of the recipient, and is mediated by the misleading influences of one's own interests and private ends.[22] In that situation (i.e., every such situation), the appropriate procedure is to defer to the authority of the sovereign.[23] The sovereign's authority, Hobbes says, includes the power of scriptural interpretation. "For, whatsoever hath a lawful power over any writing, to make it law, hath the power also to approve, or disapprove the interpretations of the same" (Lev., ch. 33, p. 380). The result then is that, whereas the sovereign may be subordinate to God, God's word—that is, what readings constitute God's word and what those readings mean—is subordinate to sovereign authority. Consequently, God, insofar as He is known through His Word, is Himself subordinate to sovereign authority. Religion, cultivated in this politically cautious manner, can become a force helpful in solidifying political authority and effectively generating political order. It loses its capacity for spawning civil insurrection, simply because the sovereign has authority over those doctrines and Divine Commands for which a rebellious clergy might want to hold him responsible.

Hobbes believes he has established a science of politics because he does not appeal to principles of association that are external to (or transcendent to) political life. There is no dualism between an "is" and an "ought" that has to be reconciled. It is fear, and correlative to that, desire for self, that provides the impetus for both association and dissociation. Nature dissociates; that is, fear and desire drive men apart, but in such a way that they are brought to see, by natural reason, that their well-being cannot be obtained without association. Religion is, for Hobbes, a force that assists the natural need for association when, because of human pride, error, or the like, fear is not sufficient.

It is the authority of the sovereign, however, that perpetuates civil order, according to Hobbes, and then only to the extent that he is able to maintain it. In this regard, Hobbes raises two reciprocally related questions: what must the sovereign be if he is to unify effectively the members of a civil association; and, given the necessarily absolute character of sovereign authority, what must the liberties of subjects be if civil association is to give the appearance of providing for both their safety and their well-being?

WHAT THE SOVEREIGN MUST BE

Prior to the moment that private individuals contract to form a civil association, whether by institution or by acquisition, no sovereign exists. His existence is generated by the very act of contracting; consequently, he cannot be party to the contract (Lev., ch. 18, p. 161). His nature is explained in chapter 16 of Leviathan, "Of Persons, Authors, and Things Personated." The nature and function of the sovereign is to mediate individual interests (i.e., natural rights) in such a way as to establish their "corporate" identity. Hobbes is no positivist; his sovereign is no mere ruler whose authority imposes itself externally upon a collection of dissociated individuals. The sovereign is the unified desire of the multitude who, in generating the sovereignty, transform human nature. Human nature is transformed as the result of man's efforts to mediate his own internally divided self-interest.

It is obvious that, according to Hobbes, individuals' interests are not always reflected in their conscious desires. In fact, one's desire to promote one's interests may be self-destructive. For example, in the interest of self-preservation one will find it necessary to acquire more power and advantages than he actually needs. They "cannot assure the power and means to live well, which [they have] present, without the acquisition of more" (Lev., ch. 11, p. 86). Men do not know with certainty the thoughts and intentions of others, whether they represent threats to their welfare or not. Neither do they know what miseries or calamities of an infinite number of possibilities await them in future time, or what remedies they will need to have available to them. Success in providing for one's welfare depends on one's ability to anticipate needs that may never arise by acquiring powers and advantages that one may never need. Preparations for the satisfaction of so many future possibilities will require men to do things that will make them appear acquisitive and power-hungry to others. To other men, equally concerned with their own well-being and their own future needs, such preparations would have to look menacing. Their own natural concerns would require that they compensate and acquire for themselves powers which would enable them to secure themselves against such a menace. Their activities would, of course, confirm the suspicions of our original man. The result is that men, in the natural condition, struggling to "assure the power and means to live well" (Lev., ch. 11, p. 86) invariably arouse the suspicion and enmity of those whose intentions they originally suspected and, in the process, create the very threats to their welfare that they originally intended to protect themselves against. Until interests are reflected in desires, that is, until desire and interest are mediated, there is no possibility of a mediation of natural right and natural law.

The mediation of desire and interest is possible only because of the peculiar character of natural man, his relational or dynamic existence. Natural man, Hobbes says, is a "person." He does not merely live in the vicinity of others, but with them. This is not to say there is a natural community of men in any sense of social homogeneity. Rather, men threaten their fellow men and are, in turn, threatened by them. They carry grudges and think thoughts of revenge; they do not forget. Creatures of other species do not threaten their own kind as a rule. Men do. Many people would consider this reason for lament. Hobbes does not. It is an integral part of the process that culminates in the sociability of man.

Hobbes explains that "a *person*, is the same that an *actor* is, both on the stage and in common conversation; and to personate, is to *act*, or *represent* himself, or another; and he that acteth another, is said to bear his person, or act in his name" (Lev., ch. 16, p. 148). To represent oneself to another in an ordinary conversation is, in effect, to impersonate oneself. The other has no direct access to one's thoughts and intentions. They have to be conveyed either in words or actions through a *persona* that one most likely will try with greater or lesser care to cultivate. One cannot even be alienated from another without "impersonating" himself.

All men, by virtue of the fact that they have identities, that is, have interests conspicuously distinguishable from the interests of others, are natural persons. Their interests get represented sometimes as mutually exclusive desires. They become civil persons, on the other hand, only when, as active parties to a social contract, their desires are made self-conscious by being integrated with the interests of the other parties to the contract. Their interests, in fact, become indistinguishable from the unified interests of the others. A civil person is a "feigned or artificial person," one who is capable of representing himself, say, in a court of law because he has been recognized as a citizen, that is, an artificial or "universalized" person, by the others. In effect, the political unity recognizes itself in him.

This transformation of the natural person into the civil person cannot take place without the mediating activity of the sovereign. Presumably, the sovereign could become a civil person, too, were it not for the fact that he cannot relinquish his place in the natural condition without losing his mediating capability and thereby throwing everything else back into the state of nature. It is only his nature as a fully natural being, with all his natural rights unmediated and untempered by any moral or social considerations, that makes it possible for him to function as the concrete unity of the political whole. Hobbes insists that "This is more than consent, or concord; it is a real unity of them all, in one and the same person. . ." (Lev., ch. 17, p. 158).

The unity of the commonwealth requires that sovereign authority be absolute, which is the same as to say that there can be only one authority. For that reason the sovereign cannot have been a party to the social contract. Likewise, he cannot be held subject to the laws he legislates (Lev., ch. 26, p. 252; cf. ch. 29, p. 312). Were he to be held subject to his own laws, that would limit his power to change the law. There would be an authority over him—his own laws—and, therefore, multiple absolute authorities. Anything less than absolute authority is no authority at all. Were there more than one sovereign authority governing a commonwealth, every subject would have to decide which authority he would obey. The subject would have to be his own authority for this decision. That would be a reconstitution of the natural condition, that is, war.

What gives the sovereign absolute authority is the fact that he has not relinquished his natural right to all things. Not being a party to the contract, he remains wholly in the state of nature, exercising his unmediated *conatus*. The price of sovereignty to the sovereign lies in the fact that he alone cannot enjoy any civil guarantees of safety. On the other hand, no property claim against the sovereign can be valid. To make a claim against the sovereign is to engage in seditious actions.

The authority of the sovereign remains absolute, however, only so long as the unity of the people endures. Hobbes explains that "In the making of a commonwealth, every man giveth away the right of defending another; but not of defending himself" (Lev., ch. 28, p. 297). Sovereign and subject both retain this right, with the distinction that the subject's right does not belong to him as a "civil person." So long as the unity of the commonwealth endures and the individual remains part of that commonwealth, he has no rights whatsoever against the sovereign. The right belongs to him only as a natural being; and, he reverts to his natural being only if and when his most fundamental natural right, his right to life, is threatened.

Strictly speaking, the sovereign is, in himself, "The People." Their unity exists only in his corporate *persona*. Any attack by one man upon another represents an attack on his sovereign person. The unity of "The People" depends on the sovereign's ability to comprehend his own interests in the natural law, which is the same as to say he must recognize his own strength and security in the security and strength of his citizenry. Hobbes realized, as did his Italian counterpart, Niccolò Machiavelli, that "the good of the sovereign and the people, cannot be separated" (Lev., ch. 30, p. 336; cf. ch. 18, p. 170; El. of Law, p. 163). With this in mind, Hobbes offered Machiavellian advice to sovereigns. To cultivate the unity of the commonwealth and simultaneously provide for his own natural self-interest, a sovereign ought to avoid inequitable taxation, provide for public charity, encourage full employment, create laws that are easily understood and which provide for the public good, select punishments and rewards that can profit the commonwealth by their example, select counsellors whose benefit will not derive from advice that conduces to civil commotion, and, finally, select commanders for his army who, if they are popular with the soldiers, are also unquestionably faithful since, as Hobbes says "[T]his love of soldiers, if caution be not given of the commander's fidelity, is a dangerous thing to sovereign power" (Lev., ch. 30, p. 341).

The suggestion made by K.R. Minogue that "The Sovereign is, in this rational system, a figure performing the same function as a Platonic philosopher-king: he supplies what is defective in the rationality of ordinary men"[24] is emphatically wrong if we understand him to mean that the sovereign must be a wise and selfless benefactor. On the other hand, if we take him to mean that the sovereign must induce in his subjects enough fear, respect and delight to preclude the possibility of collective rebellion, thereby unifying the citizenry and providing for their welfare as a means to providing for his own, then Minogue is right (cf. Lev., ch. 31, pp. 357–8). Hobbes tells us in the *Introduction* to *Leviathan*: "He that is to govern a whole nation, must read in himself... mankind" which, he says, is "hard to do, harder than to learn any language or science" (Lev., Intro., p. xii). It is hard because, Hobbes says, "naturally, the best men are the

least suspicious of fraudulent purposes" (Lev., ch. 46, p. 687), if only because they tend to read into the actions of others intentions similar to their
own. They are, consequently, easily deceived. On the other hand, the
worst of men are most inclined to be abusive and to thrust men back into
the natural condition by their threatening actions. If one is successfully to
read in himself "mankind," including the more bestial proclivities that
motivate the greater part of men, one must be able to find those
proclivities in himself. The sovereign's knowledge of human nature can be
obtained only by his taking himself as the key, and then only if he has read
himself correctly. Only by being a "wolf," that is, by adhering to what
Hobbes calls "natural reason," rather than to personal loyalty, moral sen-
timent, conscience, civil customs, political ideologies or pious religious
convictions will a sovereign be the enlightened protector of his own welfare and, therefore, provide for the unity of the commonwealth.

Why the sovereign would not abuse his powers, especially considering
the absence of any purely selfless impulses in his actions, has, in effect, already been answered. To a certain extent, there probably will be some
abuse of power since the relationship of the sovereign to his subjects is a
"natural" (i.e., not a civil) relationship. Since the sovereign is not omnis-
cient regarding the secret intentions of his subjects, and since he is
eminently aware of his own potential needs, he will sooner or later err in
the manner that any "over-provident" man in the natural condition would
err. But, Hobbes writes:

> the state of man can never be without some incommodity or other;
> and that the greatest, that in any form of government can possibly
> happen to the people in general, is scarce sensible, in respect of the
> miseries, and horrible calamities, that accompany a civil war, or that
> dissolute condition of masterless men, without subjection to laws, and
> a coercive power to tie their hands from rapine and revenge. (Lev., ch.
> 18, p. 170; cf. ch. 20, p. 195)

Hobbes's belief that, while life can never be without some inconveniences, there need be no intolerable inconveniences in civil society
had its foundations in his discovery of this symbiotic relationship of sovereign and subjects. Hobbes explains that the greatest pressures applied by
sovereigns on their subjects

> proceedeth not from any delight, or profit they can expect in the dam-
> age or weakening of their subjects, in whose vigor, consisteth their
> own strength and glory; but in the restiveness of themselves, that un-
> willingly contributing to their own defense, make it necessary for

their governors to draw from them what they can in time of peace, that they may have means on any emergent occasion, or sudden need, to resist, or take advantage on the enemies. (Lev., ch. 18, p. 170)

The sovereign may cause damage to his subjects, but he can never be accused of having injured them, because injury is illegal harm done to another, resulting from the violation of his civil rights. This no sovereign can do. He is the author of the civil laws and civil rights, and retains the right to change them. However, he may do damage to himself in the process. If his actions breed disunity, he weakens that unity on which he must depend to secure both himself and his subjects against alien powers. The sovereign, then, is not simply entrusted with procuring the safety of his people; he is, by the dictates of right reason, or by the *conatus* that defines him as a natural body in motion, dependent upon it for his own safety and welfare.

Hobbes does not limit the needs of subjects merely to security. Almost unexpectedly, he says that by the safety of the people he means not merely "a bare preservation, but also all other contentments of life, which every man by lawful industry, without danger, or hurt to the commonwealth, shall acquire to himself" (Lev., ch. 30, p. 322). Qualified by this demand, the sovereign's lot is not an easy one. The sovereign, reflecting on his own politically mediated self-interest, gets transformed into a paragon of moral virtue, much in the same manner that the radically private man in the original state of nature was transformed.

That many sovereigns are not sufficiently self-interested to see that they ought to act in this manner with their subjects is not something Hobbes would deny. Even when they are so motivated, it is not often that they arrive at the correct conclusions. Reading mankind in oneself is, indeed, hard to do. Sovereigns are especially susceptible to error because, while they remain natural persons, they also enjoy the pomp of absolute power and authority that begets illusion.

THE LIBERTIES OF SUBJECTS

What liberties are due the subjects of a sovereign authority is an issue that is important for Hobbes, especially considering the frequently defective unity of the sovereign's interests with those of the commonwealth. On this issue more than any other Hobbes's political theory has been faulted. The sovereign has been installed in order that the safety of the citizens be provided for, including the "contentments of life," as noted above (Lev., ch. 30, p. 322). The problem Hobbes's critics note is that the sovereign is not in any way "obligated to" his subjects. He remains entirely in the natural condition, wholly concerned with his own welfare, guided solely by "the morality of natural reason." The welfare and liberties of his subjects depend on the sovereign's ability to "read in himself" their interests. That is, he must be able to see a real connection between his liberties and theirs. The connection is not always obvious. When the sovereign does abuse his authority Hobbes provides for no redress of grievances, it seems, short of an appeal to the original right of nature. That is, the subjects can return themselves to the original natural condition.

Hobbes's intention was to develop a political theory that was politically realistic rather than to proselytize for idealized liberties that merely disrupt civil existence because they do not reflect the dialectical character of human self-interest. The notable absence of genuine moral progress in human history suggests that Hobbes was not entirely wrong.

Hobbes addresses the issue of political liberty only against the backdrop of "natural" liberty. He begins his analysis of liberty with definitions which, because they seem so clearly stated, tend to be somewhat misleading. Hobbes defines liberty in general as "the absence of opposition; by opposition, I mean external impediments of motion; and may be applied no less to irrational, and inanimate creatures, than to rational" (Lev., ch. 21, p. 196; ch. 14, p. 116). Liberty, defined this way, is sometimes referred to as "negative freedom." [25] Hobbes distinguishes liberty, this "negative freedom," from power. Power is the strength or wit to do what one may or may not have the liberty to do (Lev., ch. 21, pp. 196–7). In the absence of power (strength or wit), liberty provides one little real freedom. The liberty to cross a room (using Hobbes's own example) is of dubious value if one lacks the power to utilize that liberty.

Hobbes's definitions of power and liberty are incorporated into his definition of the right of nature, which he defines as "the liberty each man hath, to use his power, as he will himself, for the preservation of his own nature; that is to say, of his own life; and consequently, of doing any thing, which in his own judgment, and reason, he shall conceive to be the aptest means thereunto" (Lev., ch. 14, p. 116). Natural right belongs to every man in the natural condition where there are always external impediments to one's intended motions. While one's natural right may be violated, for example, when one is robbed, enslaved, or otherwise deprived of power, the "liberty" to use that power cannot be taken away. If it could, natural right would not be natural. The term "natural right" is Hobbes's juridical term for the human *conatus*, or endeavour, which lasts as long as life exists, by the necessity of nature.

Following his definitions of liberty and power, Hobbes defines the freeman as "he, that in those things, which by his strength and wit he is able to do, is not hindered to do, what he has a will to do" (Lev., ch. 21, pp. 196–7). In this definition, Hobbes combines power, liberty and will. Will is another term for *conatus*. Every man, according to Hobbes, has as his first and most fundamental impulse, the will to survive. There is no freedom of choice in this matter; this will exists as a natural impulse, at least to the extent that it is natural to resist those who would threaten one's well-being. Of course, the particular things for which one may have a will, inclination or desire may be such that one's specific desires betray his innermost will to survive. That, we saw, is the self-destructive nature of natural right in the natural condition.

The concern Hobbes has for the liberty of subjects is a concern for the political mediation of natural liberty which, Hobbes says, is the only liberty properly so-called (Lev., ch. 21, p. 198). Of course, it must be a political mediation of natural liberty, not a surrender of natural liberty for exclusively civil liberty. Natural liberty remains, in a certain sense, as the precondition of civil liberty.

Political mediation is fundamental because, Hobbes explains, "if we take liberty, for an exemption from laws, it is no less absurd, for men to demand as they do, that liberty, by which all other men may be masters of their lives" (Lev., ch. 21, p. 199). It is as absurd to want unmediated natural liberty as it is self-contradictory not to want politically mediated natural liberty. Obtaining the latter depends on our ability to understand both that "fear and liberty are consistent," and that "liberty and necessity are consistent" (Lev., ch. 21, p. 197). That is, it depends on the public realization that a single act of submission to sovereign authority will simultaneously impose civil obligations and provide for a politically mediated natural liberty (Lev., ch. 21, p. 203). Hobbes assures us that the submission to sovereign authority, and the consequent burden of civil obligations, do not restrict our natural liberty (Lev., ch. 21, p. 204). The act of submission simply redirects our natural endeavour, our *conatus*, onto paths that are not so clearly self-destructive. For this reason, Hobbes maintains that "The law of nature therefore is a part of the civil law in all commonwealths of the world. Reciprocally also, the *civil law is a part of the dictates of nature*" (Lev., ch. 26, p. 253). This is not a view of Hobbes's political philosophy that his interpreters often offer us. The tendency is to consider the state of nature and the civil condition as entirely distinct and separate. This comes from the equally common tendency to study Hobbes's political philosophy in isolation from his dialectical physics.

Strictly speaking, man never leaves the natural condition, even as he enters the social contract. Man remains a radically natural individual whose natural right to self-preservation cannot entirely be transferred (Lev., ch. 21, p. 208). That is the only reason that the sovereign, if he is sufficiently enlightened, will not abuse his own subjects. His absolute authority is only civil; it is authority that binds only civil persons. But it has natural limits; it does not hold against the natural rights of natural persons. Consequently, the eternal and immutable appeal that natural right has for all men is a fundamental inducement for the sovereign to establish and defend the civil rights and liberties of his subjects.

With this in mind, Hobbes explains that no man can be bound by his submission to sovereign authority to kill himself, or even to kill another except when the "refusal to obey, frustrates the end for which the sovereignty was ordained" (Lev., ch. 21, p. 208). When, for example, someone is called upon to assist in the defense of the commonwealth against foreign invasion, he would be expected to fight and, when necessary, to kill, since he does not have to fear the consequences of his provoking another (i.e., an alien soldier) to violence when that other is already committed to violence. However, it would also follow that if the victory of a foreign invader seemed certain, and if one's treatment by the invader could reasonably be assured to be better (or at least no worse) than that one has received from his own sovereign, there would no longer be a valid obligation (i.e., a rational or natural demand) to abide by the civil commitment. From Hobbes's perspective, that would be a good reason why the perspicacious sovereign would treat his own citizenry well. And, presumably, it would also be a good reason for a sovereign to temper his interest in unnecessary territorial expansion.

For similar reasons, Hobbes maintains that no man is obligated to incriminate himself by confessing to crimes, or to submit voluntarily when condemned for crimes he may have committed. Therefore, it is in the interest of the sovereign to maintain and protect the politically innocent liberties of subjects. All liberties other than those established by the natural right to self-preservation depend on the silence of law. Men may do whatever they want within the interstices of the law. When a sovereign multiplies the laws to which subjects are bound, he makes more likely the violation of laws and, consequently, obligates himself—in the interest of respect for authority (his own interest)—to convict and punish his subjects. When the innocent liberties enjoyed by subjects become crimes, subjects tend to listen more readily to the appeal of nature and have a greater inclination toward rebellion in the name of natural right. While the sovereign's authority to punish violators of his laws is received from the subjects themselves in their civil, corporate capacity, his right to punish them in their capacity as natural beings is not so received. His right to punish is a product of the fact that the sovereign remains in the state of nature, with his natural rights unimpaired by anything other than his own self interest. Few of Hobbes's interpreters have observed this, but Hobbes makes the point straightforwardly. He writes:

But to covenant to assist the sovereign, in doing hurt to another... is not to give him a right to punish. It is manifest that the right which the commonwealth, that is, he or they that represent it, hath to punish, is not grounded on any concession, or gift of the subjects. But I have also showed formerly, that before the institution of commonwealth, every man had a right to every thing, and to do whatsoever he thought necessary to his own preservation; subduing, hurting, or killing any man in order thereunto. And this is the foundation of that right of punishing, which is exercised in every commonwealth. For the subjects did not give the sovereign that right; but only in laying down theirs, strengthened him to use his own, as he should think fit, for the preservation of them all: so that it was not given, but left to him, and to him only; and (excepting the limits set him by natural law) as entire, as in the condition of mere nature, and of war of every one against his neighbor. (Lev., ch. 28, pp. 297–8)

Every subject is bound to the authority of the sovereign because he has authorized the sovereign by his own self-interested actions. However, he is not bound by the sovereign's natural right, having never contracted with the sovereign himself. Subject and sovereign stand in a "natural" relation to each other when questions of personal safety and well-being arise. Each retains his natural right to all things when this relationship is unmediated. For this reason, Hobbes advises the sovereign to exercise his right of punishing with a mind on the limits set by natural law. Hobbes's practical advice to sovereigns (an application of the natural law) is: do not make laws that you can know in advance will be violated by the general public.

There is no guarantee beyond this that a sovereign will never abuse his authority. For that reason Hobbes seems to suggest that it is important that sovereigns receive education in these matters, even before they assume office. That way, they will already have some idea of what they should avoid legislating if they wish to keep their subjects from appealing to their natural right, that is, if they wish to keep their sovereign authority intact. Hobbes clearly intends his own philosophy as the curriculum for that education (Lev., Rev. and Concl., pp. 712–13).

Perhaps the major difficulty for Hobbes's theory is the fact that sovereigns may not only resist Hobbes's efforts to educate them. They may even be uneducable owing to the very things to which Hobbes appeals in order to encourage their interest in education, that is, the insecurity and ideological dependency that seems to be an ineradicable part of public office. Hobbes himself says: "Potent men, digest hardly anything that setteth up a power to bridle their affections..." (Lev., ch. 30, p. 325). The sovereign, Hobbes says, is "*trusted* with sovereign power," with the understanding that he will procure "the safety of the people." At the same time, however, it is the very nature of Hobbes's provision for the sovereign's acknowledgment of the civil liberties of subjects (i.e., the persistent threat of an appeal to their natural right) that precludes the emergence of what Hegel later referred to as the ethical life (*Sittlichkeit*), even though the infinite character of human desire in Hobbes's account of human nature would seem to call for it. Self-interest is never fully integrated with civil society. The individual always knows his most natural interest may require that he abandon civil association.

THE UNITY OF POLITICAL, MORAL, AND SCIENTIFIC WISDOM

The most practically vital—if not the most philosophically fundamental—issue for Hobbes's political theory, then, is the education of sovereigns. It turns out that this issue is all but indistinguishable from the problem of locating good counsellors for the sovereign. Hobbes concentrates his efforts upon explaining what good counselling is and what is required of it for the successful governing of a commonwealth. He is adamant in his efforts to distinguish counsel from exhortation. The latter, Hobbes says, lacks "the rigour of true reasoning" (Lev., ch. 25, p. 243). He says: "they that exhort and dehort, where they are required to give counsel, are corrupt counsellors, and as it were bribed by their own interest" (Lev., ch. 25, p. 243). How this distinction can be maintained consistently, given the fact that all human thought and action is in the service of self-interest, is the problem Hobbes sets for himself. We are told that the virtues and defects of counsel are the same as the virtues and defects of intellect which is never selfless. The simple appeal to the neutrality of rationality is no resolution of the problem of locating honest counsellors.

Hobbes states as the first condition of good counselling that the counsellor's "ends, and interests, be not inconsistent with the ends and interests of him he counselleth" (Lev., ch. 25, p. 245). In short, Hobbes does not require of counselors that their advice be selfless, but only that their advice be consistent with the aims of government and, therefore, with those of the sovereign. In previous chapters it has been shown how and why this condition is satisfied only in the philosophical and scientific few who, because they are aware of the civil prerequisites of their own philosophical and scientific undertakings (since commonwealth is the mother of peace, and peace of leisure, and leisure is the mother of philosophy), and because political power will not satisfy their philosophical passions (directed as they are to the mastery of nature per se, not merely to dominion over men), will find that it is in their interest to promote political stability and respect for sovereign authority. In laying the groundwork for the establishment of a commonwealth, philosophers make possible the leisure which is the mother of philosophy (their own interest) and, incidentally, but not unimportantly, make possible the peace which all men perceive as their utmost natural interest.

This characteristic of the philosophical and scientific few Hobbes refers to as "a generosity too rarely found to be presumed on, especially in the pursuers of wealth, command, or sensual pleasure; which are the greatest part of mankind" (Lev., ch. 14, pp. 128–9). In chapter 27 of *Leviathan*, Hobbes makes another, somewhat oblique, reference to this generosity. He writes: "Of all passions, that which inclineth men least to break the laws, is fear. Nay, excepting some generous natures, it is the only thing, when there is appearance of profit or pleasure by breaking the laws, that makes men keep them" (Lev., ch. 27, p. 285). Profit and sensual pleasure are not the objectives of philosophical science, and therefore philosophers do not need the prod of fear, it would seem, in order to resist their corrupting appeal. Because the interest of philosophers is the "great and master delight" that accompanies the "indefatigable generation of knowledge," the philosophical and scientific few will be morally and politically generous; they will be just without coercion.

Hobbes's confidence in the justice and generosity of the philosophical and scientific few does not depend upon the selflessness of their actions and intentions. That would be a misplaced confidence that ignored what he considered to be an unavoidable fact of human nature, that its actions are always self-directed. It has been suggested, erroneously I believe, that the generous natures to which Hobbes refers represent "a kind of second nature imposed upon men by their own wills," which "is like the emergence of ethics, of civilisation, and indeed of disinterestedness."[26] To say this is to suggest that Hobbes has abandoned the foundation of his philosophical system, the *conatus* that serves as the foundation of both his physics and his psychology. Disinterestedness, superimposed by human will, is a violation of the demands of nature. The suggestion tends to turn Hobbes into an especially bad version of a pre-Kantian Kant, an advocate of the moral priority of the "Good Will." It would be more accurate to say that Hobbes arrived, partially and prematurely, at the Hegelian idea of the ethical life (*Sittlichkeit*), where the individual submerges his private identity and individuality in the life of the State, that is, where complete selfishness and perfect selflessness become absolutely identical and indistinguishable at the level of political existence. Even this approach to Hobbes's "generous natures" is misleading. The difficulty with this suggestion is that it still emphasizes selflessness more than is permissible. Political selflessness exists only in the generous few and, in them, only as the epiphenomenon of philosophical self-interest.

The philosophical sciences would not be pursued by those who have as their aim in life the acquisition of wealth, political power, or pleasure. Wealth is, in the end, only a form of power, according to Hobbes; and pleasure is only an index of its enjoyment. Science, on the other hand, promises men little that can be translated into political power or reputation, "For science is of a nature as none can understand it to be but such as in a good measure have attained it" (Lev., ch. 10, p. 75).

The more philosophically wise a person is the less his knowledge will be able to be made publicly manifest. The public cannot appreciate what it cannot comprehend. Consequently, Hobbes tells us, the philosopher-scientist will have a meager reputation and little political power. Hobbes did not foresee very well the social implications that the unity of science and technology has had, in spite of the fact that their unity is the implicit objective of his own philosophy. He saw that philosophical science would not be satisfied with political power and would not, therefore, seek it as its primary objective. He did not see that the philosopher-scientist of a much later era, no longer trusting power to uneducable sovereigns, would absorb that power as part of the philosophical project itself, without ever making that absorption politically evident. It did not occur to him that a technological science might not even recognize its own power as political.

The relationship of political power and philosophy, as Hobbes understood it, might well be stated in terms of his theory of natural equality. In a certain sense, equality is part of the very fabric of human existence. Men can always be conceived to be equal in one sense or another, but only as the function of an inequality. In the state of nature, for example, neither reason nor socially established reputation are significant forms of power. Socially and intellectually, then, men are made equal by the natural condition. It is strength that is the criterion of power in the state of nature, and men are not equally strong. Strength is made visible, however, only by battle. Consequently, authority is invisible except as a by-product of war in the natural condition. Cleverness in battle can be enough of a factor to make one who is the lesser in strength the equal to one who is stronger but not so clever. It is that inequality in cleverness that produces and sustains their equality.

Civil society, too, equalizes men in the sense that it shifts the locus of power away from physical strength. But, because of the public character of recognition as the determinant of civil power, civil society locates power in status and reputation. Physical strength is rarely significant, and, in that sense at least, men are made equals. Likewise, the sciences offer little power, since scientific rationality is not as persuasive with an unsophisticated public as is rhetoric made eloquent by passion. This is the only sense in which I can find Hobbes sincerely maintaining that "As rational beings all men were equal, whatever their civic status,"[27] though many of Hobbes's more recent interpreters would not agree. Civil society is egalitarian to the extent that its exaltation of status, reputation, or social recognition as the locus of power and authority is exclusive of the differences among men in physical strength and intelligence. *Men are made equal in those things in which they are naturally least equal by the equalizing effect of social inequality!*

Philosophical science is equalizing, since it recognizes authority in neither strength nor socially acquired reputation, but only in "the dictates of natural reason." The philosopher-scientist does not recognize the authority of political powers over his science. He remains autonomous, impervious to the demands of politics where his science is concerned. However, Hobbes realized, along with many others among his philosophical and scientific contemporaries, that one must insulate the "customary conjunctions" that unify men, that is, the customs, conventions and doctrines on which civil order is founded, from the destructive implications of philosophical science. Philosophical science must remain inconspicuous if the social order is not to degenerate to something more primitive. Civil reasonableness is not the same as scientific rationality; but scientific rationality does depend on the existence of civil reasonableness if it is to be an activity that men (however few they may be) will have the leisure to undertake. That does not mean, of course, that philosophical science should place itself in the service of doctrines, either moral or political.

The generous natures to which Hobbes refers are, clearly, not paragons of moral virtue in any sense other than a philosophically conceived self-serving one. Their generosity is derivative of a desire to invest themselves in the project to make man the master and possessor of nature. The political virtue of this project, Hobbes would maintain, is that it is not translatable into concern for political power. Nevertheless, as one can tell from a reading of *Leviathan*, it is not a selfless moral generosity that spends itself in concern for social justice, that is, for the needs of minorities, the unfortunate, the powerless, or the like.

Hobbes did not explain how philosophical counsellors might effectively gain the attention of sovereigns, or for that matter, how they would make themselves persuasive if they did capture the sovereign's attention. The problem is that sovereigns must first be made capable of following the force of reason. Hobbes does not explain how one might convince a sovereign that civil philosophy is a study worth undertaking, that is, that it is in his own sovereign interest, if he does not already see it. Neither does Hobbes explain how one might make him capable of comprehending such a science philosophically. He admitted that in the *Introduction* to *Leviathan* that civil philosophy is harder to learn than any language or science. The assumption is that we should not expect too much from sovereigns.

But then, perhaps we should not expect an answer from Hobbes to this question. After all, history has resolved the problem by providing an answer for which, to a certain extent at least, Hobbes's philosophy served as the antecedent. It is technology which has become the omnipresent authority for contemporary society—simultaneously a science and a sovereignty—without ever having undertaken consciously to acquire political power.

Hobbes concluded *Leviathan* with a carefully worded remark that his civil philosophy was written "without application, and without other design than to set before men's eyes the mutual relation of protection and obedience" (Lev., Rev. and Concl., pp. 713–14). It would appear that he had no illusions regarding its persuasiveness with those political forces that were at work reshaping the political structure of England, but only a concern that it not make him appear to be an adversary. He wrote: "And though in the revolution of states, there can be no very good constellation for truths of this nature to be born under, (as having an angry aspect from the dissolvers of an old government, and seeing but the backs of them that erect a new), yet I cannot think it will be condemned at this time, either by the public judge of doctrine, or by any that desires the continuance of public peace" (Lev., Rev. and Concl., p. 714).

His remaining interest, he declared, was to return to his investigations in natural philosophy which had now been made politically safe by the persuasiveness of his own arguments. "And in this hope I return to my interrupted speculation of bodies natural; wherein, if God give me health to finish it, I hope the novelty will as much please, as in the doctrine of this artificial body it useth to offend. For such truth, as opposeth no man's profit, nor pleasure, is to all men welcome" (Lev., Rev. and Concl., p. 714).

Conclusion

W ith this, my study is completed. Hobbes is resituated in philosophical history at the inception of a tradition that runs through Leibniz and Hegel. He remains a political realist for whom liberty is a product of order rather than chaos and a philosophical materialist for whom matter vanishes into motion, and motion into the dynamics of reciprocal individuation. The gap that ordinarily isolates bodies from the perception of bodies and, hence, physics from psychology, has disappeared. He has given us a philosophy of man that denies the radical separation of reason and desire, just as it collapses the radical difference of sense and understanding. His account of the acquisition of knowledge makes it inseparable from man's creative acquisition of mastery over nature. Hobbes's invocation to man is that he "imitate the creation," that is, invest himself in the "indefatigable generation of knowledge" that is simultaneously the "great and master delight" of the philosopher-scientist himself, and the greatest benefaction to mankind. It is this invocation that establishes the unity of scientific and moral wisdom, what Hobbes called "the morality of natural reason." All in all, Hobbes re-emerges as one who is at the threshold of the philosophical and scientific enterprise as it has taken shape in our own times.

Notes

PREFACE

1 Frithiof Brandt, *Thomas Hobbes' Mechanical Conception of Nature* (1927), 379.

CHAPTER ONE: HOBBES'S PHILOSOPHICAL INTENTION

1 *Leviathan* Introduction, in *The English Works of Thomas Hobbes*, Sir William Molesworth, ed. (London 1839; London: John Bohn 1966, reprint). All references in parentheses in the text will be to *The English Works*.
2 Francis Bacon, *Complete Essays of Francis Bacon*, Intro. by Philip H. Bailey (New York: Belmont Books 1962), 27.
3 Cf. J. Laird, *Hobbes* (London: Ernest Benn Ltd. 1934); Howard Warrender, *The Political Philosophy of Hobbes: His Theory of Obligation* (Oxford: Clarendon Press 1957); A.E. Taylor, "The Ethical Doctrine of Hobbes," *Philosophy*, 1938, reprinted in *Hobbes Studies*, Keith Brown, ed. (Cambridge, MA: Harvard University Press 1965).
4 C.B. Macpherson, *The Political Theory of Possessive Individualism* (London: Oxford University Press 1962).
5 F.S. McNeilly, *The Anatomy of Leviathan* (New York: Macmillan 1968), David Gauthier, *The Logic of Leviathan* (Oxford: Clarendon Press 1969); Gregory S. Kavka, *Hobbesian Moral and Political Theory* (Princeton, NJ: Princeton University Press 1986).
6 Cf. especially, Warrender, Gauthier, McNeilly, and D.D. Raphael, *Hobbes: Morals and Politics* (London: George Allen & Unwin, Ltd. 1977).
7 George Croom Robertson, *Hobbes* (Edinburgh: William Blackwood and Sons 1886); Leo Strauss, *The Political Philosophy of Thomas Hobbes: Its Basis and Its Genesis* (Chicago: University of Chicago Press 1936).
8 Frithiof Brandt, *Thomas Hobbes' Mechanical Conception of Nature* (Copenhagen 1927).
9 Michael Oakeshott, "Thomas Hobbes," *Scrutiny*, 4 (December 1935).
10 J.W.N. Watkins, *Hobbes's System of Ideas* (London: Hutchinson 1965); M.M. Goldsmith, *Hobbes's Science of Politics* (New York: Columbia University Press 1966); Thomas A. Spragens, jr, *The Politics of Motion* (Lexington, KY: University Press of Kentucky 1973); Hiram Caton, "On the Basis of Hobbes's Political Philosophy," *Political Studies*, XXII, 4 (Dec. 1974).
11 Strauss, *The Political Philosophy*, 94; cf. also 98, 106, 137.
12 S.I. Mintz, *The Hunting of Leviathan* (Cambridge: Cambridge University Press 1962), 20.

13 In two articles published following *The Political Philosophy of Thomas Hobbes*, Leo Strauss abandoned his exclusively "humanist" interpretation of Hobbes. Increasingly, he came to see the need for approaching Hobbes with a respect for his natural philosophy. In the chapter on Hobbes in his *Natural Right and History* (Chicago: University of Chicago Press 1953), and again in his review of Raymond Polin in *What Is Political Philosophy?* (New York: Free Press 1959), Strauss claimed that Hobbes's philosophy involves a functional neutrality to the conflict of man and nature, neutrality made possible by his "methodological" (rather than metaphysical) materialism. Nonetheless, the conflict between the two dimensions (the human and the natural) is not resolved by an appeal to functional neutrality. It is merely laid aside. Strauss does not deny that Hobbes was interested in this problem. But Strauss's later interpretation, like the earlier interpretation of Hobbes along "humanist" lines, remains vulnerable to the criticism that no entirely adequate interpretation of Hobbes's systematic intentions can be achieved if one begins with an unqualifiedly mechanistic idea of nature as central to Hobbes's thought, whether it is "methodological" or not. For Strauss's reference to his intent to "undertake a detailed investigation of the connexion between Hegel and Hobbes," see *The Political Philosophy*, 58.

14 Strauss, *The Political Philosophy*, 204.

CHAPTER TWO: HOBBES'S PHILOSOPHY OF NATURE

1 Brandt, *Hobbes's Mechanical Conception*, 340. Cf. Alan Gabbey's remark: "It is perhaps significant that the importance and subsequent influence of Hobbes and Malebranche should have been almost exclusively philosophical" ("Force and Inertia in the Seventeenth Century: Descartes and Newton," in *Descartes: Philosophy, Mathematics and Physics*, Stephen Gaykroger, ed. [New Jersey: Barnes & Nobel 1980], 304).

2 Robertson, *Hobbes*, 58.

3 Peters, *Hobbes*, 76.

4 Cf. Keith Thomas, "The Social Origins of Hobbes's Political Thought," In *Hobbes Studies*, Keith Brown, ed. (Cambridge, MA: Harvard University Press 1957).

5 Bertram E. Jessup, "The Relation of Hobbes's Metaphysics to His Theory of Value," *Ethics*, 58 (April 1984), 211. Cf. also Kuno Fischer, *Francis Bacon of Verulam* (London: Longman, Brown, Green, Longman's & Roberts 1857), ch. 13, Part I, "The Atomism of Hobbes." Cf. also Charles T. Harrison, "Bacon, Hobbes, Boyle, and the Ancient Atomists," *Harvard Studies and Notes in Philosophy and Literature*, xv (1933). Harrison takes issue with the atomist interpretations of Hobbes's physics.

6 Frederick Albert Lange, *The History of Materialism* (New York: Humanities Press 1950), I, ch. 3, 287; Hobbes, *Six Lessons to the Professors of the Mathematics*, Lesson VI, vol. VI, 340−1.

7 Cf. *The Little Treatise*, sect. 2, pr. 8, p. 201, in *The Elements of Law*, F. Tönnies, ed. (Cambridge 1889), 196.

8 Aristotle, *The Basic Works of Aristotle*, Richard McKeon, ed. (New York: Random House 1941). All references to Aristotle will refer to this volume. *De Generatione et Corruptione*, Book II, ch. 3, p. 511, 330.a.30.

9 Aristotle, *De Caelo*, Book IV, ch. 4, p. 462, 311.a.15.

10 Aristotle, *Physics*, 215.a.1.

11 Ibid., 115.a.15; *De Caelo*, 273. b.30.

12 Ibid., 215.a.1.

13 Ibid., 255.b.32; 255.a.28.

14 Ibid., 255.b.5.

15 Ibid., 241.b.24.

16 Aristotle, *De Caelo*, 300.a.25.

17 Aristotle, *De Generatione et Corruptione*, 337.a.13.

18 Aristotle, *Physics*, 253.b.9.

19 Ibid., 266.b.26.

20 Ibid., 215.a.28.

21 Aristotle, *De Caelo*, 277.a.29.

22 Marshall Clagett, *The Science of Mechanics in the Middle Ages*, (Madison: University of Wisconsin Press 1959), 520.

23 Ibid., 215.
24 René Descartes, *The Principles of Philosophy*, Part II, pr. 37, in *The Philosophical Works of Descartes*, Vol. I, E.S. Haldane & G.R.T. Ross, eds. (New York: Dover Publications 1931), 267.
25 Ibid., Part II, pr. 24, p. 265. Motion is presumed in the very idea of displacement, of course. The definition, consequently, is tautological.
26 Ibid., Part II, pr. 64, p. 269.
27 Alexandre Koyré, *Galileo Studies* (New Jersey: Humanities Press 1978), 78, 116.
28 Cf. Alan Gabbey, "Force and Inertia," 230.
29 Strauss, *The Political Philosophy*, xiv.
30 Watkins, *Hobbes's System*, 42.
31 *The Little Treatise*, Section 1, conclusion 10, 196.
32 Ibid., Section 1, conclusion 5, 195. Hobbes is using the School terminology familiar in his time. A *patient* is the passive recipient of motions from an *agent*, or active being. Today one might use the term *subject* in place of the term *patient*, except that *subject* is understood today in terms of the subject/object dichotomy and against the backdrop of the modern notion of the epistemological isolation of a perceiving subject of which the later Hobbes will be a source. However, Hobbes, still using School terminology in *The Little Treatise*, will say that the ultimate *subject* of accidents is *substance*, in which case, a *subject* (if it is a substance) would be what later philosophers and scientists will refer to as the object, not its opposite. So, *patient* should not be thought of as simply a synonym for the more contemporary notion of subject.
33 Ibid., Section 1, conclusion 15, 197. Frithiof Brandt interprets the "active power inherent" to be a concept that refers to an unmoved or first mover, explaining that it is Aristotelian, since "it is never said that this very power consists in motion..." (*Hobbes's Mechanical Conception*, 21–2). This is, strictly speaking, incorrect since the corporeal species emanating from the original agent moves locally and imparts motion to the patient. The capacity for emanating species continually and "in infinitum" is the "active power inherent" that Hobbes attributes to some agents. Actually, it would have to belong to any agent capable of provoking fear or desire in a patient. But it would also be found in agents, such as the sun, the moon, and magnets. Brandt adds that Hobbes later dropped the distinction between immediate and mediate agent, and that that forced him to abandon the notion of the "power inherent." Once again, this is not correct, though it is correct to say that the concept is altered to complement his evolving physics. It is, in effect, what will come to be the *conatus* concept in Hobbes's philosophy.
34 Ibid., sec. 2, concl. 8, p. 200. Without denying the possibility that an agent conveys motions and properties to a patient through vibrations set up in an intervening corporeal medium, Hobbes wanted to maintain that agents can influence patients by emitting corporeal (or substantial) species, small particles that move through space and "touch" the patient, thereby conveying to it, somehow, the properties or motions of the original. Why the agent would not diminish in size because of such activity was a mystery to Hobbes and others who maintained this hypothesis.
35 Ibid., sec. 2, concl. 2, p. 199.
36 Ibid., sec. 2, concl. 9, pp. 202, 203.
37 Ibid., sec. 3, concl. 3, 4, p. 206.
38 Cf. Brandt, *Hobbes's Mechanical Conception*, 103; Hobbes, *A Minute or First Draught of the Optics*, Part I, Ch. 2, para. 2, 6, British Museum, Harley ms. 3360.
39 Letter to Sir Charles Cavendish, *The English Works*, VII, 459.
40 *De Corpore*, Part IV, Ch. 26, 430; Ch. 30, 526; *Seven Philosophical Problems* in *The English Works*, VII, Ch. 7, 57–8.
41 Cf. Brandt, *Hobbes's Mechanical Conception*, 134 ff. for his remarkable reconstruction of the controversy in a series of letters exchanged between Hobbes and Descartes.
42 Peters, *Hobbes*, 77.
43 *A Minute or First Draught of the Optics*, Part I, ch. 2, para. 5, p. 8. Also cf. *De Corpore*, Part III ch. 21, art. 5, 323–4.
44 René Descartes, *Optics*, First Discourse, in *Discourse on Method, Optics, Geometry, and Meteorology* (New York: Bobbs-Merrill 1965), 70. Cf. Alan Gabbey, "Force and Inertia in the Seventeenth Century: Descartes and Newton," 238.
45 *A Minute or First Draught of the Optics*, Part I, ch. 2, p. 5.

46 On Mersenne, see Richard H. Popkin, *The History of Scepticism from Erasmus to Descartes* (New York: Harper & Row 1964), 133–40.

47 Hobbes seemed to agree that the contraction-dilation theory would imply the existence of a vacuum. In his *Minute or First Draught of the Optics* (part I, pp. 6–7) he argued that the existence of a vacuum is absurd only if one accepts Descartes' identification of space and extension, which he does not. But Hobbes's rejection of the vacuum in *De Corpore* would appear to require his relinquishing the contraction-dilation theory. He introduces the simple circular theory of motion as a substitute. The dilation-contraction theory is mentioned in *De Corpore*, but only briefly, in chs. 21 and 22.

48 Peters, *Hobbes*, 24.

49 René Descartes, *Principles of Philosophy*, Part II, pr. xxxvii, in *Philosophical Works of Descartes*, Haldane & Ross, eds. (New York: Dover Publications 1955), 267.

50 Descartes, *Optics*, 70.

51 Brandt, *Hobbes's Mechanical Conception*, 327.

52 Hobbes never argues that *conatus* is a primitive motion with no cause of its own. Cf. *De Corpore*, Part II, ch. 22, art. 17, p. 347.

53 Goldsmith, *Hobbes's Science of Politics*, p. 21.

54 *A Minute or First Draught of the Optics*, Part I, ch. 2, para. 2, p. 7.

55 Cf. S.M. Engel, "Analogy and Equivocation in Hobbes," *Philosophy*, XXXVII (October 1962).

56 Brandt, *Hobbes's Mechanical Conception*, 295.

57 Ibid., 314.

58 Ibid., 379.

59 Watkins, *Hobbes's System*, 124. "One might say that Leibniz integrated matter from psycho-physical intensities, whereas Hobbes differentiated motion into psycho-physical intensities," 131–2.

60 The inadequacy of treating Hobbes's physics as a mechanics grounded on the principle of inertia has been reflected in the observation occasionally made that Hobbes appears to treat motion, cause and reason as if they are synonymous. "Hobbes's concept of 'a cause' had no necessary connection with an antecedent motion, or with temporal antecedence at all. (He often speaks of a cause where we would speak of a reason)." K.C. Brown, "Hobbes's Grounds for a Belief in a Deity," *Philosophy*, XXXVII, 142 (October 1962). Cf. also S.M. Engel, "Analogy and Equivocation in Hobbes," 326–35. The observation suggests that Hobbes invalidly moved from physical descriptions to rational descriptions, that is, from mechanical materialism to rationalism, by equivocation. The criticism tends to dissolve, however, if the present interpretation is accepted.

61 G.W. Leibniz, *Leibniz: Philosophical Papers and Letters*, Leroy E. Loemker, ed. (Chicago: University of Chicago Press 1956), 162.

62 Loemker, *Philosophical Papers*, 218.

63 Ibid., 422.

64 G.W.F. Hegel, *Lectures on the History of Philosophy*, Haldane and Simson, eds. (New York: Humanities Press 1968) III, 325.

65 Loemker, *Philosophical Papers*, 220.

66 Hegel, *Lectures*, 338.

67 Ibid., 344.

68 Ibid., 348.

69 Ibid., 348.

CHAPTER THREE: THE LIBERATION FROM NATURAL PHILOSOPHY

1 Hobbes's early interest in Thucydides and history indicates an empirical approach that is subsequently abandoned because, like the ancient moral idealism to which it is an alternative, it is a too fallible device for promoting human "felicity." Cf. Leo Strauss, *The Political Philosophy*.

2 Cf. in this regard K.C. Brown, "Hobbes's Grounds for a Belief in Deity," 341; S.M. Engel, "Analogy and Equivocation in Hobbes," and M.M. Goldsmith, *Hobbes's Science of Politics*, 31.

3 "The train of regulated thoughts is of two kinds; one, when of an effect imagined we seek the

causes, or means that produce it: and this is common to man and beast. The other is when "imagining anything whatsoever, we seek all the possible effects, that can by it be produced... Of which I have not at any time seen any sign, but in man only; for this is a curiosity hardly incident to the nature of any living creature that has no other passion but sensual, such as are hunger, thirst, lust, and anger" (Lev., ch. 2, pp. 13–14).

4 Stanley Rosen, "Sophyrosyne and Selbstbewusstsein," *The Review of Metaphysics*, XXVI: 4, #104 (June 1973). Discussing the "intersubjective structure of self-consciousness" in Hegel, Rosen explains: "According to Hegel, the struggle for recognition between two egos makes self-consciousness manifest. This struggle is not initially "political" but expresses the intentionality of spirit as desire. We see here Hegel's assimilation of doctrines associated with Descartes and Hobbes. The "passions of the soul" reveal themselves in a pre-political "state of nature," but in such a way as to establish inter-subjectivity, and thereby to raise man from selfish desire to the level of ethical and political experience" (p. 621).

5 *Leviathan*, ch. 2, p. 11.
6 J.W.N. Watkins, *Hobbes's System*, 142.
7 Ibid., 141.

CHAPTER FOUR: THE PASSIONS

1 Macpherson, *Possessive Individualism*, 27.
2 Leo Strauss, *The Political Philosophy*, 29.
3 Leo Strauss, *What Is Political Philosophy?*, 181. Cf. Pascal, *Pensées* (Baltimore, MD: Penguin 1966). "The eternal silence of these infinite spaces fills me with dread," 95.
4 Strauss, *The Political Philosophy*, 9.
5 Cf. Lucretius, *The Nature of the Universe* (Baltimore, MD: Penguin 1951), book II, 60.
6 Peters, *Hobbes*, 135.
7 "Conception of the future is but a supposition of the same, proceeding from remembrance of what is past; and we so far conceive that anything will be hereafter, as we know there is something at the present that hath power to produce it: and that anything hath power now to produce another thing hereafter, we cannot conceive, but by remembrance that it hath produced the like heretofore... the passions, whereof I am to speak next, consist in conception of the future, that is to say, in conception of power past, and the act to come" (El. of Law, ch. 8, art. 3, p. 37).
8 Descartes, *The Philosophical Works of Descartes*, II, cixxvi, 412.
9 Ibid., 358.
10 Ibid., 359.
11 Ibid., 362, lxx, lxxi.
12 Ibid., 362.
13 Ibid., 313.
14 Ibid., 400.
15 Ibid., 358.
16 Ibid., 363–4.
17 Spinoza, *Ethics* (New York: Hafner 1974), Part III, 176.
18 Ibid., Part III, Prop. LII, 165–6.
19 Descartes, *The Philosophical Works*, I, 359.
20 Ibid., 395.
21 Ibid.
22 Ibid.
23 Ibid., 393.
24 Ibid., 372–3.
25 Ibid., 373.
26 Ibid., 395–6.
27 Ibid., lxxxvii, 369.
28 Ibid., 370.
29 Ibid., lxxxix, 371.
30 Ibid., 409.
31 Ibid., 409–10.

32 Ibid., 402.
33 Ibid., 406.
34 Ibid., 402–3.
35 Ibid., 402.
36 Ibid., xlv, 402.
37 Ibid., cxliii, 395.
38 Ibid., 409–10.
39 Strauss, *The Political Philosophy*, 56.
40 Ibid., 150.
41 Ibid., 29, 55.
42 Strauss quotes Hobbes's explanation that "magnanimity is contempt of unjust or dishonest helps" (Lev., ch. 8, p. 60). There is no justification, however, for insisting that it arises from an inner integrity of purpose or an unfailing honesty. Hobbes opposes magnanimity to "that which the Latins call *versutia*—translated into English *shifting*—and is a putting off of a present danger or incommodity by engaging into a greater, as when a man robs one to pay another, is but a shorter-sighted craft..." (Lev., ch. 8, p. 60). Magnanimity arises, then, because unjust and dishonest helps are long-range hindrances, a shorter-sighted craft, not because of individual integrity or moral sense. The magnanimous man condemns unjust and dishonest helps because his own well-being is jeopardized more than it is aided by such shorter-sighted helps. His own well-being remains his predominant concern.
43 Descartes, *The Philosophical Works*, II, clxxvi, 412.
44 *The Elements of Law*, "The Answer of Mr. Hobbes to Sir William Davenant's Preface before Gondibert," p. 453; cf. *The Elements of Law*, ch. 10, art. 18, p. 50; *Leviathan*, ch. 6, p. 45.

CHAPTER FIVE: HOBBES'S DOCTRINE OF NATURAL EQUALITY

1 C.B. Macpherson, *The Political Theory of Possessive Individualism* (London: Oxford University Press 1962), 62.
2 W.V. Glover, "Human Nature and the State in Hobbes," *Journal of the History of Philosophy*, IV (1966), 298–9; M.M. Goldsmith, *Hobbes's Science of Politics*, 90, 213–14; F.S. MacNeilly, *The Anatomy of Leviathan*, 164; Watkins, "Philosophy and Politics," 103; Strauss, *The Political Philosophy of Thomas Hobbes*, 101–2; Martin A. Bertman, "Equality in Hobbes, with Reference to Aristotle," *The Review of Politics*, XXXVIII, 4 (Oct. 1976).
3 Watkins, *Hobbes's System of Ideas*, 117; Macpherson, *The Political Theory of Possessive Individualism*, 76.
4 Michael J. Oakeshott, "Introduction," xxvii.
5 Goldsmith, *Hobbes's Science of Politics*, 63; J.W.N. Watkins, "Philosophy and Politics in Hobbes," *Philosophical Quarterly*, 5 (1955), 103.
6 Leo Strauss, *The Political Philosophy of Thomas Hobbes*, 121, 126; cf. also C.B. Macpherson.
7 Sir Leslie Stephen, *Hobbes* (Ann Arbor: University of Michigan Press 1961), 41; Samuel I. Mintz, *The Hunting of Leviathan* (Cambridge, Eng.: Cambridge University Press 1969), 13.
8 Cf. *Leviathan*, 86. Hobbes maintains that competition proceeds from desire.
9 David P. Gauthier, *The Logic of Leviathan*, 15.
10 René Descartes, *Discourse on Method*, in *The Philosophical Works of Descartes*, I, 81.
11 Actually, this argument can be found, at least embryonically, in Hobbes's *De Corpore Politico*, where he writes, "though there were such a difference of nature, that master and servant were not by consent of men, but by inherent virtue; yet who hath that "eminency of virtue above others, and who is so stupid, as not to govern himself, shall never be agreed upon amongst men, who do every one naturally think himself, as able, at the least, to govern another, as another to govern him" (*De Corpore Politico*, 103).
12 *Leviathan*, 141; cf. also *De Cive*, 39 and *The Elements of Law*, 103. Hobbes claims that equality is a function of the absolute power and authority of the sovereign, without which there is no natural equality. He writes, "As in the presence of the master, the servants are all equal, and without any honour at all; so are the subjects, in the presence of the sovereign. And thought they shine some more, some less, when they are out of his sight; yet in his presence, they shine no more than the stars in the presence of the sun" (*Leviathan*, ch. 18, 169).
13 Macpherson, *Possessive Individualism*, 68.

CHAPTER SIX: POLITICAL THEORY

1 Hegel states Hobbes's point well in his *Philosophy of Right:* "We may not speak of the injustice of nature in the unequal distribution of possessions and resources, since nature is not free and therefore neither just nor unjust. That everyone ought to have subsistence enough for his needs is a moral wish and thus vaguely expressed is well enough meant, but like anything that is only well meant it lacks objectivity" (art. 49, p. 44).

2 John Plamenatz, *Man and Society* (New York: McGraw-Hill 1963), 120; cf. *De Cive,* Author's Preface to the Reader, xv, xvi; and Epistle Dedicatory, ii.

3 Ibid., 133.

4 Once again, Hegel makes this point rather well: "The building of a house is, in the first instance, a subjective aim and design. On the other hand we have, as means, the several substances required for the work—Iron, Wood, Stones. The elements are made use of in working up this material: fire to melt the iron, wind to blow the fire, water to set wheels in motion, in order to cut the wood, etc. The result is, that the wind, which has helped to build the house, is shut out by the house; so also are the violence of rains and floods, and the destructive powers of fire, so far as the house is made fireproof. The stones and beams obey the law of gravity—press downward—and so high walls are carried up. Thus the elements are made use of in accordance with their nature, and yet to cooperate for a product, by which their operation is limited. Thus the passions of men are gratified; they develop themselves and their aims in accordance with their natural tendencies, and build up the edifice of human society; thus fortifying a position for right and order *against themselves...*" (G.W.F. Hegel, *The Philosophy of History*, trans. John Sibree [New York: Dover Publications 1956], 27).

5 *Leviathan*, ch. 15, p. 147. Also, "The law of nature, and the civil law, contain each other, and are of equal extent. For the laws of nature... in the condition of mere nature... are not properly laws, but qualities that dispose men to peace and obedience" (Lev., ch. 26, p. 253).

6 J.W.N. Watkins, *Hobbes's System of Ideas*, 76.

7 Cf. Warrender, *The Political Philosophy of Hobbes*, ch. 7, 164. Thomas A. Spragens, jr has argued that these two interpretations of *Hobbes*'s natural law are both correct, or at least are compatible with one another. *The Politics of Motion* (Lexington, KY: University Press of Kentucky 1973), 117.

8 Cf. *Leviathan*, ch. 15, 145.

9 Warrender, *The Political Philosophy of Hobbes*, 25–6.

10 Ibid., 15.

11 Ibid., 23.

12 John Locke, *The Second Treatise of Government*, ed. Thomas P. Peardon (New York: Bobbs-Merrill 1952).

13 Ibid., ch. 2, para. 14, p. 9.

14 Plamenatz, *Man and Society*, 132.

15 Francis Bacon, *The New Organon* (New York: Library of Liberal Arts 1960), Book I, Aphorism 3, cf. Book I, Aphorism 129).

16 *Leviathan*, ch. 11, p. 88, where *Hobbes* says that men who use subtlety of wit, etc., are not so likely to be victorious in times of sedition as those who "use all the advantages of force" and who "strike first."

17 Cf. chapter 4 of this work. Also cf. *Leviathan*, ch. 18, p. 169: "As in the presence of the master, the servants are equal, and without any honor at all; so are they subjects, in the presence of the sovereign. And though they shine some more, some less, when they are out of his sight; yet in his presence, they shine no more than the stars in the presence of the sun." It is the civil condition that generates civil equality by reducing to insignificance the brute difference that exists among men naturally.

18 "[A]ll signs of hatred, or contempt, provoke to fight; insomuch as most men choose rather to hazard their life, than not to be revenged..." (Lev., ch. 15, p. 140). "All signs of hatred and contempt provoke most of all to brawling and fighting, insomuch as most men would rather lose their lives (that I say not, their peace) than suffer slander" (De Cive, ch. 3, art. 12, p. 38). Cf. also *The Elements of Law*, ch. 9, art. 6, p. 43.

19 "Of the passions that most frequently are the cause of crime, one, is vain glory, or a foolish overrating of their own worth" (Lev., ch. 27, p. 283).

20 "[Th]here are no wars so sharply waged as between sects of the same religion, and factions of the same commonwealth, where the contestation is either concerning doctrines or politic prudence..." (De Cive, ch. 1, art. 5, pp. 7–8). "[T]hose hermaphrodite opinions of moral philosophers, partly right and comely, partly brutal and wild; the causes of all contentions and bloodsheds" (De Cive, Preface to the Reader, xiii). "[T]his doctrine of *separated essences*, built on the vain philosophy of Aristotle, would fright them from obeying the laws of their country, with empty names..." (Lev., ch. 46, p. 674). "But it is an easy thing, for men to be deceived, by the specious name of liberty; and for the want of judgement to distinguish, mistake that for their private inheritance, and birthright, which is the right of the public only. And when the same error is confirmed by the authority of men in reputation for their writings on this subject, it is no wonder if it produce sedition and change of government" (Lev., ch. 21, p. 202).

21 "Of all passions, that which inclineth men least to break the laws, is fear... And yet in many cases a crime may be committed through fear" (Lev., ch. 27, p. 285).

22 "It is manifest enough, that when a man receiveth two contrary commands, and knows that one of them is God's, he ought to obey that, and not the other, though it be the command even of his lawful Sovereign (whether a monarch, or a sovereign assembly), or the command of his father. The difficulty therefore consisteth in this, that men, when they are commanded in the name of God, know not in the divers cases, whether the command be from God, or whether he that commandeth do but abuse God's name for some private ends of his own" (Lev., ch. 43, p. 584).

23 "When God speaketh to man, it must be either immediately; or by mediation of another man, to whom he had formerly spoken by himself immediately. How God speaketh to a man immediately may be understood by those well enough, to whom he hath so spoken; but how the same should be understood by another, is hard, if not impossible to know. For if a man pretend to me, that God hath spoken to him supernaturally, and immediately, and I make doubt of it, I cannot easily perceive what argument he can produce, to oblige me to believe it. It is true, that if he be my sovereign, he may oblige me to obedience, so, as not by act or word to declare I believe him not; but not to think any otherwise than my reason persuades me. But if one that hath not such authority over me, should pretend the same, there is nothing that exacteth either belief or obedience" (Lev., ch. 32, p. 361). Cf. Jean-Jacques Rousseau's remark: "Of all Christian writers, the philosopher Hobbes alone has seen the evil and how to remedy it, and has dared to propose the reunion of the two heads of the eagle, and the restoration throughout of political unity, without which no State or government will ever be rightly constituted. But he must have seen that the masterful spirit of Christianity was incompatible with his system, and that the priestly interest would always be stronger than that of the State. It is not so much what is false and terrible in his political theory, as what is just and true, that has drawn down hatred on it" (*The Social Contract*, in *The Social Contract and Discourses* [New York: E.P. Dutton 1977], ch. 8, 271).

24 K.R. Minogue, "Hobbes and the Just Man," in *Hobbes-Forschungen* (Berlin: Duncker & Humblot 1968), 168.

25 Cf. Thomas Hill Green, *Liberal Legislation and Freedom of Contract* in *The Works of Thomas Hill Green* (London: Longmans, Green and Co. 1888), III.

26 Minogue, "Hobbes and the Just Man," *Hobbes-Forschungen*, 170.

27 R.S. Peters, *Hobbes*, 155.

Bibliography

◈◈◈

Aristotle. *The Basic Works of Aristotle*, Richard McKeon, ed. New York: Random House 1941

Bacon, Francis. *Complete Essays of Francis Bacon*. Intro. by Philip H. Bailey. New York: Belmont Books 1962

—*The New Organon*. New York: Library of Liberal Arts 1960

Bertman, Martin A. "Equality in Hobbes, with Reference to Aristotle," *The Review of Politics*, XXVIII: 4 (October 1976)

Brandt, Frithiof. *Thomas Hobbes' Mechanical Conception of Nature*. Copenhagen 1927

Brown, K.C. "Hobbes's Grounds for a Belief in a Deity," *Philosophy*, XXXVII: 142 (October 1962)

Brown, Keith, ed. *Hobbes Studies*. Cambridge, MA: Harvard University Press 1967

Caton, Hiram, "On the Basis of Hobbes's Political Philosophy," *Political Studies*, XXII: 4 (December 1974)

Clagett, Marshall. *The Science of Mechanics in the Middle Ages*. Madison: University of Wisconsin Press 1959

Descartes, René. *Discourse on Method, Optics, Geometry, and Meterology*. New York: Bobbs-Merrill 1965

—*Philosophical Works of Descartes*, Haldane & Ross, eds. New York: Dover Publications 1955

Engel, S.M. "Analogy and Equivocation in Hobbes," *Philosophy*, 37 (October 1962)

Fischer, Kuno. *Francis Bacon of Verulam*. London: Longman, Brown, Green, Longman's & Roberts 1857

Gabbey, Alan. "Force and Inertia in the Seventeenth Century: Descartes and Newton," in *Descartes: Philosophy, Mathematics and Physics*, Stephen Gaykroger, ed. New Jersey: Barnes & Noble 1980

Gauthier, David. *The Logic of Leviathan*. Oxford: Clarendon Press 1969

Gaykroger, Stephen, ed. *Descartes: Philosophy, Mathematics and Physics*. New Jersey, Barnes & Noble 1980

Glover, W.V. "Human Nature and the State in Hobbes," *Journal of the History of Philosophy*, 4 (1966)

Goldsmith, M.M. *Hobbes's Science of Politics*. New York: Columbia University Press 1966

Green, Thomas Hill, *Liberal Legislation and Freedom of Contract* in *The Works of Thomas Hill Green*. Vol. III. London: Longman's, Green 1888

Harrison, Charles T. "Bacon, Hobbes, Boyle, and the Ancient Atomists," *Harvard Studies and Notes in Philosophy and Literature*, 15 (1933)

Hegel, G.W.F., *Lectures on the History of Philosophy*, Haldane and Simson, eds. New York: Humanities Press 1968

—*The Philosophy of History*, trans. John Sibree. New York: Dover Publications 1956

Hobbes, Thomas. *The English Works of Thomas Hobbes*, Sir William Molesworth, ed. London 1839; London: John Bohn 1966, reprint

—*The Little Treatise*, in *The Elements of Law*, F. Tönnies, ed. Cambridge 1889

—*A Minute or First Draught of the Optics*. British Museum, Harley ms. 3360

Jessup, Bertram E. "The Relation of Hobbes's Metaphysics to His Theory of Value," *Ethics*, 58 (April 1984)

Kavka, Gregory S. *Hobbesian Moral and Political Theory*. Princeton, NJ: Princeton University Press 1986

Koyré, Alexandre. *Galileo Studies*. New Jersey: New York: Humanities Press 1978

Laird, J. *Hobbes*. London: Ernest Benn 1934

Lange, Frederick Albert. *The History of Materialism*. New York: Humanities Press 1950

Leibniz, G.W. *Leibniz: Philosophical Papers and Letters*, Leroy E. Loemker, ed. Chicago: University of Chicago Press 1956

Locke, John. *The Second Treatise of Government*, ed. Thomas P. Peardon. New York: Bobbs-Merrill 1952

Lucretius. *The Nature of the Universe*. Baltimore, MD: Penguin 1951

McNeilly, F.S. *The Anatomy of Leviathan*. New York: Macmillan 1968

Macpherson, C.B. *The Political Theory of Possessive Individualism*. London: Oxford University Press 1962

Minogue, K.R. "Hobbes and the Just Man," in *Hobbes-Forschungen*. Berlin: Duncker & Humblot 1968

Mintz, Samuel I. *The Hunting of Leviathan*. Cambridge, Eng.: Cambridge University Press 1962, 1969

Oakeshott, Michael J. "Introduction" to *Leviathan*. New York: Crowell-Collier 1962

—"Thomas Hobbes." *Scrutiny*, 4 (December 1935)

Peters, R.S. *Hobbes*, Baltimore, MD: Penguin 1967

Pascal. *Pensées*. Baltimore, MD: Penguin 1966

Plamenatz, John. *Man and Society*. New York: McGraw-Hill 1963

Popkin, Richard H. *The History of Scepticism from Erasmus to Descartes*. New York: Harper & Row 1964

Raphael, D.D. *Hobbes: Morals and Politics*. London: George Allen & Unwin 1977

Robertson, George Croom. *Hobbes*. Edinburgh: William Blackwood and Sons 1886

Rosen, Stanley. "Sophrosyne and Selbstbewusstsein," *The Review of Metaphysics*, XXVI: 4, no. 104 (June 1973)

Rousseau, Jean-Jacques. *The Social Contract and Discourses*. New York: E.P. Dutton 1977

Spinoza, Benedict de. *Ethics*, James Gutmann, ed. New York: Hafner 1974

Spragens, Thomas, A., jr. *The Politics of Motion*. Lexington, KY: University Press of Kentucky 1973

Stephen, Sir Leslie. *Hobbes*. Ann Arbour, MI: University of Michigan Press 1961

Strauss, Leo. *The Political Philosophy of Thomas Hobbes: Its Basis and Its Genesis*. Chicago: University of Chicago Press 1936

—*Natural Right and History.* Chicago: University of Chicago Press 1953

—*What is Political Philosophy?* New York: Free Press 1959

Taylor, A.E. "The Ethical Doctrine of Hobbes." *Philosophy,* 1938, reprinted in *Hobbes Studies,* Keith Brown, ed. Cambridge, MA: Harvard University Press 1965

Thomas, Keith. "The Social Origins of Hobbes's Political Thought," in *Hobbes Studies,* Keith Brown, ed. Cambridge, MA: Harvard University Press 1957

Warrender, Howard. *The Political Philosophy of Hobbes: His Theory of Obligation.* Oxford: Clarendon Press 1957

Watkins, J.W.N. "Philosophy and Politics in Hobbes." *Philosophical Quarterly,* 5 (1955)

—*Hobbes's System of Ideas.* London: Hutchinson 1965

Index